TechnoTouch

Here's hoping the journey is good to you. I'm glad our paths crossed.
- Marlene

Other Products by Marlene B. Brown

Books:
*TechnoTouch II: Combining High Tech Advertising with
   High Touch Marketing for High Return Sales*
Magnetic Marketing: Advertising & Marketing Secrets
The Incredible Internet: Making it Pay Off for Big for You
Techie Time/Techie Talk: A Humorous/Serious Approach

Video Training Programs:
The Challenge of Change
Shared Leadership Through Empowerment
Communicating Successfully

Audio Tapes:
TechnoTouch: Managing Change for 21st Century Ldrsp.
Techie Time/Techie Talk: A Humorous/Serious Approach
Better, Better, Best: The MarmeL Theme Song

Binder with Forms & Diskettes:
Success System for Entrepreneurs/Small Business Owners

Screen Saver:
Thought Master by Marlene B. Brown

CD-ROM:
TechnoTouch: An Interactive Multimedia Book

Newsletter:
TechnoTouchTrends: A leading-edge bi-monthly newsletter

TechnoTouch
*Managing Change for
21st Century Leadership*

TechnoTouch Copyright 1994, 1997 by Marlene B. Brown. *All rights reserved.* No parts of this book may be used, reproduced or utilized in any form, or by any means, electronic or mechanical including photocopying, recording, or by any information storage and retrieval system, without written permission from the Publisher, except in the case of brief quotations embodied in critical articles and reviews. Inquiries should be addressed to the Permissions Dept., Sunrise Publishing International.

This book is designed to provide information in regard to the subject matter covered. It is sold with the understanding that the publisher and author are not engaged in rendering legal, accounting or other professional services. If legal or other expert assistance is required, the services of a competent professional person should be sought. The purpose of this book is to educate and entertain.

FIRST EDITION

Library of Congress Cataloging-in-Publication Data
Brown, Marlene B.
　Technotouch: The Journey to Twenty First Century Success/ by Marlene B. Brown
　　　p. cm.
　　ISBN 1-56728-015-3　　　LC 92-090740
　　1. Change　2. Future Success　3. Leadership　4. Technology
5. Empowerment　I. Title
　　HD　　　　1994　　　　CIP
　　Printed in Canada
　　　　　　10 9 8 7 6 5 4 3 2 1

SECOND EDITION

Second Printing 1997 Revised

DEDICATION

To my children, Brad, Vanessa, Christina, Melanie, and Stacy, for their faith in me and support of me. They will always be my greatest productions as well as a continuing source of endless pride and love

To my grandsons, Jeremiah, Josha, and Trevor, and to my special granddaughter, Rachel Marie. Their unconditional love was the source of much of my inspiration

To my father, who taught me a love for humanity, the importance of giving, the power of humor

To my mother, who taught me perseverance, the importance of family, the power of inner strength

To Earl and Geoff, for their quiet devotion, loyal support, objective feedback, computer expertise, and administrative assistance

And finally, to the thousands of people from my audiences, and my loyal customers, who saw value in and took action on the ideas I shared with them

ACKNOWLEDGMENTS

Writing a book is a solitary effort by the author made possible by many people whose professionalism and support, both before and during production, play an important role in the book's successful completion. Individuals who deserve special recognition for various roles they played are: Earl Lewis, Brad Brown, Vanessa Inn, Christina Brown, Melanie Caron, Stacy Brown, Robert Stark, Geoff Caron, Tim Butcher, Jim Buschmann, Anne Gennings, Martin Inn, Dan Poynter, Del Biddle, Patti Lester, Fred Burrows, Jamie Osborne, Catherine Brown, Fred Behning, Richard Frank, Ken Kogut, Dana Jerrard, John Zhang, Slim Fiore, Janice Lim, Sandi Burrows, John Ryder and Chris Young.

Most of all, I'm grateful for my "families" who provided much of the creativity, perspectives, and experiences that were the foundation for this book. Among these "families" are my children and grandchildren, my supportive team at MarmeL Consulting, my colleagues in NSA, the special upper management and human resource people who are clients of mine, and all those meeting planners, directors of training, and audience participants I had the pleasure of working with.

A heartfelt thanks to not only these people, but to all others who've been there when I needed them.

Contents

Chapter 1	Getting off the Bank	11
Chapter 2	The Journey Begins	15
Chapter 3	The Pond's Technology Facility	19
Chapter 4	The Pond's Telecom Facility	23
Chapter 5	Management VS Leadership	27
Chapter 6	Education on the Pond	33
Chapter 7	Heading Down the River	37
Chapter 8	Out Into Open Water	43
Chapter 9	Companies on the Open Seas	49
Chapter 10	Mapping the Mission	55
Chapter 11	Technotouch Begins	59
Chapter 12	Different Ships, Same Boats	65
Chapter 13	Operating Systems and Control	71
Chapter 14	The Being as Programmer	77

Contents, *cont.*

Chapter 15	*A Spirit Full of Energy*	83
Chapter 16	*Waves And Sea Walls*	89
Chapter 17	*Unplugging the Pond Mentality*	93
Chapter 18	*What the Tide Leaves Behind*	99
Chapter 19	*Super Conductors/Digital Teams*	103
Chapter 20	*Technotouch Defined*	109
Chapter 21	*The Tide Will Turn*	115
Appendix	*Twenty-one Technotouch Trends*	119

Preface

In my seminars and keynotes, I often engage participants in an exercise designed to get them to identify and analyze the roadblocks that are preventing them from living a happier, more productive life. The settings vary, both geographically and culturally, but the underlying theme behind the responses doesn't vary much.

How do you survive and thrive in a world that's constantly changing, where security and predictability are gone? Why should I give my all, when I may be outsourced tomorrow? How do we leaders get our people to buy-in to the vision? Where's the joy in the workplace? How do we managers and supervisors who are playing dual roles become guides and coaches? How do those of us on the front lines and in the field pull together as self directed work teams? And where's the balance in life?

Perhaps these and similar questions are ones you're asking yourself as you struggle to cope with the real life challenges facing all of us as a new millennium arrives.

To remain competitive in the global economy of the 21st century, we have to restructure, reorganize, and reengineer ourselves, our companies, and our people.

What can you do about all of this? How much control do you have over events in your life? How can you take charge of the direction your future is heading in?

The book you're about to read is a novel with business applications. It is composed of original ideas and concepts that have been brewing in my head for the past three years as I presented them to clients, refining them along the way.

I believe the message is one that will help you, the reader, find answers to the feelings of anxiety and lack of control over your world caused by the rampant and unpredictable changes that are occurring to all of us.

It's important that we not only understand why the changes are occurring, and what the future holds, but also how we can gain some semblance of control and even live life more fully than we have been.

When I started to write, the book flowed and was completed in six days. I had no idea the book would come out in the form of a dialogue between two characters, a guide and a disillusioned bank sitter. It was as though the channel was open, and the message needed to come out and be heard.

Those who have read it have commented on the fascinating fast-paced way it's written, with the reader wanting to keep reading to find out what happens in the next chapter. They've also appreciated the fresh approach to a troubling issue, as well as being able to laugh out loud whenever the humor surfaced.

I hope you're as excited as I am about learning how to stay afloat in constant sea change where the surf's always up. Are you ready to discover what's meant by Technotouch and how it can help you be successful today and throughout the 21st Century? If so, pull on your life jacket and let's begin the journey!

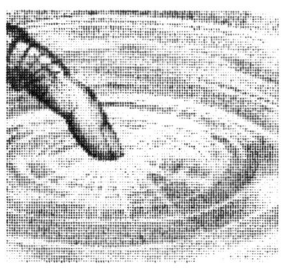

Chapter One:

Getting off the Bank

" *W*hen I was a child, I would sit on the bank of a stream on our farm, watching twigs and leaves meander merrily on their way. When I was a young mother, I would sit on the bank of the stream in back of our house watching my children wade in the creek, delighting in the ripples their tossed pebbles produced."

"What's that got to do with 21st Century Success?"

"Well, it's occurred to me midway through my life, that it's not easy to convince people to embrace the challenge of getting off the bank and participating in the river of life."

"The bank's a safer place. You can watch the action from there, and not have to risk falling overboard."

"This may be true, but don't you find that boring?"

"May be boring to you, but what do you expect in a world where the direction of the river keeps changing and you never know what's around the next bend?"

"That's part of the challenge of change. Change is a constant. And when change occurs, one of three things happens. We either inherit the change, or the change is forced upon us, or we create the change to stay competitive."

"The second one happened to me."

"Hey, what do you say you take a trip with me to explore what lies out there for us?"

"I know what lies out there for us. Uncertainty, unpredictability, all warranties, no guarantees, and no satisfaction."

"Depends on what you define as satisfaction."

"I'd like to know that I'm going to have a secure job with a secure income - one where if I give a company my expertise and loyalty, they'll reward me by periodically promoting me, giving me an increase in pay, with a decent benefit and retirement package, so when I want to go sailing down that river of life, the waters will be calm."

"The only place you see calm water for any length of time is in a pond. Ever sat on the bank of a pond where the water had stagnated for awhile?"

"What's your point?"

"My point is that wherever there's stagnation, there's stench. Unless the water keeps somehow moving and circulating, it's not vital and alive. Even the tadpoles would have problems flourishing."

"Well, I'll take calm, predictable, boring water any day over white water rapids that unexpectedly upend you, or hurricane gales with forty foot high waves that destroy everything in their path."

"Is that how you view the world you live in today?"

"Yep! As I said before, all warranties, no guarantees."

"How about coming on a journey with me?"

"Where to?"

"Down the river of life. Let's take a look at some places where the water is calm, and some places where it's not, and see if we can change your paradigms."

"Oh, yeah, that word. My uncle says he'd rather have four nickels."

TechnoTouch

"Well, I'm glad to see that your sense of humor hasn't left you. What do you say? How about letting me be your guide for a while? I'll even give you a lifejacket and hold out a lifeline until you tell me it's okay to let it go."

"What the heck. I haven't got anything better to do except watch life go by from up here on the bank. And the way the water's rising, it may not even be safe up here much longer!"

"Good point. Let's go. Here's your official guidebook. Help me put the vessel in the water and we'll venture forth."

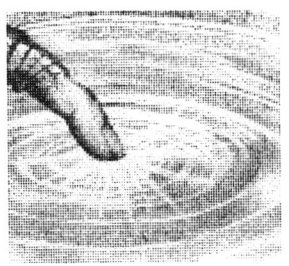

Chapter Two:

The Journey Begins

"Where are we going first?"

"Where would you like to go?"

"You're the one who convinced me to go on this journey with you. I was content sitting on the bank. So you tell me!"

"Fair enough. Let's head down stream until we come to a place that looks worth exploring."

"How will you determine that?"

"By the current."

"Why the current?"

"Well, as you know, a current is defined as a moving stream of water, air, or electricity."

"And..."

"Do you know the meaning of voltage?"

"What's this, a test?"

"Not really, but bear with me. Voltage is a unit of electrical force."

"So now we've got a moving stream of water and an electrical force. What's next - the thunderstorm?"

"Well, I'm sure that it may appear to some that the clouds are menacing... what's your definition of power?"

"That's an easy one! My boss on payday. My other half in life when they want things done their way. My children when they throw a tantrum in public."

"My, we are a bit cynical, aren't we?"

"You would be too if it happened to you. It's kind of like that song lyric that goes something like this - it's my life and I'll whine if I want to."

"Glad to see the sense of humor is still alive. Actually, power can be defined as a physical or mental strength, or energy."

"Okay, okay, I'm confused. What does this have to do with this journey designed to convince me it's better out here than safely on the bank?"

"Well, let's go measure it and find out."

"I suppose now you want to know if I know the meaning of measure?"

"You're learning quickly."

The Journey Begins

"I can remember my grandfather saying, measure twice and cut once. It seems to me that today's motto is measure once and cut twice!"

"A little realistic sarcasm there, but that's understandable. Actually, measure is a standard of determining quality by comparison."

"Oh, now we're into that famous, or infamous, word - quality. That's the movement that started this whole mess."

"Explain."

"We were doing fine until the so-called quality movement began. Then the downsizing, what the gurus cutely call rightsizing, began. That's when I wound up out of a job, struggling to survive."

"And choosing to just sit on the bank."

"What'd you expect?! Oh, let me guess. Plunge in, *change,* adapt, don't be like the dinosaur."

"What are the alternatives? Unless becoming extinct is part of your life's plan."

"Now who's getting cynical?"

"Touché... Let me ask you a question. When scientists wanted to get a spacecraft on the moon, what did they aim at?"

"Oh, this is a tough one! They aimed at the moon, naturally."

"That's what you might reasonably think, but they actually aimed the rocket for the spot where the moon would be by the time the rocket got there."

"What does this have to do with adapting?"

"The world we are navigating in today means figuring out where you think the moon will be and aiming for it. That means stretching our imaginations, our perceptions."

"Let's tune into Moon River while we're at it. Hey, how come we left the river?"

"We've come to the pond to take a look at how they run their businesses here."

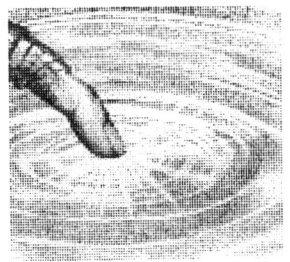

Chapter Three:

The Pond's Technology Facility

"What do you mean by a technology facility?"

"In one of the buildings, they design hardware and software. In another, they sell it, plus manufacture it. And in yet another building, they package it up for shipment to the customers."

"And who are the customers?"

"Almost everybody today. Office buildings, homes, schools, health care, utilities, hospitality, anyone who wants to travel the *technotouch byway*."

"Oh, so we've coined another phrase, have we?"

"Only if it fits. Leave your lifejacket on. It'll keep

TechnoTouch

you hidden from the view of others as we continue our adventure."

"First it was a journey. Now it's an adventure!"

"Well, actually that's what life is. An adventurous journey to destinations yet unknown."

"I can hardly wait!"

"Computers revolutionized the way we lived at the end of the 20th Century. Technology, the Internet, and the World Wide Web will do that for the 21st Century."

"Just what I needed, a revolution, and spiders."

"Well, some search engines on the Web do use spiders!"

"Hey, wait a minute - you're confusing me."

"I thought your eyes were beginning to glaze over. Not to worry. You'll start to understand."

"You mentioned a revolution. What are we going to do, dump some tea bags in the harbor?"

" No. A revolution can also mean a total change of conditions, and it can be for the better. Fiber will be in the home. Beepers, faxes, wireless telephones, mobile communication, televideo conferencing, will all be as commonplace as the computers are today".

"I've just begun to understand how to turn a computer on."

"Well, pretty soon you're going to see computers linked to printers, linked to the Internet, enabling you to do some pretty neat communicating."

The Pond's Technology Facility

"The only communicating I want to do is in person or by telephone."

"Well, you'll be able to talk on the phone via your computer. We'll see a swing to a digital network through the country and then globally."

"Hey, talk about a swing! I just noticed something. We've been on a calm waterway."

"That's because it's a pond. But remember what I told you about ponds as we observe what kind of life is growing here. Let's take the elevator up to the top floor."

"The Ivory Tower, right?"

"Sometimes."

"This looks familiar. Big office rooms, expensive furniture, lots of assistants, regional directors, and vp's. Where's the head honcho?"

"Way back in the corner room."

"Oh, the *really* big one - the one with the view."

"Now, why do you suppose that's where their office is?"

"So they can count their stock dividends and get their manicures and not have to be bothered with what the little people think."

"May appear so. Let's head down the hall to the Sales and Marketing department."

"Boy, is this stress valley or what? All these people, sitting at their desks, one hand glued to the telephone, the other hand reaching for the antacids."

"And why's that?"

"If they don't reach their quota, they're surplus, they're history."

"Let's head to engineering."

"This is an equally miserable looking bunch of people. They've got orders piled high and dry. Look at that, some of the target deadline dates are weeks old!"

"Why do you suppose that is?"

"Beats me. Where we heading now?"

"Let's drop in on the manufacturing department."

"There's not a smile on any of these people's faces, either. They look like robots in an assembly line. And it looks like they're behind schedule too."

"Our last stop here is the shipping department. What do you think?"

"Well, they look like they're as unhappy and behind as the other departments."

"Let's head out of the building and go across the pond to another place."

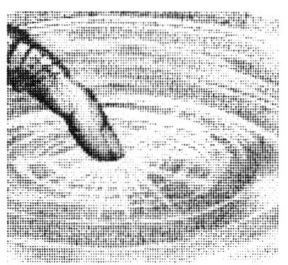

Chapter Four:

The Pond's Telecom Facility

"*I*nteresting. Looks a lot like the place we just left, only a lot more wires and cables."

"Very observant. Why do you suppose that is?"

"You tell me. It's your journey - excuse me, your adventure."

"Uh - oh, the cynicism's rearing its ugly head once again. This is the Utilities Facility. They're involved with such things as conductors, cables, and watts."

"Conductors and cables? Are we on a city by the bay or in a pond."

TechnoTouch

"Ah, ha! The humor returns. Okay, I'll plunge in and take a chance. What do you suppose we mean by conductors?"

"Easy. They're the ones that operate the cable cars!"

"Funny. What do we mean by conductors when referring to utilities?"

"I give up. What do we mean."

"A conductor is a substance that transmits heat and electricity."

"And a watt is what follows a who in the old Abbot and Costello routine."

"Very good! A watt can also be a unit of electrical activity or power."

"You know, even though this place is involved in a different business, the structure and layout of the building and the looks on people's faces are almost the same There's even some hanging out by the water cooler, appearing to be dogging it."

"Astute observation. Why do you suppose that is?"

"Why do you ask so many questions?"

"Because that's the only way I'm going to get any answers."

"Now you're beginning to sound like an old school teacher I had."

"Take a look at the cables they're using. Notice the thickness of them. These are actually standard

The Pond's Telecom Facility

copper cables, comprised of many pairs or wires, separated from one another."

"That's what my old boss did with all of us. Put us in cubicles where we seldom had time to communicate with one another."

"Now, that's a good analogy, except that if the wires in this copper cable did communicate, it would be what's termed 'cross talk', and you'd have mumbled, poor communication over the wires."

"What's the answer then?"

"Now who's asking the questions? ... Sorry... Maybe the answer lies partly in fiber optics."

"And now I'm supposed to know or ask what fiber optics are."

"That's part of the communication process, of importance to all leaders and team players. Sharing what we know, and asking to learn about what we don't know."

"Okay, I know that fiber optics are supposedly an essential part of the information superhighway, or waterway, as you call it. But I don't know how."

"Fiber optic is a receptacle through which light travels at a faster rate of speed, thus transmitting voice and video electronically."

"Why do we need light to travel faster?"

TechnoTouch

"With the advent of the microchip, information has been decentralized. Fax modems and online services, combined with cellular phones and the Internet, have made information instantly available anywhere."

"You mean we're on line most of the time?"

"That we are. Let's go down to the end of the pond and visit another facility where we can see what's going on with leadership and teamwork."

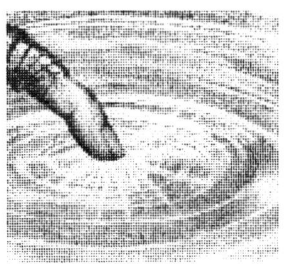

Chapter Five:

Management VS Leadership

"Notice any difference here?"

"Other than that it's quieter, and most people are wearing white uniforms, it still seems structured the same way. Why's that?"

"You've probably heard about the hierarchical structure."

"Yeah, but enlighten me, guide."

"The pyramid way of doing business dates back 2,000 years. It's actually based on a war leader's model."

"Sounds like the place where I worked!"

"The old hierarchical system functioned with power over. We didn't realize it, but we taught people to leave their brains at home, to come to work and mechanically produce with no joy and no passion, to make no decisions, to not think for themselves, to have to be told what to do."

"Like a bunch of robots."

"Actually, this system worked well for a number of years, especially for big businesses after WWII."

"Why's that."

"When we left the agricultural era, which we had been in for thousands of years, and entered the industrial era where things were produced in assembly line fashion, work was organized by management and directed by a supervisor. The job of employees was to do what they were told, no more and no less."

"That doesn't make much sense."

"Maybe it doesn't today, but the scientific management strategies of the 20th century sought to eliminate bottlenecks and inefficiencies in production by scrutinizing and timing every workers' every motion."

"Not much trust here."

"Exactly. What this created was a mindset of 'us' against 'them' that still exists today, a mindset that makes people resist change."

"And not want to come down off the bank."

Management VS Leadership

"Oftentimes. The old hierarchical system functioned with power over. What we can refer to as an *'IP* organizational pyramid."

"*'IP*? What does that stand for?"

"At the top of the pyramid were the *VIP's.*"

"Those who thought they were *very important people*, right?"

"They're the people who've traditionally been the leaders. They made most of the decisions and kept most of the information to themselves."

"Yeah, you sure didn't dare mess with the chain of command!"

"And in the middle we have the *FIP's*, meaning?"

"*Fairly important people?*"

"You catch on fast. These are the layers of management. And at the bottom we have the *SIP's.*"

"Let me guess. These must represent the *slightly important*, or *somewhat important people*."

"Not bad. They represent the lemmings, who blindly do what they are told, and march out to sea to their demise."

"Not a cool pyramid! What do you see in its place?"

"The *TechnoTouch Byway*, a fluid, easily navigable environment built around information systems, teams, and networks. One where communication flows freely, forward progress is continuous, and people look to their customers for feedback."

"Think we're going to get that overnight?"

"No, but forward looking companies who want to stay competitive know that this is the direction they need to go in. Remember, though, that it took us 2,000 years to develop the pyramid structure. It will take more than an occasional training session or a few weekend retreats to adapt to the new environment. Like anything else, it's an ongoing process."

"I never had much of anything in the way of training that made a difference."

"Perhaps you weren't offered it, or perhaps, if you were offered it, you resisted."

"Now what's resistance got to do with it?"

"Resistance is the degree of an opposing force, the extent to which a conductor impedes the flow of the current."

"So we're back to the current again, are we?"

"Kind of. And back to paradigms. As you can see in the labs here, there are a lot of people working on ways to save lives and cure diseases. Almost every scientific breakthrough was preceded by a shift in one's way of thinking, from Edison's belief that voice could travel over wire to Kennedy's belief that we could land a man on the moon."

"Makes sense."

"Good! What do you say we continue the adventure by heading down to the opposite end of the pond and checking out an Educational Facility?"

"Lead the way. Now you've got me intrigued!"

TechnoTouch

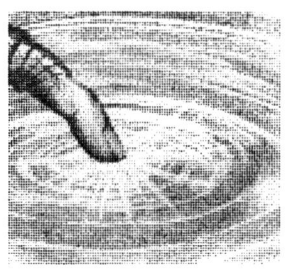

Chapter Six:

Education on the Pond

"*This* looks a lot like school did when I was there."

"How do you mean?"

"Teachers and principals laying down the rules, and students supposed to blindly obey them. Do as you're told, and don't question authority. Seems a bit like that 20th century scientific management principle you told me about earlier."

"Interesting comparison."

"I remember hearing an educator talk about something called 'in parentis loci' which means that while the child is in the school setting, the educational system is responsible for them - that the teachers and administrators are acting in place of the parents."

"While that is probably true, and maybe should be, what do you see as you look around?"

"The same thing I saw when I was in school. Some people looking interested, most looking bored and uninterested. Just waiting for the bell to ring."

"To go where?"

"Someplace that's fun."

"Can't learning be fun?"

"Now you're really going out on a limb here! That's not the main purpose of education."

"Maybe not the main purpose, but isn't it a major component?"

"Okay, interpret again, please."

"Keeping a sense of humor is critical to maintaining balance. As we go down the river of life, we encounter challenges and discover things that need improving. That usually requires personal change, and change sometimes may be perceived as doing things that aren't fun."

"Yeah, like some days you're the bug, and some days you're the windshield."

"Interesting way to look at it. What's important is to take our job seriously and ourselves lightly and not be afraid to risk."

Education on the Pond

"Do you really think people will risk what little security they have left?"

"As we head to the new millennium, leadership is unchartered terrain, full of risk taking, adventure, and discovery. We have to be continuously changing and improving our game. What's your favorite hobby or past-time?"

"Sitting on the bank."

"Come on, don't let me down now. What do you really enjoy doing with your spare time?"

"Well, I like to golf in the summer and ski in the winter."

"Is your golf swing good enough?"

"Of course not."

"Are you trying to improve your golf game?"

"Well sure, who isn't?"

"How do you do it?"

"I don't know. Practice. Watch the pros. What are you driving at? No pun intended!"

"Do you enjoy practicing and watching the pros?"

"Yeah."

"Then I rest my case. Learning can be fun when you empower yourself."

"Oh, here we go! I knew that buzz word would show up sooner or later."

"While we're observing what's going on here, why don't you tell me what empowerment means to you?"

"Glad to. It means if we had three people doing the job, and two get the pink slip, then that one lucky son of a gun has to empower themselves to do the work of three! Without getting paid any more, I might add. And they should feel fortunate they've still got a job so don't complain."

"What's that do to your energy?"

"What little energy I had left was spent just trying to keep my head above water and survive, and even then I wound up being tossed out of the boat when they decided the craft was still too overloaded."

"And that's when you headed for the bank."

"Yep. Who wouldn't?"

"Truly empowered people wouldn't."

"You're going to have to go some to get me to buy into this one!"

"Time to leave the pond."

"Yeah, the stench is starting to get to me."

Chapter Seven:

Heading Down the River

"By the way, do you think that any of what we saw today is applicable in the homes of these people living along the riverbank?"

"What do you mean?"

"Power over, control, pyramid structure."

"Sure. When I was growing up, all I ever heard was such things as 'you'll do what I say as long as you're living under my roof'!"

"Why do you suppose that's so?"

"Probably because of another saying I heard a lot, 'as long as I'm paying the bills, you'll do as I say.'"

"What do you think of those sayings?"

"Are you kidding? People don't want to be told what to do. That's treating them like children, who have no mind of their own. People want to be respected."

"Don't you think most parents want that also, for both themselves and their children."

"I'm sure they do."

"And don't you think most employers want that for their employees?"

"Probably. Then what's the rub?"

"Every organization, every family, goes through similar phases of changes and growth, or lack of. The first one is formation. That's the beginning, when we develop a better product or service. It's the honeymoon stage where energy is high and communication is intense and frequent. Everybody's doing what needs to be done, adapting and flexible."

"Like getting used to the other person leaving the toilet seat up."

"Kind of. By the way, approximately 1 out of 100 companies actually outlast this phase. The next phase is expansion, consisting of marked growth, with systems and procedures in place, and financial success achieved."

"Oh, they buy a house with two bathrooms, right?"

Heading Down the River

"Clever. Problem comes when rigid policies and assembly line thinking set in, and people become attached to yesterday's solutions. When you're the only one who has what the market wants, then anything works. In today's intensely competitive world, that's no longer true for any of us."

"So what's the solution?"

"Every growth cycle has a peak. This phase is *peaksion*. This is the phase where many companies decline."

"Because if you do what you've always done, you'll get what you've always got?"

"That's it. And we see their obituaries everyday in the media. But we can plan ahead, catch the next wave, move into a new expansion cycle, revitalize, and make strong again."

"How do we do that?"

"By returning to the same spirit we had in the formation phase, when we were excited and challenged."

"A second honeymoon?"

"Or we give people the tools to become Super Conductors."

"Has that got any connection with the Super Bowl?"

"Well, not directly, but that raises an interesting point."

"Which is?"

"Who gets into the Super Bowl?"

"The best two teams."

"Ah ha!"

"Oh, I am so glad to see that my brilliance overwhelms you."

"You said teams. You didn't say individuals."

"Right. Meaning?"

"Meaning that it really isn't individuals who accomplish great things with their lives. It's the contribution each person makes to the team's end goal. So they've first got to come up with the goal, right?"

"Right."

"And who determines what that goal is?"

"It would be nice if it was the team, but usually it's the boss."

"Let's look again at the analogy of the Super Bowl team. Who sets the goal here?"

"Well, probably the team and the coach."

"And maybe also the stakeholders?"

"Meaning the fans?"

"Not only the fans, and the suppliers, who are the essential external customers, but anyone who has an investment in the successful achievement of the goal,

Heading Down the River

including the coach, the owner, and the players - all those people who are the internal customers."

"That makes sense."

"You're with me. Good. We're heading into the open water now. Hold on!"

TechnoTouch

Chapter Eight:

Out Into Open Water

"Notice anything different?"

"Yeah, it's choppier."

"You're impossible, but I'm not giving up on you yet! How about the environment?"

"Well, now that you mention it, the air does smell fresh and clean. The water is clearer. It's more lush and beautiful."

"There's hope for you yet!"

"Don't push your luck! I'm not sure I want to stay out here."

"Why not?"

TechnoTouch

"If the wind whips up, or a tropical storm heads our way, we could be overboard in a second."

"But remember, I told you at the beginning of our journey that I'd let you keep the lifejacket on, and I'd extend the lifeline to you as long as you needed it."

"Okay, I'll hang on for a while longer."

"Good. What we're going to do now is to tour the same type of facilities out here in the open sea as we did back on the pond. They'll all be doing essentially the same things. Let's see if you notice any differences."

"Am I getting graded, teach?"

"Remember, I'm only acting as your coach. You'll teach yourself. 21st Century leaders understand the importance of *VPAC*."

"Is this the victory pak that'll help us win the Super Bowl?"

"The Super Bowl of your choice, yes."

"Okay, explain."

"The V stands for *Vision*. You can think of it as an active matrix travel video, a picture of the highest level of performance possible in each area of your business, the ideal picture of what the company could be if it fulfilled its potential and the human potential of all its people. Visions are flexible, able to adapt to changing ideas, new technology, and circumstances."

"What makes you think this would work?"

"It will work if it's a vision that inspires and motivates, capturing the imagination and creating a sense of ownership, commitment, and energy among the people involved, thereby increasing performance and productivity."

"Why would people want to commit to this?"

"Most people want to commit to something they're proud to be a part of, something they believe is worth going for. Vision is a deep voyage into the heart and soul of an organization, unlocking people's self-directed energy, drawing them into using their own talents and initiative."

"Well, this visioning thing is nothing new. Successful athletes worldwide have discovered the value of mentally rehearsing a performance before the actual competition."

"Exactly. Visioning focuses on the end state, not the means of getting there. Then we must come up with a plan."

"The map for the journey?"

"Yes. The plan spells out the details of who, what, when, where, how."

"Oh, we're back to goals now, are we?"

"In a way. It's essential that the plan be written so everyone can be in agreement as to the why. To be successful, the plan must include a specific statement of the team's goals when realized. Then we move to the *Action* step. Unless we start taking action, the vision will remain just that, a dream, but not a reality."

"Kind of like Moby Dick."

"Which brings us to *Continuity*."

"Of course. That's logical!"

"Once we're in the Action stage, we should start all over again with the vision stage, so that the process is on-going."

"A little dizzying, isn't it?"

"To some, but necessary if we're going to stay competitive and keep moving forward."

"Okay, break out the sea-sickness patch!"

"This is a good time to finish our Super Bowl analogy. Are we in agreement that it's a shared goal, that they're all focused on making the same goal a reality?"

"Yep."

"If teams are going to stay focused, they need a model to follow, a guide in this tumultuous journey. They begin with Expectations. And these are the expectations of anyone who has a stake in the outcome. In the facilities we've toured, this could include such things as high quality, schedules met, cost performance. And the expectation for the Super Bowl would be?"

"Earning the title, and getting to wear those rings."

"You've got it. With clear expectations, teams can then write their Mission, a statement describing each team members unique contribution to the objective. In the case of the facilities we're going to visit now, it could be a number of teams' unique contributions. But in each case, this statement describes the product or service and is endorsed by the entire team. You still with me?"

"So far."

"Then the team comes up with a Vision, a target, where the team wants to be at some future time. Concrete measurements are then developed and used to record the team's progress. The measurements not only reflect results, they show where improvements are still needed. In the case of the Super Bowl team, it could be yards run, passes completed, touchdowns made."

"Okay, I'm with you there. How do you measure that in all the facilities we're visiting?"

"How has productivity, quality, or customer service really been enhanced."

"How do you determine that?"

"By surveys, feedback, various means of tracking the results of whatever the team established as their expectations. Then an Action Plan must be designed that will address who, what, and when, specifying people who will take specific actions. This means hitting the bull's-eye, accomplishing those goals the team is trying to achieve. This is a Continuous Process which begins all over again the next season. Let's stop at one of these facilities and see it in action."

Chapter Nine:

Companies on the Open Seas

"Keep in mind that the waves that have washed over the marketplace in the last 20 years are common to all: global competition as well as competition from smaller companies located within that same country, wave after wave of new information, technology creating thousands of new products and services, transforming the way we live and the way we work."

"And creating enough stress and anxiety to make people say bye-bye to the rapids and head for the calm bank, or be forced there."

"Yes, it has created stress in the form of pressure to match competitors' prices, quality, higher levels of service convenience, friendliness and speed. Everyone has been forced to introduce new products or services fast enough to match the competition while installing new production and information systems. To innovate successfully is to learn how to do things better, cheaper, and faster. For some, it was too much and their companies struggled or were bought out."

"And you call that progress?"

"It's all a part of the journey."

"A journey that's not so pleasant for some of us."

"It depends on your perspective."

"Which probably puts us back to paradigm shifting again, huh?"

"In a way. Most companies did just that and started looking for new methods and new techniques to help them run their company better. Seminars and training brought new ideas which provoked action. People on management teams began to acquire the leadership skills in their areas of expertise necessary to help their companies strive to become first in their industry."

"Boy, I wouldn't sit on an upper management team and tell them what to do!"

"It's not so much telling them what to do, as it is helping them to embrace a different perspective and find answers to - for instance - how they can manage the new technology available to them."

"So how did they do this?"

"Teams were designed to break down barriers. Managers started getting out of their offices, walking around and asking questions of their customers.

"Nobody's asked me yet."

"Until now. Remember, employee involvement is one of the components essential for successful navigating."

"Okay, okay. But I can tell you that I never had any real power to influence or control my workday life."

"And that's probably part of the reason why you didn't 'buy in', why you didn't commit to the organization's goals. Employee empowerment really means that employees - at all levels in the company - commit their best efforts, rather than simply putting in time."

"Well, don't most people live by the motto, 'what's in it for me'?"

"It appears as though that's the wave length most people are tuned into, yes. That's why we now see organizations adding authority, accountability, and flexibility to the responsibilities of the workplace.

They find that this increases productivity and profitability, and the resulting surge of positive energy translates directly to the bottom line."

"So all they really care about is the bottom line."

"Not really, although for any business to remain in business, they must eventually be showing a profit. Remember all those stakeholders. For example, if the goal is to win the Super Bowl, they've got to discover how to get everyone not only empowering themselves to give their best, but also pulling together as a team for that common goal."

"Not every team can win the Super Bowl."

"True, and that may not be the goal of every team. But if you're in the NFL, it probably is. The point is that finding one's work spirit lies at the foundation of the empowerment process."

"Oh, now we're into spirit. Gone religious on me, have you?"

"Spirituality and religion may seem alike but they're really two different things. "

"How so?"

"Spirituality has to do with meaning and purpose in life, why we're all here."

"What's it all about Alfie stuff?"

"Kind of. More and more people are searching for their reason for being, trying to find out what their unique gifts and talents are and then

Companies on the Open Seas

integrating that into not only their work place but also into their entire life experience."

"I don't recall that being a top priority when I was ushered out the door."

"I understand. But realize also that life isn't always fair. But it is..."

"I know, I know - an adventurous journey where the surf's always up."

"What may seem like part of that unfairness is actually a realistic, essential move. There is no alternative to radical change. Competition is so intense, customers quality demands are so stringent, and product development is so fast that a traditional hierarchical organization simply can't keep track of it all."

"When's it all end?"

"It probably won't. Being an innovative, high quality, low cost manufacturer of goods or services is not a one shot effort. Anybody who's still running a business on the hierarchical model in the 21st century isn't going to be in business."

"What's the payoff of all this radical change, this chaos?"

"Let's go visit some places where it's working and see for ourselves."

TechnoTouch

Chapter Ten:

Mapping the Mission

"How do you live with constant and rapid change?"

"By having a changeless core inside of you."

"Is that similar to an apple core? And wouldn't that cause heartburn?"

"Your humor is apt. What is necessary is to have a sense of who you are, what you are about, and what you value."

"How do we find that?"

"By writing our personal mission statements."

"I thought that was just for companies?"

"Used to be, but that has also changed. We cannot separate our job from self. Once we have our own personal sense of mission, know what we want to contribute and achieve, we have the vision and values that will help direct our lives."

"Kind of like our own map of the waterway?"

"Exactly. Once we've mapped out our travels, we can then make the decisions concerning the most effective use of our time, talents, and energy. If our center doesn't empower us, then it's depowering us."

"Where do we start?"

"By looking at our various centers, such as family, friends, work, financial, recreational, social, community, educational, religious or spiritual, as well as our self center, and determining where we need to create more harmony."

"Any guidelines, oh worthy guide, for this personal mission statement?"

"A few. It should include a purpose that will never fully be accomplished, one that may change. It should also be one that, when we look back on life, has made a positive difference in the lives of others. And it should be one we feel passionate about, one that inspires and uplifts us. Something we think about and strive for on a daily basis."

"A sort of burning in the belly?"

"That'll do. It should be written out, in a short, simple, memorable phrase. Then you keep it near

Mapping the Mission

you at all times, referring to it often - at least daily - until it becomes a part of all that you do."

"You said it may change?"

"Yes, as everything else does and will. It's a process and you'll want to review it regularly and make minor changes as you gain more insight or circumstances change. When you can relate everything you do to your mission statement, you no longer are at the mercy of the waterfalls of change."

"How do you deal with the stress and anxiety all these waves of change are causing?"

"By controlling the controllables, negotiating the negotiables, and dropping the bananas."

"So we've gone from waves to monkeys in one fell swoop."

"Whenever events happen in our lives that stress us, it helps to ask ourselves three quick questions."

"Which are?"

"First question, 'is this a life or death situation'? We could probably answer 'no' to 98% of the stressful events we face each day. Now obviously, if the answer is 'yes', then we need to do something about it. The second question, 'will it make a difference in five years'? Again, most times, the answer will be 'no'. In fact, most things we allow to drain our energy we won't even remember next week, let alone in five years."

"That makes sense."

"The third question is, 'how much control do we have over the situation'? If we have very little control, but we give it a great deal of time and energy, we're trying to sail through the harbor when the water's frozen solid. We can then determine how much time and energy we wish to devote to those things over which we have control."

"What do bananas have to do with it?"

"They catch monkeys in India by putting a cage with a banana in it near the edge of the jungle. The monkey reaches into the cage to get the banana. They don't have the human skills to realize they need to turn their paw sideways in order to bring the banana out, and they don't want to let it go."

"I know humans who don't have those skills."

"The point is, the net drops down, and the monkey gets caught while he or she is free."

"So much for banana lovers, huh?"

"What this means is that we have to let go of those things over which we have no control. The key, again, is to control the controllables, negotiate the negotiables, and drop the bananas."

"Sure beats slipping on peels, doesn't it?"

"And enables us to spend our energy on things and people worthy of it. Let's go check it out."

Chapter Eleven:

TechnoTouch Begins

"Boy, these places sure aren't as quiet as the ones on the pond."

"Why do you think that's so?"

"I'm not sure."

"When we're out on the open seas, navigating for 21st century success, we don't have much control over our environment. And when we don't have control, things tend to seem more chaotic, noisier. So what's the solution?"

"Ear plugs?"

"The real secret of effectiveness is to concentrate on inner control. Managing self is the only place we have any real control anyway. Instead of reacting to the danger, we can concentrate on grasping the creative opportunity that is offered."

"As the 20th Century comes to a close, companies large and small must come to terms with the most powerful and far-reaching changes in 200 years. Management struggles to adapt, but tangled bureaucracies smother vision, growth, and change. Even our most successful companies are fighting to survive. Yet with this change comes extraordinary opportunity. To steer our companies into the 21st Century, we need a new way of thinking about a new world."

"That's what happens when we chart these new seas?"

"The Chinese symbol for change is actually made up of two words, danger and opportunity. This translates into the saying, 'crisis is opportunity riding the dangerous wind'."

"I still don't understand how all these changes can be called opportunities."

"We can either say we're in trouble at the present time, or we can say we can take advantage of this situation and immediately act. We can say we're going to be in trouble, or we can say in the

TechnoTouch Begins

future we could be in a position to profit from what's going to happen."

"Now we're back into the paradigms, I take it."

"In a sense. We've got to be constantly reframing, changing the way we see our markets, our businesses, our internal customers, our external customers. In order to do that, we must be able to relate our daily actions to an over-arching purpose to which we're committed. Without this, we lack the constant feedback and communication that allows us to stay the course, and thrive in the midst of whitewater."

"What does purpose have to do with whitewater?"

"You can compare purpose to the mental line a kayaker draws in the rapids. You see, purpose is different than goal or destination. What do you suppose the kayaker's purpose is?"

"To get there safely!"

"Not just to get there, but to experience the challenge and the excitement of the journey."

"I'm more interested in surviving. What's wrong with that?"

"Nothing, as long as it's combined with a purpose, one that is constantly growing and evolving. Without a purpose, we're only coping, making it through. With purpose, we have meaning and significance for the quality of the journey."

"So we're back to quality, are we?"

"Quality is about personal mastery, a lifelong journey of learning, changing, evolving, and getting better at everything we do. Purpose, and new action, flow from inward change. We have to have faith that when our purpose is right, we'll be able to do our best to overcome the odds, and the rest will somehow be taken care of."

"Easy for you to say."

"It's not as difficult as it may seem, if we're able to let go of outer control and power over, be willing to remain flexible and take risks."

"And who do you think is going to take a risk in an uncertain world?"

"Again, what's the alternative - sitting on the bank? Letting life pass you by? Or participating in the journey. "

"Management says they want us to participate, but do they really?"

"Remember when we talked earlier about moving from thousands of years of an agricultural era, where events were relatively predictable, to an industrial era where machines and robot like action were the norm ?"

"Yes."

TechnoTouch Begins

"We moved next into an Information era. We're now in an Information-Plus era, where the knowledge base is doubling at a fantastic rate. We've got to have a way to manage this information, plus manage our lives and our workplaces, efficiently and effectively."

"And how do you propose we do that?"

"By something I call *TechnoTouch*."

"You mean that with all this new technology, there won't be any need to reach out and touch anybody."

"No, quite the contrary. All this new technology is merely a wonderful tool to enable us to store and retrieve information and communicate in a quicker, better manner. Let's walk through and I think you'll see how this is becoming a reality."

TechnoTouch

Chapter Twelve:

Different Ships, Same Boats

"Let's begin in this information technology facility."

"This is definitely different."

"In what way?"

"There's only one level. There's no offices with closed doors. People appear to be working in small groups where everyone actually looks enthused and interested in what they're doing!"

"Notice the sayings decorating the walls."

"Yeah. One says, *You tell us how it's supposed to be done.* Another says, *What are you doing to help the team today?* Still another says, *What are you held accountable for?* And assorted others say things like, *What information do you need?* and *What information do you owe the rest of us?* What's all this? More administrative flavor of the month?"

"Take a look at the signatures on them."

"*TechnoTouch 1, TechnoTouch 2, TechnoTouch 3.* What does that stand for?"

"The names of the teams. Look at this sign. *You're a full participant in decisions as to what the basic policy of the company should be.*"

"Well, I've got to admit it's certainly a different approach than I was used to. I'm not sure it'll work everywhere, though."

"It won't work back on the pond. It'll only work in a constantly changing environment like the open sea."

"Why? Because it's easier to get rid of the bodies out there?"

"I understand your cynicism. Whenever we move from our present state to our desired state, we have to go through a transition state. This is a period of high insecurity and ambiguity, where people are unfrozen from their current ways of thinking and doing things and are drawn into a new frame of reference."

"Hold it. Who said we wanted to go through this transition state in the first place?"

Different Ships, Same Boats

"It isn't a case of wanting to, as much as a case of having to."

"Now you're beginning to sound like a parent."

"Sorry about that. Bear with me. Why, then, would a person or an organization depart from the present state for a transition state of insecurity?"

"Beats me!"

"Because the pain of maintaining the status quo is too great."

"Says who?"

"Have you ever broken a bad habit?"

"Yeah, one or two."

"Why did you break it?"

"Didn't really have much choice."

"Didn't you, though? Every day is a series of choices, some good for us, others not so good. When we choose to change something about ourselves, we usually do it because the pain of going through the change far outweighs the temporary pleasure of staying where we are."

"I'm not sure I'm buying into that one."

"The process of change is painful, but staying stagnant will prove to be even more painful. Those companies who are choosing to go through the painful transition period are growing and prospering. Those who chose not to begin the change when it first became apparent it was necessary are taking longer to prosper. And those who aren't making the transition are doomed to even more pain and may not survive."

"You mean they'll jump ship?"

"We didn't all come over on the same ship, but we're all in the same boat today. Predictability and security as we've known it are gone. The workplace is changing, with technology exploding, and mergers and acquisitions commonplace. The workforce is changing, with women and immigrants entering the workforce in increasing numbers."

"That's part of the reason I was on the bank. Good old quota concept!"

"I understand your frustration. But we need to utilize the talents of everyone, no matter what their culture, no matter what their gender."

"Even if that means putting some of us out on the bank?"

"As we continue to move into *TechnoTouch*, and the open sea concept, people will stay as members of a team only as long as they are contributing to the team's effort."

"Otherwise they'll be benched?"

"Probably. They'll also be paid for performance, and rewarded with a share of the profits. And, of course, be paid by internal satisfaction."

"What makes you think this will work?"

Different Ships, Same Boats

"It won't work unless four crucial components are involved. First, people at all levels have to be able to make decisions. Second, people need the information necessary to make intelligent decisions. Third, people at all levels need training to gain the skills necessary. And fourth, people need to have a stake in the outcome of their decisions."

"What are they going to do, give everybody who buys into this change Super Bowl rings?"

"If that's what their goal is, and they earn it. Many of these facilities we're touring right now have created a feeling of ownership."

"Yeah, right! I never felt I owned a piece of the rock where I worked!"

"That's all changing, also. Most facilities and companies are creating this feeling of ownership by some form of bonus or profit sharing."

"Hey, I just noticed something else."

"What's that?"

"It appears as though we've entered a facility that's operating the way you've been describing."

"You're right, we have. Let's check it out, shall we?"

"Yeah, I'm ready!"

TechnoTouch

Chapter Thirteen:

Operating Systems & Control

"Everywhere you look, people actually appear to be enjoying what they're doing!"

"Kind of like improving their golf game?"

"Oh, another reference to joy in the workplace, I suppose."

"You could say that. Remember that we learned earlier that the task of 20th century companies was to organize work so it could be carried out by wage labor, by pairs of hands that could be replaced at a moment's notice. The changing marketplace has made that approach obsolete."

"Okay, I can buy into that even though I may not like it."

"A 21st century company's task will be to organize work so it can be carried out by men and women who can take responsibility and who share in the risks and rewards of enterprise."

"And you think that's going to be easy to do?"

"Nobody said it was going to be easy. Let me ask you a question."

"Go ahead."

"Have you ever washed a rental car?"

"Are you crazy? Why should I wash somebody else's car?"

"My point exactly. We only take pride in those things we feel a sense of ownership about. We create that ownership by employee and team involvement."

"And what makes you think people are going to fully commit and get involved in the first place?"

"Everybody has certain identifiable driving forces that shape their work and their life. When we know what these are, and we gain as much control over them as possible, then we live a more empowered, fulfilled life. One of the keys to doing that is do find out where the real power lies."

"Let me guess. With the person who has the fastest horsepower or the biggest hard drive?"

"Sense of humor again, huh? Let me ask you a question. At work, we listen, we talk, we think, and

Operating Systems & Control

we do. Of those four, where does the real power lie?"

"For me, it used to be listen and do, in school, at home, and then at work."

"That's *pond power*. The real power, the real levers of change, lie in our thinking. Our creativity, our passion, our satisfaction, our fulfillment, all of these are determined by our thinking. We each have within us all we'll ever need to become all we want to become. Whether we're open to owning and accessing that power depends on how willing we are to think about our thinking."

"How do you think about your thinking?"

"By thinking about your being, and the vehicle it's traveling on."

"Now you've really lost me."

"Okay, let me try to explain. On a computer, data moves on hardware called a bus. You can think of it as an electronic highway. The operating system is the vehicle, the basic software that controls computers."

"This is too complicated for me."

"Let me try once more to simplify it. The operating system controls all the input and the output by telling the hardware what to do."

"Now that sounds like my old boss!"

"However, you can control the output by controlling what you input, and by the various applications you choose to load on your hard drive."

"What's that got to do with it?"

"Once again, it depends on what your goal is. If your goal is to use a computer just to type, then the only application you'll need is a word processor. But if your goal is to present a computer-driven full-blown multimedia presentation, you're going to require a system that will give you the power to multi-task, allowing you to import and export text, sound, animation, even video. A very useful tool indeed for education facilities. And remember, we said earlier that training was one of the four crucial components."

"Why would I need all of that?"

"We know that most of our people do not have the skills and the knowledge they need to be productive in the 21st century. We also know that people process information differently. Some do so visually, they've got it when they see it. Some process it through their auditory senses, they've got it when they hear it. And still others are kinesthetic, they've got to touch it and feel it."

"You're talking about senses."

"Right! And the more senses we appeal to, the easier it is for people to process the information they need to understand what it is we're asking them to do."

"I think I'm into system overload."

"Let's sit down over here and see if we can find more space on your hard drive!"

TechnoTouch

Chapter Fourteen:

The Being as Programmer

"You comfortable?"
"Yeah. A bit confused still."
"Ready to continue our journey?"
"Why not."
"That's the spirit! Thousands of companies are struggling to reduce their workforce, boost productivity and improve quality. But changing a corporate culture will never work unless managers learn to trust others on the management team, along

with the workers, and empower everyone to be able to make decisions."

"That wasn't the case where I was."

"Workers must prove that they are trustworthy, can take the initiative, and won't abuse the power, authority, and responsibilities awarded to them. Everyone must learn to cooperate, to think win-win, to understand one another."

"That's like expecting a dried up sponge to come back to life."

"If it's watered properly, it could. Let's look at it this way. Our brain is like a computer, the hardware, with our mind the software, and our being the programmer."

"That's a cool way of thinking of it!"

"Or we could look at it another way. Our brain is a TV set, with our mind the TV program, and our being the writer, director, and producer."

"Kind of what you put in is what comes out?"

"Exactly! Great student!"

"Well, you're a pretty decent guide."

"Thank you... Remember as children how open our minds were? We eagerly absorbed everything that came our way."

"Yeah, until somebody told us we weren't supposed to color outside the lines."

"Exactly. And after years of being bombarded by other's criticism, negativity, and doubt, we

The Being as Programmer

developed ways to protect ourselves. Our being shut down, and when it did, it separated us from our own creative power."

"That's called survival."

"Maybe. But surviving isn't going to cut it in the 21st century. We've also got to thrive."

"Makes sense."

"We may temporarily lease our bodies and our minds to our company but when we lease our being we're going to run out of energy."

"So what's the answer?"

"The key to shaping our work and our lives in the ways we want them to go is knowing how to excel, not how to just merely survive. To do that, we have to examine our needs, and our desires, and then look at what the fears are that are preventing us from getting what we desire."

"How does this tie in to thinking?"

"We can start by looking back at our lives and examining why we made the choices we did. What was our thinking that caused us to make the decisions we made. When we understand why we made those choices and take responsibility for them, then we can let go of them."

"Why do we have to let go of them?"

"Because it's only by letting go of the old that we can make new, better choices."

"Is that what you call empowerment?"

"Yes, it is. When we declare what we want to create for ourselves, we set a powerful new electromagnetic energy field in motion that opens up new possibilities. We can then get in touch with our vision, our passion, our purpose, and take action."

"That makes sense."

"I'm glad. When you think back to the facilities in the pond, the rigid hierarchical way of organizing work and thinking have limited the ability of people and organizations to behave in natural ways. The transition is painful, leaving the calmness and predictability of the pond, but the results promise to be worth the pain."

"In what ways?"

"The workplace will be healthier, saner, more creative, and even more chaotic, just as the forces of nature are. Businesses will benefit from a vastly more responsible workforce. Those in the force will get more respect, and their work will become more meaningful."

"How?"

"By being involved, by thinking, by contributing their ideas, which are eagerly sought out. And anyone who wants to survive the sea change needs to start preparing to leave the stagnation now. And

The Being as Programmer

one of the most important trends futurists see is a new determination of people who state, 'I'm in charge of my life.'"

"What do they have to commit to?"

"A lifetime of learning, including exploring new job possibilities, taking an inventory of their skills, adding to them every single year. Committing also to being flexible people who can ride the waves successfully, moving easily from one function to another."

"How do we learn how to do that?"

"By acquiring the tools to work well in teams, the so-called soft skills, which are actually essential people skills."

"So it's back to school, huh?"

"School's never out for the learner. And if we're not a learning organization, we're a drowning organization."

"So how do we acquire this learning?"

"21st century success will be achieved by companies who invest in their people, training them in new skills, giving them the tools to manage the change. 21st century success will also be achieved by people who, in exchange for these tools, give their companies 150% of their talents and commitment... If you're rested enough, let's continue our journey

TechnoTouch

by going in and out of various other facilities on the open sea."

Chapter Fifteen:

A Spirit Full of Energy

"It appears to me that no matter what kind of a facility we're in, be it telecommunications, utilities, healthcare, education, various corporations, and associations, they've all changed."

"In what way?"

"Well, it seems that the traditional roles, those of boss, supervisors, even managers, are gone, and employees have more responsibility than maybe they want. Even the role of CEO's seems to be changed. And now there's MIS's and CIO's?"

"CEO's have to share information, and someone has to advise the company on the role technology systems play in accessing current and new information. The process of change is usually not comfortable. Sometimes it's even painful."

"Sounds like a bunch of masochists to me."

"Not when you consider that staying as one is is even more painful."

"Clue me in on that! I rather like my comfort zone!"

"Most people do. But that wound you up on the bank, didn't it?"

"Not a bad place to be."

"True, if it's the time in life when you choose to be there, and you have the means to be able to enjoy it."

"You've got a point there."

"Remember, people are willing to depart from their present state for a painful temporary transition state when the pain of maintaining the status quo is too great."

"When the pond's drying up?"

"Exactly. It's when the change related pain is either current or anticipated. You see, current pain is the level of discomfort a person experiences when their goals are not being met. Anticipated pain is the pain felt when their goals are not expected to be

A Spirit Full of Energy

met, due to the status quo."

"So when do they accept the change?"

"Only when it is proven to those affected that the present way of doing things is more painful than the pain that accompanies transition."

"Buy-in's required, huh?"

"Yes, buy-in of acceptance of the change needed as well as the funds necessary to make the changes a reality."

"Money too, huh?"

"You can look at it that way, or you can look at it as a necessary investment in the future of the company."

"Good point."

"It's important to realize that people don't resist change as much as they resist not being involved in the change. These facilities and businesses we're seeing who have chosen to go through the painful transition are growing and prospering, even though the seas are unpredictable. Those who aren't are doomed to even more pain and may not survive."

"Like those back on the stagnant pond, huh?"

"You never cease to amaze me. What else do you notice different in these facilities?"

"The people out here seem to really love their work, and take pride and joy in doing their jobs in a truly excellent manner."

"They do. As you can see, these work places have a work spirit full of energy, positiveness, purpose, vision, an open state of mind, a full sense of self, where they're living in the moment, fully participating in the product or service, displaying a sense of oneness in the outcome."

"I never would have thought this concept possible."

"Why"

"It seemed to me to be too utopian."

"Does it look like it's working?"

"Yeah, I've got to admit that it does. People appear to be genuinely happy, and it looks like, from the charts and stuff on the walls, that they're more accountable and productive."

"Most people are when the work place itself is a more enjoyable place to come to each day. When people align their personal interest with their work, choosing to work for a particular company, they become a valuable productive resource."

"I always felt like just a cog in the paddle wheel."

"Most people did under the *pond system*. Out here they set their own mini goals, doing tasks they've never done before. They're connecting to their work, which is a natural way for all of us to express who we are."

A Spirit Full of Energy

"So it's the responsibilities of the *open sea facilities* to give us job satisfaction."

"It's their responsibility to create the kind of environment where that will happen, yes, but each of us must take responsibility for our own job satisfaction. It's not the company's or the boss's job to make us happy and fulfilled - it's our own job."

"Does this mean that we're going to be guaranteed a job?"

"No. But it does mean that managers will be sharing more power with their people. Companies will continue to invest in their employees, thus offering their workers increased employability in return for hard work and commitment."

"Explain that one."

"The only tie that will bind employees and employers will be a common commitment to success and growth. While companies can't guarantee permanent jobs, they will give their employees opportunities to develop talents that will serve them whether they stay with that company or move on."

"I must admit it sure beats what we had, when it comes to enjoying what you're doing, but I'm still not a convert to a work place that offers no security."

"Let's take a short voyage out to a nearby island and discuss it. Ready?"

"Why not. I've come this far on the journey with you."

"That's the spirit."

"Next thing you know, we'll be seeing ghost busters!"

Chapter Sixteen:

Waves and Sea Walls

"How are you going to get people past the fear, resistance, and cynicism?"

"By involving them in the process. People don't argue with their own statistics. This means we need to involve people at all levels. Those at the bottom of the current hierarchical structures will be blocked from being empowered and involved, if those at the top still have organizational obstacles in the way."

"Kind of like a wave dashing against a sea wall."

"Great analogy. And any gains will leak away unless employees not only had a hand in creating it, they also are compensated fairly and trained well. Changing the culture is difficult but essential. The goal is to create an entire environment where people feel good about themselves, where everyone has something to contribute because they have significant life experiences, where everyone is constantly updating their skills. Self-directed work teams will be the norm."

"What's the rationale behind self-directed work teams?"

"For starters, managers can no longer handle the responsibilities that rapidly changing technology and complex organizational problems create. And workers are no longer satisfied with blindly taking orders and using only a fraction of their abilities."

"So they let us test the water, huh?"

"Not in true SDWT's. These teams are responsible, within guidelines, for managing work processes to achieve results. Team members continually identify and solve problems. They select the best solution, implement it, and monitor the results. Managers have little to do with the day to day activities of the team. People closest to the action have the authority to make decisions based on a shared understanding of the company mission.

They learn to ask questions rather than assume the answers."

"And you're telling me that turns people on? It seems to me as though it would increase fear and anxiety."

"It is the anticipation of these changing roles that makes people fearful. Workers are worried that they will have to assume more responsibility and will be punished for mistakes. Managers fear they will become unnecessary to the company and lose their jobs."

"Well, isn't that what's happening?"

"Letting go of some of the obvious levels of power and delegating responsibilities is seldom easy. The problem here is one of lack of understanding about SDWT's. Adults learn through experience, not conceptually. If people haven't experienced teams, they don't understand them or have the tools to work well within one."

"Such as?"

"Communication, problem solving, knowing how to manage conflict, understanding the differences in people, and understanding the decision making process."

"Which brings us back to continued learning."

"Yes. Or what we refer to as LifeLong Learning."

"You're kidding! I live by the motto, 'no more classes, no more books, no more teachers dirty looks.'"

"Learning didn't end when we left school. All successful people and all successful companies know that, and they keep learning, growing, training, and retraining. They know that the best investment they can ever make is in themselves and in their people. That on-going process of always doing better today what you did your best yesterday."

"Is that the song I heard playing in many of the facilities we were in?"

"Yes. The one that goes *Better Better Best, No Matter What Your Quest.* The only way to survive the journey, and enjoy the process of it, is to learn how to provide products and services the customers deem of value in a better, faster manner."

"Hey, I can hardly wait to see this in action. Let's go!"

Chapter Seventeen:

Unplugging the Pond Mentality

"*I* must admit there was a spirit of cooperation among those teams back there."

"That's because they mutually trust and respect each other, and thrive on being creative and innovative."

"I never was encouraged to be innovative. I always had to do things like the other kids at home, and I got hollered at in school when I did something creatively."

"I understand. And, again, that's *pond mentality*. It stifles people."

"I sure have met my fair share of dried up pond puppets!"

"What did you notice about communication?"

"That was real different. Sometimes people were working together as teams, but they weren't sitting down in old boardroom type settings. They were usually standing, excitedly doing and sharing at the same time. Other times they were working alone on projects, but there seemed to be a great deal of movement."

"Fluidity?"

"Like the sea, huh."

"Yep, like the sea. Where everything, including information, flows freely, and giving customers A-1 quality service is a top priority."

"Why do we have so much trouble communicating with one another?"

"Partially because we were never taught the skills necessary to listen effectively."

"What's listening got to do with it?"

"Everything. Listening is at the center of any communication. We need to share with others what we know, get feedback from them, have empathy or understanding for their viewpoint, and ask open-ended questions."

"Open-ended? You mean, questions designed to keep them talking nonstop?"

Unplugging the Pond Mentality

"No. Questions that can't be answered with a simple yes or no. If you really want to know what another person is feeling or thinking, you've got to communicate like a reporter."

"Be nosy?"

"Not really. Ask them what, how, and why questions. These questions gently probe and provide others with the opportunity to help us, through close reflective listening, understand what their needs and wants are."

"What made the pond people stagnate?"

"They felt depowered."

"Explain that one."

"They felt as if they, personally, didn't matter. Therefore, they kept their ideas to themselves and did only what they were supposed to do."

"They sure weren't very excited about their jobs."

"Maybe they felt as though they were renting them?"

"Yeah, and we already know we don't wash rental cars!"

"Empowered people know they not only make a difference, they know they're a part of a team where everyone is expected to use their full talents and abilities. They have control over how they do their jobs and they are responsible for the end results."

"Is that why the people in the open sea facilities appeared to be taking action to do things better?"

"Yes, because empowerment is a total shift for the better in how we do business and how we work together."

"I never felt confident enough to do that."

"Most people in the pond don't, and confidence is a key. Empowerment only exists when employees feel free to speak up, take ownership of their work, and make the changes necessary to improve their jobs and better meet the needs of their customers."

"How do you suggest I begin?"

"Think about, and make a list of, all the skills, talents, abilities, special knowledge, and character traits you bring to the company."

"That wouldn't take me long!"

"Now, that's *pond mentality*. We're out on the open sea now. Trust yourself and everything you have going for you. Then determine those you're most proud of, those you especially enjoy, and think about ways you could make greater use of these strengths to help the team and the company achieve their goals."

"Does this apply to just the workplace?"

"Not at all. Just as an empowered workplace team uses all their talents, abilities, and skills to serve their customers by exceeding and anticipating their needs, an empowered family team works at creating that same type of environment in their relationships with each other."

"We were going to discuss security."

"So we were. Let's alight and discuss digital beings."

"I'm so plugged in, I can hardly wait!"

TechnoTouch

Chapter Eighteen:

What the Tide Leaves Behind

"Peaceful island, this. Now, getting back to security."

"Oh, yes. That seems to be an important issue with you."

"Isn't it with most people?"

"It has been. Let me ask you a question."

"Shoot. I may not have an answer, though."

"Some answers we don't have yet. That's why we need to keep learning and growing. But many of the answers we need are right inside of us. We just don't usually take the time to give ourselves permission to ask and then to listen."

"Makes sense."

"What is it that you value most in life?"

"I'm not sure what you mean."

"What are the things that are most important to you, your top priorities. The things in life you'd like to look back on and say you've accomplished?"

"Well, being financially secure, having time to do the things I want to do."

"What would you like said about you at your wake?"

"Boy, that's a morbid thought!"

"Not really. Look at these waves surrounding us. As the tide rolls in, it leaves various things in its wake. As we go through life, we do the same. Remember, there is a season for everything."

"Is this a cooking lesson?"

"In a way. We're born in the spring of our life. In the summer, we're usually involved with the work we've chosen to do and our family structure. In the fall, we're changing colors and moving to different roles. And we die in the winter of our life. What do we take with us and what do we leave behind?"

"Now I know I'm going to hear that oft-quoted, you can't take it with you!"

"Have you ever seen a U-haul or a Brinks truck hooked up to a hearse?"

What the Tide Leaves Behind

"That's a good point. You're pretty witty, you know that?"

"Thank you. But that doesn't mean we don't want to strive to accomplish good things in our lives. It just means that we need to take the time to make sure the journey's not over before we've got our priorities straight, before we're balanced enough inside to leave behind what we want to."

"I thought you said we can't take it with us?"

"Although I didn't say that, we really can't. But we can leave behind some very valuable things."

"Such as?"

"Photographs, writings, memories others have of us. For some of us, our genes."

"I think I see where you're heading."

"When the winter of your lifetime comes, and others gather for that process, what is it that you want them to remember about you? And it usually isn't the fact that you contributed significantly to the bottom line, or that you kept a spotless bathroom. People remember the relationships, the ways in which you impacted on them or their world. And those memories, those relationships, need to be thought about and worked on constantly to make them positive ones. The only real security we have is that which is inside of us."

"That's beginning to make sense."

"You see, all people have internal power. If organizations or people themselves don't eliminate the resistance, they'll burn out."

"Now you've lost me again."

"Ever heard of Ohm's Law?"

"Yeah. I think it means E = I over R."

"And translated that means?"

"Voltage equals current over resistance."

"Very good. Let's get back in the vehicle and travel along the shore line as I explain what that has to do with managing change for 21st Century leadership."

Chapter Nineteen:

Super Conductors & Digital Teams

"How many watts are there in a standard light bulb?"

"Usually sixty."

"And in a Christmas tree bulb?"

"I'm not sure."

"Seven. And parking lot bulbs?"

"Got me there, but I met it's a megabunch!"

"Five hundred is the average. Why do you think that is?"

TechnoTouch

"So it can light up the way for more people?"

"Excellent. Now how many watts do you think most people are functioning with?"

"Well, I can remember when I was cruising at a thousand watts! Today, I'm probably down there with the Christmas bulb."

"Let's look at how we can increase wattage in our workplace teams and on our family teams. Remember when we said earlier that a conductor is a substance that transmits heat and electricity?"

"Yep."

"What do you suppose a *Super Conductor* is?"

"Ah, I've got it! Either the most popular cable car operator, or the coach of the winningest football team."

"Close. Resistance creates heat and that's why wires and cords burn up. A *Super Conductor* is the only wire that doesn't cause resistance. Can you see the tie in between the *pond mentality* and the *open sea mentality?*"

"Well, let's see. If resistance equals voltage times current, then resistance slows the moving force. Does that apply to our personal lives as well as our professional lives?"

"Sure. They're really not that separate. Who we are and what we choose to do with our gifts and talents is a large part of our lives."

Super Conductors & Digital Teams

"Okay. But if we're talking about *Super Conductors*, then we're back to talking about just the boss, right?"

"Not in the open sea. Here, people know that no matter what position they hold, they can choose to increase their internal wattage whenever they wish. As digital beings, we each have a *brighter switch* we can control."

"A *brighter switch?*"

"What most people would refer to as a dimmer switch."

"You know, guide, your sense of humor isn't so bad, either!"

"Thank you. With the *brighter switch,* we can choose on our own to turn up our internal energy level."

"Does that mean that everyone will become *Super Conductors?*"

"Probably not. The world will always need guides for the journey, and team members who take part in the journey."

"What's the difference?"

"The guides, the *super conductors,* connect vision with action, individual needs with group success, and the ability to change with the chances for success. They will be the visionaries who will guide their people into the future, down waterways not yet explored."

"How do you become a *Super Conductor?*"

"You go from being a manager and a supervisor to being a guide and a coach. Instead of concentrating on only doing things right, you concentrate on doing the right things."

"I'm not sure I understand the difference here."

"Change leaders need to understand two things. One, what's changing and why. And two, how to implement the change and survive the accompanying stress. As they're guiding their people down the river, management focuses on efficiency in getting any ice jams broken up and out of the way. Leadership determines whether that's the best route to take in the first place."

"And the team members?"

"Employees will need to be proactive, open to change, rather than reactive, resisting the change. They will have to be involved in process innovation and process redesign."

"What's that?"

"More commonly called reengineering, but what I like to call *techno-redesigning.* If done well, these processes will deliver extraordinary gains in speed, productivity, and profitability, all essential for the journey. It means starting from the future and working backward. It's asking, 'if we were beginning this company again, how would we structure and run it?'"

"You mean don't keep manufacturing paddle wheel boats when the customers want speed boats."

"Exactly. You take a look at what business you are currently in and what business you want to be in. Then you look at what you need to do to make that business successful. Once you've done that, how would you determine that success?"

"Having never done it before, I'm not sure."

"You'd do some benchmarking. One of the best ways to do that is to talk to customers and ask them how well you're currently meeting their needs. Also ask them what needs they have that you're not meeting, as well as what future needs they may have that you might be able to provide."

"I can't recall anybody ever asking me this."

"All that has to change now. Another way is to learn where our competitors are ahead of us. Not that we want to emulate them, but we want to leapfrog them by anticipating and exceeding the needs of our customers. That means wearing our customers' life jackets for the whole journey."

"What's going to make all this work?"

"Let's head back to the dock, and I'll share that with you."

TechnoTouch

Chapter Twenty:

TechnoTouch Defined

"*B*y the way, what do you mean by *Techno-Touch?*"

"The explosion of new technology has changed the basic flow of information, thus changing the way our companies are organized. You can now communicate with your customers more easily and more often, becoming more responsive to their needs. You can communicate with both your office and your home while traveling. You can even communicate with your office from your home."

"Making telecommuting a more attractive alternative?"

"Yes. And of course, all of this changes the traditional command and control methods of management. Information, no longer concentrated in the hands of a few, is now distributed and available to a much larger group of people."

"Will this E-mail thing be used even more?"

"Yes. As companies set up and refine their Intranets and Extranets, E-mail will be used by internal and external customers alike. A lot of information that used to be available only in paper form will now be quickly and conveniently accessed in digital form."

"Whoa! I have some idea of what the Internet is, and what it can do, but what do you mean by Intranets and Extranets?"

"Management is realizing that there are no 'non-knowledge workers'." People on the front lines are making decisions every day that affect the business and if they don't have the information, they're going to make the wrong decisions. When team members get communications online, it's quicker and the company knows everybody got the same information."

"Is this information accessible to anyone?"

"No. Fire walls are used to keep selected information secure from outside intrusions and

TechnoTouch Defined

password controls are used to restrict access where needed internally."

"How will this benefit the company?"

"Employees can access more information more rapidly when they need it. Administrative costs are lowered as the business process becomes more efficient. Thousands of dollars in paper and mailing costs can be saved. And an Intranet that links everyone in the organization to a single communication network may finally help companies achieve flatter, less hierarchical communications and make quicker better decisions needed to stay competitive."

"Okay, what are extranets?"

"Extranets are collaborative networks that use Internet technology to link businesses with their customers, suppliers, and other businesses that share common goals. The result is a complete electronically integrated supply chain. As the market evolves, and security and cross-platform issues get resolved, the principle goal will be to dynamically publish relevant information to individuals. This will mean a reduction in staff costs and an increase in sales."

"That's sure going to bring added change."

"True, and all hardware, software, and peripheral companies are faced with the same challenges."

"What's that?"

"They must produce applications that deliver on individual strengths but also work well together."

"More open systems, I take it."

"Yes. We must be able to not only get the information to the people that need it, but deliver it in a usable form, where people can not only access it, but share it as needed."

"Is this what's referred to as cross-functional workflow automation?"

"That's it. Workflow automation will manage complex, interlocking tasks and the information they utilize and generate. The whole thrust of technology has shifted toward connecting people and their knowledge. Leading-edge companies focus on the importance of building long-term relationships while getting the task done. They do this by combining high tech with high touch for high return."

"*TechnoTouch?*"

"*TechnoTouch.*"

"Wow. Incredible."

"We've only just begun. The old journey of starting on the bottom rung of the career ladder, doing what you were told, waiting your turn, eventually being tapped to rise, are gone. It will never return."

TechnoTouch Defined

"And in its place will be perpetual change?"

"Waves and waves of it. Dynamic change. Proactive people adding value to their companies, taking charge of their own destiny, giving their companies their best. Proactive companies transforming themselves by replacing management layers with fast-moving technology-utilizing teams, building partnerships with customers and vendors."

"What will the role of management be?"

"As we've said before, they will be coaches and guides. They will also be involved in developing new strategies and new business, further expanding and testing their strengths. Their assignments will be broader than ever before. They will be challenged to always be doing something that contributes significant, positive change to the organization."

"So it's either take control of your life or someone will do it for you."

"Pretty much. *TechnoTouch* people will derive their identity from their occupation, not from their attachment to a single company."

"Creating their own opportunities."

"Yes. And communicating constantly."

"No more stagnant, dried up pond companies."

TechnoTouch

"Only fast changing, easy adapting, ever growing, open sea companies and people. Well, here we are at the dock. Shall we alight?"

Chapter Twenty One:

The Tide Will Turn

"*I* have a feeling this part of our journey is almost over. So what else is needed?"

"This changing culture will never work unless managers and employees are ready to accept the change and work to improve themselves both personally and professionally. We've been used to hierarchy and control. Now we have to teach trust, communication, and teamwork."

"How important is trust in all of this?"

"Trust is the emotional glue that bonds people together. Leaders earn trust with their integrity in not only defining and constantly renewing the vision, but in also living it consistently."

"The old walk your talk routine, or in this case, row your boat."

"Another good analogy. 21st Century Success rests on continuously improving the existing work processes, and continuously advancing great innovative ideas. Empowered teams need to know how to problem solve. Managers who came up through the ranks face the toughest adjustments, that of learning how to be open to feedback and suggestions."

"Is that how you break down the inevitable internal resistance, the sea change walls?"

"That's part of it. We fear the unknown. You wouldn't want to walk on the bottom of the ocean unless you had been given the tools to do so."

"And a lifeline to hold onto!"

"Yes, it's important to know that the on-going support we need when learning anything new and constantly changing will be provided. We also need to build change in waves, creating a few success stories early on, rewarding those who succeed, and communicating this to everyone so the energy stays high."

"Back to *Super Conductors* and *Digital Teams*."

"Right. 21st Century organizations will be composed of true leaders, *super conductors* who

The Tide Will Turn

enable their teams to become empowered and involved, helping their energies flow. They will guide *virtual digital teams* composed of empowered employees transmitting high energy, producing positive results, lighting up their companies, and connecting the world."

"Wow, a true multimedia experience! 'Watt's' next, oh wise one?"

"Lao Tse, an ancient philosopher, tells us to stay centered and balanced. He wrote that nothing is weaker than water, yet for attacking what is hard and tough, nothing surpasses it. That means we need to stop clinging to fixed methods and keep adapting and changing according to our customers needs."

"Let go of the rocks and let the current carry us?"

"Flow, rather than flee or fight. But continue to persevere."

"Ten percent inspiration and 90 percent perspiration?"

"As Harriet Beecher Stowe once said, 'when you get into a tight place and everything goes against you, till it seems as though you could not hold on a minute longer, never give up, for that is just the place and the time that the tide will turn'."

"Makes sense, but in which direction?"

"In the direction of *TechnoTouch*. When we empower ourselves, our families, and our workplace, we find a spirit, an energy, and a power that's greater than us. When we know what our purpose in life is, and we commit ourselves to a life full of meaning, where we interact with others and add more love to the world, every day becomes even more precious. Because in the long run, we're here to improve the quality of life for others, by serving."

"Oh wise one, you have served me well on this journey. What do I owe you?"

"Only one thing. Your promise that you will continue on the journey, serving others, and becoming a guide to them."

"Is it time to let go of the lifeline?"

"We'll just extend the length of it, so you can continue your journey unencumbered. You'll find others on the journey who will reach out and guide you along the way."

"Thanks for helping me to understand the adventure. See you around the bend?"

"See you around the bend."

Appendix A.......Twenty-one Technotouch Trends ©

1. Adopt an Open Sea Mentality: ever moving, circulating, vital, alive, growing.

2. View life as Technotouchers do: an adventurous journey to destinations yet unknown.

3. Travel the Technotouch Byway: a fluid, easily navigable environment built around information systems, teams, and networks.

4. Technotouchers set the goal by the stakeholders, plan ahead, catch the next wave, revitalize, and make strong again.

5. A Technotouch Vision: a deep voyage into the heart and soul of an organization that unlocks people's self-directed energy.

6. Map out your travels, then make the decisions concerning the most effective use of your time, talents, and energy.

7. Give very little time and energy to a situation over which you have little control: don't try to sail through the harbor when the water's frozen solid.

8. Make personal mastery your lifelong journey: learning, changing, evolving, getting better at everything you do.

9. Use the new technology tools to store and retrieve information, and communicate knowledge in a quicker, better manner.

10. Technotouch Companies organize work so it can be carried out by men and women who can take responsibility, and who will share in the risks and rewards.

11. Technotouchers know school's never out for the learner: they're futurists who take charge of their lives instead of being at the mercy of the waterfalls of change.

12. The only way to ride the waves successfully and survive the journey is to learn how to provide products and services the customers deem of value in a better, faster manner.

13. In Open Sea Facilities communication flows freely:people trust themselves and everything they have going for them.

14. Digital Teams are composed of people who choose to control their internal brighter switch.

15. Super Conductors are visionaries who will guide their people into the future, down waterways not yet explored.

16. Break down the Sea Change Walls by being open to feedback and suggestions.

17. Technotouchers will be challenged to always be doing something that contributes significant, positive change to the organization.

18. Technotouch Leaders will be coaches and guides who earn trust with their integrity in defining and constantly renewing the vision, and by living it constantly.

19. Digital Teams are composed of empowered employees transmitting high energy, producing positive results, lighting up their companies, connecting the world.

20. Empower yourself, your family, and your workplace to find a spirit, energy, and power that's greater than any of us.

21. Technotouchers welcome the adventure, and look forward to what's around the next bend!

I wanted to leave you with the lyrics to the MarmeL Theme Song, which I co-wrote and produced in 1993. May the words help you to continue the journey.

Better, Better, Best - No Matter What Your Quest

Better, Better Best; No Matter What Your Quest. (chorus)
Today you're gonna do it; you're gonna be your best.
Traveling your path, on the Journey called Success.
A never ending challenge to be, Better, Better, Best.

You are like the butterfly, inside the cocoon.
You are like the flower, just about to bloom.
It is all inside you, there is no time to rest.
Empowering yourself to be, Better, Better, Best.
(chorus)
Contribute to the Vision, with purpose and with passion.
Walking your own talk, in your own fashion.
Everything in your life, is an opportunity.
You can make it happen, act and it will be.
(chorus)
Choose your own window, of opportunity.
With everything you do, make it quality.
Owning your own space, stand up to the test.
Enjoy what you do, be Better, Better, Best.
Add to your worth, with life long learning.
Add to your value, to increase your earning.
Orchestrate your life, but stay in harmony.
Be the change in the world, you would like to see.
So come on get on board, it's time to really live.
Using all your gifts, to find a way to give.
You can make a difference, by serving up success.
Helping other people to be, Better, Better, Best.
Better, Better, Best, No Matter What Your Quest
Today you're gonna do it, you're gonna be the best.
Traveling your path, on the journey called success.
A never ending challenge to be, Better, Better, Best!

INDEX

Action Plan, 46, 48
Adventure, 20, 23, 118
Automated work flow, 112
Balance, 101
Benchmarking, 107
Better, Better, Best, 92,121
Brighter Switch, 105
Cables, 24, 25
CEO, 83
Change
  a definition, 12, 67
  acceptance of, 85
  control of, 57, 58
  coping strategies, 67, 85
  corporate culture, 60, 89
  fear of, 66, 116
  future of, 81, 113
  humor and, 16
  leaders, 106
  pain, 84
  phases of, 38, 39
  power and, 104
  resistance of, 26
  results of, 12
  risk taking, 79
  transistion, 66
CIO, 83
Coach, future 113
Communication
  digital, 21
  fluid, 94
  ineffective, 25
  power of, 25, 94
Commitment, 45, 72, 81
Computers, 20, 73
Customers
  service/satisfaction, 97, 107

Control, inner, 60
  lack of, 59
Decision making, 69, 78, 79
Digital teams, 116
Depowered, 95
Downsizing, 117
Edison, Thomas, 30
Education, 33, 34
E-mail, 110
Employee
  empowerment of, 36, 51
  involvement of, 96
Empowerment, 35, 36, 51, 80
Energy, 16, 105
Enginnering, 22
Extranet, 110, 111
Family, 37, 97
Fiber Optics, 25
FIP's, 29
Force
  current, 15
  voltage, 16
Goals
  reaching and, 40, 48
Growth cycles, 38
Guides
  as leaders, 113
Hierarchical
  structure, 27, 28
  pyramid, 30, 80
Humor
  importance of, 14, 38
  use of, 24
Information
  era, 63
  processing, 74
  superhighway, 25

Innovation, 50
Internet, 20, 111
Intranet, 110, 111
IP Pyramid, 29
Joy in workplace, 71
Lao Tse, 117
Leadership
  definition of, 35, 106
  skills, 50, 84
  20th Century, 27, 29
  21st Century, 102, 113
Lifelines, 14, 44, 118
LifeLongLearning, 92
Listening
  communication and, 94
  importance of, 95
Management
  scientific principles, 28
Managers
  vs. leaders, 106, 113
Manufacturing, 22
Meaning in life, 62
Measure, 16, 17, 97
  progress, 47
Microchip, 26
MIS, 83
Mission
  building of, 47
Mission Statements
  importance of, 55, 56
Ohm's Law, 102
Open Sea concept, 87, 105
Open Systems, 112
Organizations
  phases of, 38, 39
Paradigm, 13, 30
  shift in, 50, 61
Perceptions, 18

Power
  enhancement of, 24
  lack of, 51
  sharing of, 87
Pond Mentality, 73, 93
Pride, 72
Priorities, 100
Proactive, 113
Process improvement, 116S
Productivity, 52
Purpose, 61, 118
Quality, 17, 62
  measure of 474, 48
Re-engineering, 106
Relationships, 101
  long-term, 112
Resistance, 85
  change and, 28
  fear and, 30
Robots, 28
Sales and Marketing, 21, 22
Sea Change, 116
Security, 12, 35
Service
  customers and, 47, 94
  of self to others, 118
SIP's, 29
Spirituality, 52
Stakeholders, 40
Stowe, Harriet Beecher, 117
Stress, 57
Super Bowl
  analogy to, 39, 40, 44, 46
Super Conductors, 39, 104, 116
Supply Chain, 111
Survival, 84
Teams, self-directed, 90, 91
  training of, 69

Teamwork, 72, 90
Technology
  importance and, 19, 51, 63, 109, 112
  information, 65
TechnoRedesigning, 106
TechnoTouch©, 63, 66, 109, 112, 118
TechnoTouch byway, 19
Telecommunications, 110
Televideo Conferencing, 21
Training, 51, 81
  importance of, 91, 92
  lack of, 74
Trust, 77, 115
Twentieth-Century companies, 72, 81
Twenty-first Century companies, 71
Us vs.Them Mentality, 28
Utilities, 23
Virtual teams, 117
VIP's, 29
Vision, 44, 47
Visionary Leaders, 105
VPAC, 44, 45
Watts
  and power, 103
Workflow automation, 112
World Wide Web, 20

About the Author

Marlene B. Brown is a leading edge visionary who has had a tremendous impact on the lives of the 1,000's of people whose paths she has crossed.

Founder and CEO/President of MarmeL Consulting Firm, and TechnoTouch Marketing, Marlene specializes in helping corporations and associations move their people into the new millennium with enthusiasm, passion, and focused purpose.

Her company mission is to provide top-quality service and on-going value that exceeds and anticipates her customers needs and expectations, by presenting ideas designed to positively and productively influence their thoughts and their actions.

Her client list includes a wide range of industries, among these IBM, GTE, AT&T, CIA, Xerox, Hewlett-Packard, Anionics, Kauai Resort Hotel, Federal Reserve Bank, Metropolitan Insurance Co., University Hospital, ASAE, PCMA, MPI, AMA, APWA, USPS, PSI, ASFSA, USAF, various school districts, numerous members of Congress, the Capitol Hill staff.

Marlene produces a variety of publications, including Technotouch Trends Newsletter, and is the author of several audio and video learning programs and books, as well as electronic products such as screen savers, success systems on floppy diskettes, and interactive educational CD-ROM's.

Marlene B. Brown is a graduate of Utica College of Syracuse University and the University of Cortland. She began her professional life as an innovative Senior English and Psychology teacher. She is a former instructor for the American Management Association.

She went on to raise a family of five, and found and manage three businesses. As a much sought-after speaker, Marlene has spoken in over 43 states and 4 countries to date. She is one of less than 5% of the National Speakers Association's 4,000 International members who have earned the CSP (Certified Speaking Professional).

When not consulting, speaking, or writing, Marlene can be found improving her technological skills, playing the keyboard, or enjoying her grandchildren. She loves to read and research, write, listen to music, dance, meditate and work out at the health club.

Services Available

Marlene B. Brown speaks to conventions and organizations all over the world. She also has her messages available on audio and video tapes, disks, and CD-ROM.

In addition, Marlene conducts seminars and in-depth consulting in the areas of managing change, future trends, leadership, sales & marketing, and technology productivity.

For further information on Marlene's programs and services, contact:

MarmeL Consulting Firm
53 White Street, Suite 305
Clark Mills, NY 13321-0083
Tel: (315) 853-1318 x1
Fax: (315) 853-4636

If you would like to share any comments, experiences, or ideas about Technotouch, feel free to write Marlene at the following address:

Marlene B. Brown, CEO
MarmeL Consulting Firm
P. O. Box 83
Clark Mills, NY 13321

or

E-mail: marlenebb7@aol.com *or* marlene@borg.com

Visit our Web page at : http://www.technotouch.com/

Yes! I Want to be Successful Today & Tomorrow!
Please Ship the following Products Immediately!

QTY.	ITEM DESCRIPTION ORDER FORM	INVESTMENT	TOTAL
____110	Technotouch:Managing Change™ Book	$14.95..........	$_____
____725	TechnoT2: HighTech/HighReturn Mktg™ Book	29.95	$_____
____130	Techie Time/Techie Talk™ Book	14.95	$_____
____135	Technotouch:Managing Change™ Audio Book	12.95	$_____
____215	ThoughtMaster by Marlene Brown™ ScreenSaver	24.95	$_____
____210	Better, Better, Best: MarmeL Song™ Audio Tape	12.95	$_____
____530	Entrepreneur/Small Biz System™ Binder/Diskette	59.95	$_____
____310	The Challenge of Change™ Video/Audio/workbook	75.00	$_____
____315	Shared Leadership™ Video/Audio/workbook	75.00	$_____
____320	Communicating Success™ Video/Audio/workbook	75.00	$_____
____420	Becoming All One Can Be 12 cassette audio progr m	74.95	$_____
____410	Technotouch Trends ™ 1 year/6 issues Newsletter	49.00	$_____
____900	TechnotouchPlus™ Special $520.value, 1of @only	397.00	$_____

Shipping: $3.00 for 1st product; $1.50 for @ addt'l product. Air Mail: $5 @ $_____

NYS residents add 8% sales tax .... $_____

TOTAL PURCHASE AMOUNT .... $_____

THREE EASY WAYS TO PLACE AN ORDER:

1.) *Call* 1-315-853-5092 x5 *or* 2.) *Fax* the completed order form to: 1-315-853-4636 *or* 3.) *Mail* order form along with payment to: Sunrise Publishing International,
P.O. Box 840, Clark Mills, NY 13321

_____ Enclosed is my check, money order, or credit card (below) for payment in full, plus shipping and handling, & applicable tax.
Make checks payable in US funds only to: **Sunrise Publishing Int'l**

or

Charge My Credit Card: VISA_____   MasterCard_____   Exp. Date____/____

Credit Card Account Number:_____

Signature _____

Name (please print) _____

Company / Title _____

Address _____

City _____ State _____ Zip_____

Phone _____

Fax _____

Email/Web page _____

Language Teaching Insights From Other Fields: Sports, Arts, Design, and More

Edited by Christopher Stillwell

tesol press

Typeset in ITC Galliard and Vag Rounded
by Capitol Communications, LLC, Crofton, Maryland USA
and printed by Gasch Printing, LLC, Odenton, Maryland USA

TESOL International Association
1925 Ballenger Avenue
Alexandria, Virginia 22314 USA
Tel 703-836-0774 • Fax 703-836-7864

Publishing Manager: Carol Edwards
Cover Design: Citrine Sky Design, Edgewater, Maryland USA
Copyeditor: Sarah J. Duffy

TESOL Book Publications Committee
        John I. Liontas, Chair

Maureen S. Andrade	Joe McVeigh
Jennifer Lebedev	Gail Schafers
Robyn L. Brinks Lockwood	Lynn Zimmerman

Project overview: John I. Liontas
Reviewers: Jennifer Lebedev and Gail Schafers

Copyright © 2013 by TESOL International Association

All rights reserved. Copying or further publication of the contents of this work are not permitted without permission of TESOL International Association, except for limited "fair use" for educational, scholarly, and similar purposes as authorized by U.S. Copyright Law, in which case appropriate notice of the source of the work should be given.

Every effort has been made to contact the copyright holders for permission to reprint borrowed material. We regret any oversights that may have occurred and will rectify them in future printings of this work.

ISBN 9781931185073
Library of Congress Control Number 2013940183

Table of Contents

Introduction

Chapter 1: Enhancing Teaching With the Fruits of Distant Fields 3
Christopher Stillwell

Recontextualizing the Language Classroom

Chapter 2: How Would a Bartender Create a Safe, Social, and Supportive Classroom Environment? 11
Andrew Boon

Chapter 3: What Can We Learn From Martial Arts Masters About Practice Techniques and Learning Environments? 23
Anne Paonessa

Chapter 4: How Would a Role-Playing Game Master Engage Learners in the Quest for Knowledge? 35
Roger Dupuy

Dealing With Challenges

Chapter 5: What Does It Mean to Be a Whitewater Language Teacher? 51
Karen Blinder

Chapter 6: How Would a Zen Master Bring Compassion, Equanimity, and Choiceless Awareness to the Language Classroom? 59
John Spiri

Teaching the Four Skills

Chapter 7: How Would a Restaurant Reviewer Critique Student Writing? 69
    Sylvia Whitman

Chapter 8: What Can We Learn From Certified Ski Instructors About Teaching Academic Speaking Skills? 77
    Li-Shih Huang

Chapter 9: How Would an Actor Teach Language Learners to Improvise and Fluently Speak the Speech? 89
    Christopher Stillwell

Chapter 10: How Would an Architect Such as Frank Gehry Design Language Learning Tasks? 101
    Tim Stewart

Chapter 11: How Would a Basketball Coach Get a Team to Talk the Talk? 111
    Sylvia Whitman

Chapter 12: How Would a Social Activist Promote Critical Literacy in the Language Classroom? 125
    Rawia Hayik

Developing as a Professional

Chapter 13: How Would a Public Speaker Hook 'Em Every Time? 141
    John Schmidt

Chapter 14: How Would a Document Designer Create Classroom Materials? 155
    Tammy R. Jones and Gabriela Kleckova

Chapter 15: How Would a Researcher Conduct a Language Course Evaluation? 171
    Cynthia Quinn and Gregory Sholdt

Index 183

Introduction

CHAPTER 1

Enhancing Teaching With the Fruits of Distant Fields

Christopher Stillwell

We would not have to go very far to find current examples of insights from one field being used to inform another. Navy SEALs train Olympians, Disney experts mentor hospital managers, ballet professionals give football players pointers, and brain scientists advise everyone from architects to astronomers. Though it may seem that language teachers lack the resources for similar coaching, we must remember that all teachers have what Cosh (1999) has referred to as a valuable and free resource in their midst: other teachers. Many of these language teachers started out working in other fields and studying other subjects, and even when studying to become teachers, they have typically been required to enroll in courses outside their language teaching concentration. No matter how distinct these other areas of experience may be, chances are that these teachers regularly and naturally draw on this experience to address everyday challenges of teaching. We might wonder: What would language teachers discover if they could tap into this living library of their colleagues' knowledge and experience? Would a martial arts master be effective at maintaining an orderly, productive classroom atmosphere? Would a restaurant reviewer know the secrets of critiquing essays? And what insights might come from discussion of teachers' hobbies? Might role-playing game masters know a thing or two about making lessons exciting?

Though the diversity of language teachers' experience is something that should be trumpeted, it is sadly rarely discussed. Unless your school has been visited by a chatty substitute with a lifetime of fascinating stories to share, it is unlikely that anyone in your teachers' room has ever asked, "Did I ever tell you about the summer I spent with the carnival? Gives me a whole different perspective on the three-ring circus that is seventh-grade Spanish, Period 2." That is a shame, for just such a conversation could provide the foundation for our continuing creativity and growth as teachers. As Csíkszentmihályi (1997) notes, one core component of creativity is crossing borders and making discoveries from the resulting mix of ideas. Brain scientists might add that this border crossing is likely to help us learn more and improve our practice, because the brain is built for exploration and learns best from information we find interesting (Medina, 2008). The more we explore foreign ideas in relation to language instruction, the more interesting discoveries we might make, and the more creative, informed, and exciting our teaching may become.

AN INVITATION TO A CONVERSATION

Many of us have sparked conversation in our classrooms with questions like "Who would you invite to your dream dinner party?" As language teachers looking for insights on teaching, what might our own answers be? If we broke bread with a panel of language teachers who also happen to have extensive experience in other fields, where would the conversation go? In a sense, the volume now in your hands represents a book-length conversation of that nature, a gathering of some of the more interesting dinner guests a language teacher might ever care to meet. In one corner, the social activist and the document designers exchange views on subtle aspects of texts that influence the way learners perceive what they read, while in another corner the martial arts master and the whitewater paddler reflect on their philosophies of language instruction. Meanwhile, numerous other such conversations take place in a unique space where language teachers can benefit from one another's varied backgrounds.

It is worth remembering that the most important guest at this particular meal is you, dear reader, for only your engagement and insights will truly bring this gathering to life. Before we begin, you may find it useful to have a quick look at the guest list in the Prereading Brainstorming Exercise (Figure 1), asking yourself what you might expect to hear from each of these professionals. Whether your guesses are on target or not, chances are that you will come up with a number of additional ideas to bring to the conversation.

For instance, you might wonder, what would a bartender have to say about language teaching? Bars tend to have the lights rather low, you might think to yourself, at least until it is time for everyone to go home. At that point the lights come up brighter than the brightest day. Why is that? Do patrons feel more secure and comfortable chatting and spending time in the relative anonymity of the low light? Do the bright lights at the end of the night extinguish this comfort, making patrons feel exposed, vulnerable, and eager to scurry out the door? If so, how might this idea apply to the classroom? Might lowering or raising the classroom drapes have an impact on conversation activities? Through this exploration you may stumble on insights that are not even mentioned in the chapter, but that are no less worthwhile for the opportunities for creativity and insight that they afford. And whatever your guesses, each chapter will likely yield surprises that

Prereading Brainstorming Exercise

List three insights a language teacher might learn from each of the following professions.

Bartender
Martial arts master
Role-playing game designer
Whitewater paddler
Zen master
Restaurant reviewer
Ski instructor
Actor
Architect
Basketball coach
Social activist
Public speaker
Document designer
Researcher

Figure 1. Guest List

translate to new ways of thinking about your teaching and new ideas to try in your classroom. This breath of fresh professional air may even help keep burnout at bay.

A FOUR-COURSE MEAL

It can get a bit noisy with 14 people talking at once, so for this book the guests' perspectives have been separated into chapters that fall into four sections: Recontextualizing the Language Classroom, Dealing With Challenges, Teaching the Four Skills, and Developing as a Professional. However, just as these conversations crash the gates of disparate fields typically concealed from language teachers' view, the focus of each perspective often spills beyond the boundaries of its section. Thus, a chapter that is primarily focused on teaching advanced speaking skills may very well have useful comments to make on beginning classes well, or course planning, or professional development.

In Recontextualizing the Language Classroom, we begin with a visit to the local pub, as Andrew Boon reflects on his experience as a bartender and shares what that work taught him about creating a comfortable environment for language learning. Anne Paonessa draws from her experience as a martial arts master and owner of a martial arts school to demonstrate techniques for disguising repetition in practice activities, establishing an environment that fosters respect and learning, and getting families involved in students' education. And Roger Dupuy shows us that if a role-playing game master were in charge of a language class, the quest for learning could be enhanced by such game elements as a set-up to contextualize the learning, avatars to facilitate risk-taking, and character sheets to record and reward students' progress.

In the Dealing With Challenges section, Karen Blinder takes us to the river, asking us to consider how a whitewater paddler would approach the rapids of language instruction by finding ways of using the current to his or her advantage and remaining willing to adjust course at a moment's notice, among other things. Meanwhile, John Spiri enlightens us with principles of a Zen master, showing the usefulness of cultivating a kind of mindfulness without judgment, or "choiceless awareness," for interactions with students in class.

Chapters in the Teaching the Four Skills section bring us to an even broader range of contexts, as former restaurant reviewer Sylvia Whitman considers culinary approaches to critiquing student writing, and ski instructor Li-Shih Huang explores parallels between skiing black diamonds and developing advanced speaking skills. I draw from my previous experience in theater, looking into ways that actors' techniques for developing improvisational skills might be adapted to helping learners build fluency, and Tim Stewart notes intriguing overlaps between the work of language teachers and that of architects, exploring the power of visuals for enhancing teaching and learning. Sylvia Whitman returns to imagine expert basketball coaches' drills for getting students to talk the talk, and social activist Rawia Hayik closes this section with a view on how educators can "transcend the mere teaching of language skills and address social issues in the language classroom" through the use of social justice picture books and participatory documentary photography.

In the final section, Developing as a Professional, public speaker John Schmidt identifies the tricks of the Toastmaster trade and shows how they can be applied to communicating lesson content effectively. Tammy Jones and Gabriela Kleckova look to the field of document design to find ways that language teachers can make materials that "communicate information not only through textual content but also through carefully crafted visual design elements that scaffold the overall meaning." Finally, Cynthia Quinn and Greg Sholdt take classroom surveys to a more rigorous level, showing what a language course evaluation might look like if it were conducted by a professional researcher.

METAPHORS, BRAINSTORMS, AND A CAVEAT OR TWO

It should by now be evident that many of these chapters provide new metaphors for language teaching. They encourage us to prepare for the whitewater rapids of our lessons, to provide novices with practice runs on the bunny slopes of language, and to critique writing as cooking instructors would provide insight to budding chefs, early enough to make a difference before the dish is burnt. In these metaphorical visits to distant fields, we can see our work through new lenses. As Jones and Kleckova recount in their experience of a course of study outside language teaching, "because of our backgrounds in TESL/TEFL, it was natural for us to focus on classroom contexts and materials," and this act of examining their language teaching work through a new lens provided "a minor professional epiphany." In addition to such epiphanies, identifying parallels between our work and that of these other artists may also help us better appreciate the artistry of our own craft.

A few words of caution. Although the insights shared in this volume should provide ample food for thought and can hint at useful directions for future exploration and research, they are best considered as complementary to the existing professional knowledge contained in our own field, with all the context-specific solutions that have been found in response to our particular context-specific challenges. And although great effort has been made to verify the accuracy of the professional knowledge from other fields here represented, it should be acknowledged that in some cases we may lack the training necessary to fully understand these strands of wisdom that are divorced from their original context.

Still, just as the most outlandish fable can teach us something about ourselves, reflection on even imperfect understandings of other fields can provide useful frames for understanding what we do as language teachers. At heart, this is a book about exploration, about seeking inspiration from beyond our routine contexts. If you are intrigued by any of the possibilities you find, you have only to seek information by reading further, inviting other professionals to join the party, and generally continuing to fill your basket of teaching techniques with the fruits of distant fields.

REFERENCES

Cosh, J. (1999). Peer observation: A reflective model. *ELT Journal, 53*(1), 22–27.

Csíkszentmihályi, M. (1997). *Creativity: Flow and the psychology of discovery and invention.* New York, NY: Harper Perennial.

Medina, J. (2008). *Brain rules: 12 Principles for surviving and thriving at work, home, and school.* Seattle, WA: Pear Press.

AUTHOR BIOGRAPHY

Christopher Stillwell is a PhD student at University of California Irvine's School of Education, with an MA in TESOL from Teachers College Columbia University. He has taught ESL/EFL for 18 years in such places as Spain, the United States, and Japan, including work at Teachers College as instructor of an MA practicum in TESOL and at a university language program in Japan as assistant director. He received two 2011 Best of JALT awards for invited presentations on peer observation and on conflict resolution techniques for language learning, and he is listed on the U.S. Department of State's database of English Language Specialists. (StillwellC@aol.com)

Recontextualizing the Language Classroom

CHAPTER 2

How Would a Bartender Create a Safe, Social, and Supportive Classroom Environment?

Andrew Boon

Whether you are a priest, a psychologist, an entertainer, or a teacher, you never forget a good bartender. Like teaching, bartending is a multifaceted art, a craft, a profession that involves an individual responding to multiple variables and possibilities as they unfold in real time, with the end goal of providing the utmost satisfaction to the customer. The bartender is not only there to serve drinks and to take the money (providing customers with a wide knowledge and selection of beers, wines, spirits, and cocktails from which to fill their empty vessels) but also works to ensure that the customer has a wholly enjoyable and rewarding experience from start to finish.

As with the language teacher meeting students for the first time and thereafter on a regular basis, the bartender's personal touch is essential. No matter how busy the bartender or how crowded the bar, it is always very welcoming for customers when they enter the establishment and the bartender greets them with their name, knows their preferred drinks, and knows something about their lives. Being sociable, friendly, and approachable is of paramount importance. Like the language teacher, the bartender must be able to initiate, develop, and modify conversational topics according to the needs of his or her customers. Moreover, the bartender must listen carefully to the customers and work to make each of them feel an accepted, valued, and important part of the social experience. Finally, like the language teacher, the bartender needs to smile, be happy, and be motivating. Like stepping into the classroom, stepping behind the bar is a stage where one gives a public performance. The friendly, organized, confident, energetic bartender will help make his or her customers feel at ease, supported, and wishing to return for more.

"So you used to be a bartender?" you, the reader, ask.

"Yes, that's right," I, the author of this chapter, reply. "I worked part-time at a local pub down the road from my house and at the Students' Union bar at university. This helped me pay my way through school. In fact, when I graduated, I found myself at a crossroads having been offered both a career in pub management and a place on a postgraduate certificate in education course."

"So you chose the teaching route?"

"Yes, that's right. I finished my teacher training course (still working part-time as a bartender, of course!), then I got a job offer to teach English in Japan. And 15 years later, here I still am. Kampai!"

A BARTENDER'S TIPS FOR LANGUAGE TEACHERS

Tip 1: Build rapport.

Remember your customers' names. Remember their drink preferences. Know something about their interests and their lives, and use this to engage them in conversation. Doing this will make your customers feel welcomed, attended to, and an important part of the whole social experience.

Similar to the bartender's interaction with customers in a bar, Dörnyei and Murphey (2003) state the importance of a teacher "knowing a student's name, and the student knowing that the teacher knows it" (p. 27). This helps each student in a class not feel invisible, faceless, and excluded. Through the use of his or her name (a symbol of that person's individual and social identity), the student instead can feel he or she belongs to, is recognized and valued by, and has an important role to play in the group.

Also, making the effort to get to know each student can help to build rapport between teacher and students and students and students in the group and establish an environment where group members feel motivated to learn. For example, the teacher commenting on a student's new haircut, playing a student's favorite song on YouTube at the beginning of the class, or incorporating a student's favorite sports team into the lesson can help to show the teacher cares, is paying attention to the students, and is personalizing the learning experience for group members. According to Dörnyei (2001), "teachers who succeed in establishing relationships of mutual trust and respect with the learners are more likely to inspire them in academic matters" (p. 36).

One tip to help the teacher and the class members begin to remember everyone's names and learn about one another is to get students to complete a class survey (see Table 1) in the first lesson, walking around the classroom and interviewing each other:

First, the teacher asks students to come up with four of their own questions

How Would a Bartender Create a Safe, Social, and Supportive Environment?

Table 1. Survey: Interview 10 Students in Your Class

Questions	Student's name	His or her answer
1. Where are you from?		
2. Where do you live?		
3. Do you have any brothers or sisters?		
4. What do you like to do in your free time?		
5. What kind of sports do you like?		
6. Who is your favorite singer?		
7. _____?		
8. _____?		
9. _____?		
10. _____?		

and write them in the space provided on the worksheet (Questions 7–10 in Table 1). Then, students are encouraged to interact with one another by asking one survey question to 10 different classmates, filling in their names and the answers they give on the worksheet.

After students have completed the survey activity, the teacher introduces a game in which class members share their answers. First, the teacher puts the class into teams. Using the class register, the teacher instructs the first student on the list to stand up. The teacher then asks the class to give some information about this student. When students answer, their team is awarded one point. For example:

> "Can you tell me anything about Yuta?"
> "Yuta lives in Saitama!"
> "Team 1—great! One point!"
> "He likes playing soccer."
> "Team 6—one point!"

The teacher repeats this process with each student on the class register. As each student stands up, the teacher draws a seating map on a piece of paper. For example:

TEAM 1	TEAM 2	TEAM 3
Yuta Tatsuya	Jun Saori	Yuki Mika S
Yoko Ami	Kota Mika	Daiki Kenta

By doing this, the teacher can begin to connect the names on the class register to the faces of individual students as they stand up during the activity. After the activity has finished, the teacher can give the students individual class work to reinforce the learning that has taken place. For example, students can write sentences or paragraphs about group members via the information collected from the survey. While students are doing the individual work, the teacher has time to refer to the seating map and memorize the students' names. After that, the teacher should inform students that there will now be a test—but the test is for the teacher. The teacher should then try to name all the students in the class. This very public display not only shows that the teacher is making an effort to remember students' names but also puts the teacher under the pressure of making potential mistakes in front of everyone, a situation that students will go on to face in the upcoming lessons in the process of learning the second language (L2). In other words, it shows that risk-taking is an important and accepted part of the classroom environment.

Another tip for remembering names is for the teacher to give students a piece of paper toward the end of the first lesson and ask them to write their name (in large letters) on it. The teacher then uses a digital camera (with the students' permission) and goes around the class taking quick profile pictures of students as they hold their names in front of themselves. After the class, the teacher can create a class photograph sheet to help facilitate name recognition in subsequent classes.

Alternatively, the teacher can provide students with a blank postcard and ask them to write their name, attach a photograph, and write a short introduction about themselves on the postcard for homework (see Figure 1). Once the postcards have been completed, the teacher can then use them for remembering student names, finding out more information about the class, grouping students

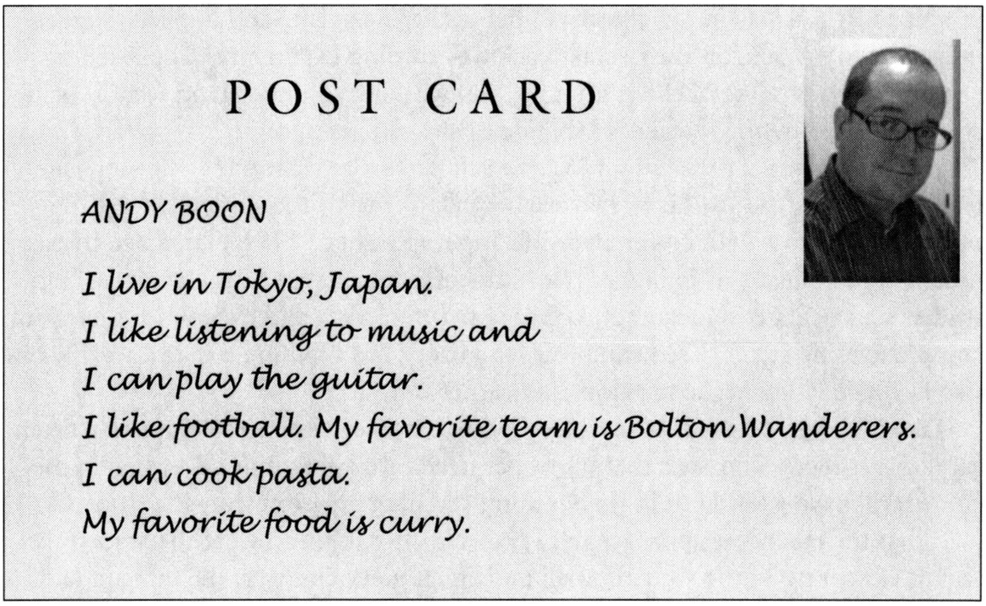

> **POST CARD**
>
> ANDY BOON
>
> I live in Tokyo, Japan.
> I like listening to music and
> I can play the guitar.
> I like football. My favorite team is Bolton Wanderers.
> I can cook pasta.
> My favorite food is curry.

Figure 1. Example Postcard

randomly during lessons (shuffle the cards and pick four students), and other communicative activities (e.g., shuffle the cards, one student picks a card, finds the corresponding student, and begins a conversation with that student related to their interests).

Tip 2: Address their needs.

As a bartender, always address the needs of your customers. Make sure they are having a good time and that their glasses are always full. Listen to them when they want to be listened to. Make conversation with them when they want to talk. Converse about a variety of topics, but be ready to modify the topic according to the needs, wants, and interests of each particular customer. Build their trust in you, and you will be successful.

As a language teacher, the first stage of addressing students' needs is to understand what students may want to learn during lessons, may lack in terms of L2 proficiency, and may be required to know in order to succeed in a particular context, and then to design and implement a course that helps them achieve their goals (Nation & Macalister, 2010). However, because "needs are in a constant state of flux" (Boon, 2011a, p. 168), it is important for the teacher to keep the channels of communication open throughout the duration of a course so that adjustments can be made to materials, lessons, methods of delivery, and the syllabus if necessary.

Therefore, like the bartender, the language teacher needs to be a good listener; listening to (and giving feedback on) not only the language being produced by learners in the classroom but also the explicit (and implicit) suggestions they may make on the overall teaching–learning experience. The teacher needs to show that he or she is listening and working to understand what is being communicated by the learners so that he or she can act upon it.

Like the bartender selecting topics to suit particular customers, the language teacher must also adjust his or her teacher talk to match the students' level. By providing students with comprehensible input (Krashen, 1981), language that is modified to be just a little higher than students' current level, teachers may help students participate in meaningful classroom interaction and experience success in comprehending the L2 (reducing learner anxiety and building self-efficacy). It can also facilitate language acquisition and learner output.

Like the trust between a bartender and a customer who feels completely taken care of, a student who feels that his or her needs are being fully addressed in the course will have great faith in the teaching–learning environment. If a student feels that the teacher is approachable, available, attending to what the student is saying, accepting of the student as an individual grappling with the difficult and face-threatening task of learning another language (Dörnyei, 2001), and accepting of and working hard to advance the student's current L2 level, that student will quite simply be motivated to learn.

As well as conducting an initial needs analysis with students at the start of a course, one tip is to establish a medium whereby students can provide regular feedback to the teacher regarding aspects of the teaching–learning environment. For example, the teacher can set aside time at the end of each class for learner self-reflection (Boon, 2012). Here, students can reflect quietly on their learning experiences by making notes as to what they enjoyed or did not enjoy about a particular lesson and write their suggestions for any course modifications they may desire. The teacher can discuss the reflective comments with individual class members or collect them in student notebooks to read later. Alternatively, the teacher can ask students to provide feedback via email or posting comments on a class blog or Facebook group. This shows that the teacher is listening to ideas from the students.

Regarding the teacher adjusting his or her use of language to suit the level of the class, this skill tends to develop naturally as the teacher becomes exposed to more and more classroom teaching. One tip, however, is for the teacher to check his or her comprehensibility in the classroom by recording classes and listening back to the interaction between teacher and students. It can often be a rude awakening for teachers to realize both the quantity and level of teacher talk that is articulated during lessons.

As an example, the following is a short extract from a lesson I recorded years ago. The interaction takes place between myself as teacher (T) and an intermediate student (M) who is taking private classes at a conversation school. The target of the lesson is to use past modals to express regrets or talk about actions that were advisable in the past. The interaction follows from a warm-up activity about personal regrets and precedes an examination of the specific grammar rules. The activity in progress is from Unit 5 of the textbook, *Northstar High-Intermediate* (Ferree & Sanabria, 1998). The student is asked to examine the language that appears on a pamphlet about the environment (*We should have protected the earth. We shouldn't have allowed the environment to become so polluted. We could have kept the water a lot cleaner. We could've avoided a lot of environmental problems.*) and to answer three questions about it. I begin to check the student's answers by asking the first question from the textbook:

1. T: "Do the sentences focus on things that were done or things that were not done?"
2. M: (8 secs) Erm . . .done.
3. T: Things that were done?
4. M: Err . . . already done but . . .erm . . .they're, they are thinking not should have done.
5. T: Okay. If I say, "We could've kept the water cleaner" . . . did they keep the water cleaner or did they keep the water clean?
6. M: (11 secs) PARDON? (laughter) . . . ONCE AGAIN!
7. T: No problem. . . . "We could've kept the water and air cleaner in the past." Did they keep the water clean?
8. M: Keep the water clean?
9. T: Yeah.
10. M: Keep the water clean is . . . ?
11. T: In the past . . .
12. M: . . . In the past? (laughter)
13. T: DID they keep it clean?
14. M: Erm . . . (5 secs) . . . I think so.
15. T: "Things that were done or things that were not done . . ."
16. M: . . . Done or not done.
17. T: "We should have protected the earth." "We shouldn't have allowed the environment to become so polluted." "We could have kept the water a lot cleaner." "We could've avoided a lot of environmental problems." Let's take these sentences one by one. . . . What do they mean? "We should've protected the earth"?
18. M: . . . We should've protected the earth.

This extract illustrates a crisis in the flow of a lesson due to the teacher's use of language. The teacher's first question in Line 1 ("Do the sentences focus on things that were done or things that were not done?") leads to an incorrect response by the student in Line 2 ("Erm . . . done") and, after an attempted clarifying move by the teacher in Line 3 ("Things that were done?"), is reinforced by the student in Line 4 ("Err . . . already done"). The teacher makes the immediate decision of trying to elicit the correct answer from the student rather than just supply it. The subsequent questions asked by the teacher (Lines 7, 13, and

17) create a great deal of confusion for the student. The student's repetition of the questions being asked (Lines 8, 12, 16, and 18), long pauses (Lines 2, 6, and 14), and laughter (Lines 6 and 12) are signals of confusion and fear of making further mistakes. This intensifies the crisis for the teacher by threatening to derail the activity completely.

By recording and transcribing the class, seeking to understand what is happening in the exchange, and reflecting on the issues that arose, the teacher here can increase awareness of how the poorly structured questions created a linguistic overload in which M was trying to process the meaning of each lexical item rather than understand the illocutionary force of the questions themselves. In a follow-up interview, M stated, "At times I was completely lost. . . . I was stuck on the word and forgot the question."

The teacher can then use the information drawn from the recordings to pay greater attention to certain aspects of teacher behavior and language in subsequent lessons (in this particular case, the teacher can work on improving teacher questions). For more information on collecting and analyzing classroom data, please refer to Richards (2003).

Tip 3: Stay positive.

As a bartender, stay positive, smile, and be friendly. No matter how you feel on any given day or night, you are there to serve your customers and create a pleasant and enjoyable environment. The bar is a stage where people are constantly watching your every reaction. Your positivity and enthusiasm becomes your customers' positivity and enthusiasm; it is truly infectious. So take a deep breath, open the door, and give it your best shot.

Like the bartender, the language teacher performs in a public arena, in this case under the watchful eyes of the students. The teacher who is genuinely enthusiastic, energetic, and expectant of students' progress with the L2 will generate a much higher level of effort and motivation among class members than the teacher who is faking it (Csíkszentmihályi, 1997; Dörnyei, 2001). After all, teacher positivity quite simply equals student positivity. This is why, as Bess (1997) suggests, "teaching . . . requires extremely high energy, focus and total commitment" (p. xii).

One tip for staying positive is to reflect on daily teaching experiences (Boon, 2011b) and to enjoy moments of success (secretly punching the air in triumph as we leave the classroom) when the lesson goes better than expected. Reflection is also a time to focus on the teaching puzzles; those aspects of a lesson that did not seem to work. It is a time to think of possible solutions to experiment with in subsequent lessons. Keep a teaching journal, a meditational space in which to write about one's classes, to explore issues that arise, and to record and celebrate one's successes. Learning and growing from what we do is, after all, the perfect tonic to successful teaching and the continual source of our energy.

CONCLUSION

This short chapter has shown a number of parallels that exist between bartending and language teaching from my own experiences as a bartender and as a teacher. It has explored the importance of teachers building rapport and trust with learners, addressing and understanding their ever-changing needs, and creating a teaching–learning environment in which learners can feel safe, supported, and secure. It has also touched upon the reciprocal nature of the classroom for both parties involved: As the students grow, the teacher grows; as the teacher grows, the students grow.

Let's take a moment to return to the bar and reflect. Take out a piece of paper, and draw a line down the middle of the page. On the top left, write the word *Satisfied*, and on the top right, write the word *Dissatisfied* (see Figure 2).

Now, make a list of the food and drink establishments you have visited as a customer. Write the name of each place under the Satisfied or Dissatisfied column. Now, think more deeply about each specific bar or restaurant you have written down. Why did you place it under the column you did? Is it a place you frequent regularly or have never returned to? What is it about this particular environment that is or was hospitable or off-putting? What can you take away from your experiences here that would help you provide an even better service to students?

Morrell (2008) provides the following advice for the bartender:

> It is really a good idea to think of your customers as guests. This drives home the idea that the people that walk into the establishments we work in are not merely random people coming in to get food and drinks. Instead, it fosters the idea that these people are valuable and more like family coming for a visit. (p. 102)

SATISFIED:	DISSATISFIED:

Figure 2. Reflection Paper

For the language teacher, our "family" comes to visit on a regular basis. It is up to each of us to discover innovative ways to provide the teaching–learning "fizz" to our students rather than the "Death in the Afternoon."

REFERENCES

Bess, J. L. (Ed.). (1997). *Teaching well and liking it: Motivating faculty to teach effectively.* Baltimore, MD: Johns Hopkins University Press.

Boon, A. (2011a). Negotiated syllabuses: Do you want to? In I. S. P. Nation & J. Macalister (Eds.), *Case studies in language curriculum design* (pp. 166–177). New York, NY: Routledge.

Boon, A. (2011b). The reflective teacher: Towards self-actualization. *The Language Teacher, 35*(4), 27–30.

Boon, A. (2012). Here we are, now motivate us. *Modern English Teacher, 21*(1), 56–61.

Csíkszentmihályi, M. (1997). Intrinsic motivation and effective teaching: A flow analysis. In J. L. Bess (Ed.), *Teaching well and liking it: Motivating faculty to teach effectively* (pp. 72–89). Baltimore, MD: Johns Hopkins University Press.

Dörnyei, Z. (2001). *Motivational strategies in the language classroom.* Cambridge, England: Cambridge University Press.

Dörnyei, Z., & Murphey, T. (2003). *Group dynamics in the language classroom.* Cambridge, England: Cambridge University Press.

Ferree, T., & Sanabria, K. (1998). *Northstar high intermediate: Focus on listening and speaking.* New York, NY: Addison-Wesley Longman.

Krashen, S. (1981). *Second language acquisition and second language learning.* Oxford, England: Pergamon Press. Retrieved from http://www.sdkrashen.com/SL_Acquisition_and_Learning/index.html

Morrell, T. (2008). *Bartending basics: A complete beginner's guide.* Vancouver, British Columbia, Canada: Pratzen.

Nation, P., & Macalister, J. (2010). *Language curriculum design.* New York, NY: Routledge.

Richards, K. (2003). *Qualitative inquiry in TESOL.* Hampshire, England: Palgrave Macmillan.

AUTHOR BIOGRAPHY

Before embarking on a career as an English language teacher in Japan, Andrew Boon was a bartender in the United Kingdom for 7 years. This part-time job contributed to the financial support of his undergraduate degree (BA, with honors, in English with philosophy) and postgraduate studies (postgraduate certificate in education). It also helped him develop such important skills as communication, listening, organization, observation, problem solving, flexibility, initiative, and professionalism that have proven to be invaluable in his approach to teaching and to establishing a safe, social, and supportive learning environment for students. He looks forward to continuing to develop as a teacher and contribute to the field until the bell is sounded and "time" is finally called on his career.

CHAPTER 3

What Can We Learn From Martial Arts Masters About Practice Techniques and Learning Environments?

Anne Paonessa

In over a decade of teaching and running my own martial arts school, a school where no one was required to attend and I alone had to pay the rent each month, I learned how to use the techniques of a martial arts master to motivate students to commit to their training and improve their skills. Publishing articles in martial arts industry magazines and speaking on school ownership, self-defense techniques, and effective instruction while appearing on the Chicago news and Oprah several times helped me reflect on my teaching and arrive at my own philosophy for effective education. As a teacher in both a bilingual classroom and an English language learner (ELL) classroom, I have found myself drawing on my martial arts background to reach and engage students.

There are many connections between the principles of teaching martial arts and teaching language. Instructors in both disciplines concern themselves with lowering students' affective filters while building students' confidence and self-esteem. Just as martial arts students progress through a logical sequence of movements that build upon each other, language students similarly attempt to progress to higher levels of proficiency. Martial arts' use of belts for rankings helps students concentrate on their own progress and mastery of the skills as opposed to comparing themselves to others. This chapter shows how language students' individual growth, at their own pace, can be fostered, charted, and celebrated in a similar fashion. In addition, it explores ways that both fields involve establishing comfortable, engaging learning environments with clear expectations and respect for all.

A MARTIAL ARTS MASTER'S TIPS FOR LANGUAGE TEACHERS

Tip 1: Have a routine framework.

Having a routine framework is a principal part of a martial arts class, following Eastern traditions that are thousands of years old. The master and the students know what to expect and do at the beginning and end of each class. At the start, students know where to go to line up and show that they are ready to begin. The master and students bow to the U.S. and Korean flags in the room and then to each other. The beginning of class also frequently includes a brief meditation, clearing the mind of any other events of the day and preparing students for the class that is about to take place. This *empty mind* helps students focus and avoid external distractions as well as to set aside internal fears.

Next, the master declares the objective for that day's class session so that the students will have a clear focus for their learning. Even though the instructional content of each class may vary, procedures are in place for a wide range of activities that happen on a regular basis. Students know how and when to use the training equipment available to them, and they know what they should do if they arrive at class late or if they need to use the bathroom. They know and understand the expectations for asking questions and working with other students. These standard operating procedures minimize distractions and help the classes run smoothly. At the end of the session, the students bow to signal respect to each other for the work that has been accomplished. This final bow is often followed by a reflection on what was learned in the class.

A routine framework can also help language classrooms run efficiently and allow everyone to make the best use of their time together. Teachers and students can work together to establish routines to set the stage for learning from the start (including discussion of the content and language objectives for each session) and to reflect on progress at the end, and they can also establish standard operating procedures for the most common activities in their classroom. Documenting these routine procedures through pictures and captions in students' native languages can help all students follow the routine, including those students with lower levels of proficiency and those who join the class after the school year has started. Finally, the language teaching master can even make meditation part of the routine, teaching students to take deep cleansing breaths to relax, focus, and give their best effort.

Tip 2: Have respect.

The basic foundation of any successful martial arts program is grounded in a tradition of respect for self and others. Students show respect through listening, supporting their fellow students, and always trying their best. This respect is mutual. The martial arts master shows respect for students by always trying to provide the best possible training experience, knowing students as individuals, and guiding them to build off of their unique strengths. Respect is given for the students' effort and hard work, even when they may be slow to progress. This respect for students is evident through the master's patience and strong leadership. High expectations for all students are clearly set. The master has a belief in the students' abilities, often before they can see it in themselves.

It is imperative that the language teacher, like a master, establishes a learning environment based on mutual respect for all members. Such an environment can help lower students' affective filters and make them comfortable taking risks with English. This foundation also builds a sense of community and gives a feeling of importance to the learning that is taking place. When each and every individual in the learning process can actually feel respected, students are motivated to try their best and encourage others. They feel like they are a part of something special and form an identity as a group that is supportive and protective of its members.

Tip 3: Remember: Appearances matter.

The appearance of a martial arts school is important for many reasons. As mentioned earlier, the master/school owner has to cover a wide array of costs associated with owning and operating a business, whereas no student has any obligation to come pay the necessary tuition to make the school viable. To maintain and develop a successful school, masters must pay attention to the appearance of all areas of their school, keeping them clean and organized. No one will want to give money to a school that appears dirty or cluttered, because that would not project a professional appearance and would not garner trust in the school's ability to provide quality instruction. A professional appearance can establish a learning environment where all members are prepared to participate, have a sense of purpose, and rise to the level of the professional atmosphere.

A martial arts school that has a set location for equipment and a place in the lobby for announcements, newsletters, signs, and other means of communication will win more new students than a school that appears haphazard or scattered in its delivery of information or instruction (see Figure 1). In addition, a martial arts school that uses its lobby to display pictures of its students and staff can create a sense of community and pride in its members. A clearly posted motto or mission helps to provide an overall focus for all. For instance, in my school this motto is "A place to challenge yourself."

Teachers of any subject should take the time to critically evaluate their learning spaces. Even a talented teacher's effectiveness could be seriously diminished through lack of organization or poor arrangement of the physical space. Ask yourself: If students did not have to be there, if you operated in a highly competitive industry where students had a choice of which classroom to attend, would they choose yours? Can elements of a successful martial arts school be useful for you,

Figure 1. Orderly Appearances at a Martial Arts School

such as effective use of limited space, an area for signs and announcements, and display of a classroom motto and photos of your students? In what ways can you project professionalism and provide tools for engaging learning? What changes would you make to your physical space if students and their parents were "shopping" classrooms the way that most families will visit several martial arts schools before deciding where they would like to begin their training? How would carefully setting up your classroom benefit both you and your students?

Tip 4: Use a belt system.

As Mason (n.d.) notes, the martial arts belt system provides a concrete way that students and others can recognize hard work and progress. The master establishes a set curriculum for each belt level, so the students know what they need to learn to get to that next level. When students reach a higher level, they wear their new belt color with great pride and a real sense of accomplishment. Generic compliments such as "good job" are unnecessary, because everyone knows and naturally respects the effort involved in order to earn the right to wear this new belt color. This system also allows students to watch and follow students of higher ranks as examples of how things should be done. Students can look at the belts of others and know who they should ask for help.

As language teaching masters, we should also pause to celebrate students' growth. Very often, the students themselves do not recognize their own growth and accomplishments because they are focused only on reaching that next level. Language teachers should provide tangible ways to help students document their progress and reflect on their growth as a result of their hard work. One option is to assemble portfolios of dated student writing with self-assessments, recordings of students' speech to track growth in oral fluency, and sample reading passages with running records of any errors or self-corrections (such as repeating a word to correct pronunciation or realizing a word didn't seem to make sense in the context of the sentence and re-reading to address the error). All of these saved samples will help students specifically see their accomplishments. You may consider developing a checklist appropriate for students' grade and proficiency level to promote effective self-assessment.

Belt system principles can also be adapted for the language classroom by creating opportunities for students to recognize their strengths and to help others who need aid in those areas. In a martial arts studio, this happens when a Green Belt knows to ask a higher ranking Blue Belt for help with kicks or board break. Identifying language students as "experts" in certain areas can similarly give them a chance to develop leadership skills, to gain confidence in those areas of strength, and to be recognized by peers as valid resources for learning.

Tip 5: Facilitate effective practice.

An effective master uses a wide range of techniques to help each and every student practice and reach his or her full potential. These techniques include stating clear objectives, modeling, providing opportunities for free practice, and offering feedback specifically tailored to each student.

The master models techniques for students for several reasons. Many students are visual learners, and modeling helps them clearly see and understand the technique they are trying to learn; it also gives them a highly proficient level to strive for. In addition, modeling allows masters to share the struggles that they encountered and insights they gained while they were trying to learn the technique as students themselves. Masters may share different breakthroughs they experienced as the technique continued to become more advanced, fluid, powerful, and technically correct.

Most important, the martial arts master understands that students learn best by doing. The master therefore provides ample opportunity for scaffolded practice. Students may work on just the initial segment of a technique before they add the next steps, or students may work on the technique as a whole. The master will carefully watch students and see where they are progressing and where they are struggling. With this information, the master will design specific practice opportunities to help each student progress. If a student is developing a kick but executing it too low, the master may use a target in a different way by having the student kick over it or between two targets held at a higher level.

Understanding the theory behind the movement or being able to explain it is not the same as getting a feel for the movement and having the opportunity to get better at it. Students need time to work when there is no feedback offered, with freedom to make mistakes and explore the new material. Later, students may be asked to evaluate their own execution by responding to guiding questions.

The master will offer specific feedback after the student has had time to come to conclusions independently, pointing out what the student is doing well and suggesting areas for further practice.

Naturally, language teachers can use similar techniques, allowing students to practice freely and reflect prior to being given individualized feedback. For language teachers to be effective models for students, it is important that we continue in our own practice and development of skills, pushing ourselves to face new challenges in writing, reading, listening, and speaking for a variety of purposes and audiences. Continued personal challenge helps us better understand and relate to students as they strive to learn.

Tip 6: Be patient.

Patience is a virtue that assists both the teaching and learning that are taking place. For a martial arts master to demonstrate this virtue with his or her words, actions, and body language is imperative. If you say, "It's OK to make a mistake, you are learning," but your face shows exasperation or frustration, students will feel your disappointment and feel pressure and anxiety to please you, all of which may impede their progress.

Demonstrating patience with yourself as a learner and talking about it with students can be invaluable. Students should be made aware that they owe themselves kindness because acquiring a new language takes time. Without patience, students can feel like they are failures, that they are taking too long, or that they are not capable of learning. These feelings can cause them to shut down or give only surface-level effort to appease the teacher. A language teaching master will demonstrate the impact of patience on learning. This can be done by discussing examples of young children trying to learn a new task, such as tying their shoes or riding a bike without training wheels. How would the children progress if the people around them showed frustration? How fast would they accomplish the task if they shut down and stopped trying, only focusing on what they can't do yet rather than on the progress they are making? (For a related perspective on the impact of a teacher's patience on students' learning, see Chapter 6, in which John Spiri discusses the techniques of the Zen master.)

Tip 7: Disguise repetition.

Martial arts classes involve building a solid foundation in basic skills and continually building on that base in order to achieve more difficult tasks. No matter how many years students have been training or what their current belt rank may be, there are many basics that they must continually review and strengthen. A White Belt, or beginning-level student, will practice a basic front snap kick to try to build a basic level of proficiency by raising his or her knee high enough and snapping the foot out (Figure 2). A more experienced Red Belt will still practice the front snap kick, but this student's purpose for practicing is to add speed, balance, and power to this kick. Students may repeat the same technique thousands of times during their training time.

To keep students making their best effort and discovering nuances in their techniques, it helps to use a variety of equipment and instructional delivery methods. Students will perform a side kick differently when they are doing it in the air, on a hand-held target, or on a bounce-back bag. Students can also practice this kick with each other while they are both wearing sparring equipment, or they can simply have a different focus for practicing the same kick. During one class they may focus on speed, and in another class, power. During some classes they may work alone to improve their kicks, whereas in others they may work with a partner or small group. This variety helps the students stay engaged and approach the same technique in a fresh way. Disguising this repetition enables students to grow and develop in ways that they may not experience if they were expected to repeat the same move in the same way over and over again.

Figure 2. Walking Front Snap Kick

In the language learning classroom, there are many skills that we want students to build in order to gain fluency and increase their confidence and proficiency levels. If we expect them to practice these skills in a routine, repetitive manner, we will see limited results, but if we can identify the key skill we want them to focus on and find a variety of meaningful ways for them to engage in practice, students will enjoy the lessons more and we will see far more growth as a result.

This variety in delivery should be intentional and planned. Just as a martial arts master knows the training equipment that is available and plans accordingly, a language teaching master will know the techniques that he or she can use to provide both instruction and opportunities for application. For example, students may practice questions through role-playing that they are at a dinner party or a job interview, or they may practice as reporters interviewing characters from history or a book. The students may also interview people who work at the school, such as a custodian, bus driver, teacher, or principal. Variety in activities keeps students engaged and interested in their learning and allows them to build fluency and confidence. Too often in a language learning classroom, a class has a focus followed by an all-too-brief opportunity for the students to engage in the necessary practice. Disguised repetition encourages true acquisition of the target language.

Tip 8: Make progress visible: Break boards!

The martial arts master has students break a wooden board with a different technique at the end of each level of their training. This is a tangible way for the students to test their knowledge and apply it to a real situation. Many are nervous before breaking a board, but each time students succeed, they seem to walk a few inches taller and exude a new sense of accomplishment. The students often collect the boards they have broken as trophies, and they look to their next challenge as soon as they achieve the one that was right in front of them.

For many students, it will take more than one attempt to be successful. Experiencing failure before ultimately succeeding teaches students that if they persevere and self-assess regarding what they need to do differently, they will most often still reach their goal. The greater the challenge, the greater the gain in self-confidence students get when they see they can meet their goal.

Giving language students similar challenges can provide opportunities for them to see the improvement in their abilities. Specific tasks can be offered for students to try at different levels and in all domains of language. On Challenge Day, students select the domain and level of challenge for their task, which may be color-coded in a similar way to a martial arts belt system. An example of this may be in the domain of presentational speaking, which would involve delivering information in a speech with wide ranges of difficulty.

Prior to the start, it is important to remind the students that everyone brings a different level of knowledge and language experience to the classroom and learns at a different pace. Language teachers continually need to point this out; otherwise, students may feel competitive with others instead of themselves, and some students end up feeling superior and others inferior. This is definitely not the goal!

If students keep some sort of class ID on their desks during every lesson, colored stickers might be affixed to it to record completed challenges. If not, students can collect Challenge Cards for successfully completed tasks and keep them in their portfolio. Keeping the cards in their portfolios helps the students see their growth and provides a valuable reference point for parent conferences.

Tip 9: Get families involved.

Another secret of the martial arts master's success is that of involving the family in the student's development as a martial artist. Students do not develop in isolation at the martial arts school itself. Dougherty (2010) suggests that family involvement helps to ensure that students practice at home, attend classes regularly, stay focused on their goals, and maintain a sense that others care about their development and successes.

A language teaching master can work to build ties with the students' parents or guardians through effective and frequent communication focused on student accomplishments and how students can be helped at home to make even further growth. The language teacher can also involve families in projects in which the adults share experiences or stories with their children, possibly in their native language. In addition, language teaching masters can serve as advocates for the ELL families they encounter, ensuring they feel comfortable and welcome in their schools and making them aware of resources available to them.

Tip 10: Provide energetic leadership.

True martial arts masters understand that their passion and energy level will feed the rest of the class. Therefore, masters clear their minds of any other distractions they may have and bring enthusiasm, focus, and commitment to every class. If a master stood in front of the class and led with minimal energy, the students would directly reflect that and place an equally minimal amount of energy into their own efforts. This low energy level would negatively impact their enjoyment of the class and their motivation to try their best to reach those next levels.

True masters will bring the same high level of energy to each class, whether it is the first or fifth class they have taught that day. They will smile, make eye contact, and show excitement for what they are about to teach and the training opportunities the students are about to have.

Masters of martial arts and of language teaching remain leaders at all times. If they see something isn't working, they step in and make necessary changes. They are proactive, making decisions and executing them rather than just letting things go. They renew their own love for what they do and strive to have some balance in their lives so that they do not burn out. They have fun while they are teaching and share that enthusiasm with their students. This enthusiasm is contagious, inspiring students do their best.

CONCLUSION

There are a number of reasons language teachers might look to martial arts masters for examples of effective teaching practices. Martial arts masters are typically recognized experts in their field who are not afraid of hard work. They are dedicated to their own development, and they are dedicated to the development of students. They hold high expectations for students and work with them until those expectations are met. Masters do not see students as having limits; they see them as people who want to learn and achieve, and masters take responsibility to help them reach their goals.

Martial arts masters also need to be prepared to teach students with a variety of needs. This may include blind students, highly functioning autistic students, and students with missing limbs. In each case, the master must adapt and learn new techniques with the students. Masters also remember that they have much to learn from such students, such as true determination, belief in oneself, and the ability to maintain a positive outlook in spite of challenges.

Of course, language teachers work with a wide range of learners as well. Students come to us from a variety of countries, with unique personal and academic backgrounds. We can utilize the principles of the martial arts master to give students language learning experiences that last long after their time in class is over, by fostering respect and patience, establishing a routine framework, carefully planning the appearance of our classrooms, using systems with clear expectations and challenges, disguising repetition, involving families, and structuring learning events to show students their growth.

ACKNOWLEDGMENTS

I would like to thank Dr. Stephen Krashen, a fellow Tae Kwon Do Black Belt, for reviewing my work and sharing his insights. Further acknowledgment goes to the many inspiring martial arts masters, students, and ELLs that I have had the privilege of working with.

RESOURCES FOR FURTHER EXPLORATION

Hyams, J. (1982). *Zen in the martial arts* (Reissue ed.). New York, NY: Random House Digital.
> The author, who trained with masters such as Bruce Lee, shares from his more than 25 years of martial arts training. He reveals how Zen principles can be applied to enrich several aspects of your life, including controlling pressure and improving relationships.

Lawler, J. (2011). *Dojo wisdom*. London, England: Penguin.
> Martial artists learn more than to throw the perfect punch. This book shares insights, even if you never train in martial arts, on ways to tap into an inner warrior power you may have never known you have.

Martial Arts Industry Association: www.masuccess.com
> This website for one of the leading martial arts industry consulting firms provides access to free issues of *MA Success Magazine*, which covers a variety of topics.

Morgan, F. E. (1992). *Living the martial way*. Fort Lee, NJ: Barricade Books.
> This book is a step-by-step guide for applying the Japanese warrior's mindset to daily life. It explores history, philosophy, spirituality, and strategy and tactics to be used by a martial artist.

Mostofizadeh, K. (2011). *25 principles of martial arts*. Los Angeles, CA: Mikazuki.
> This book shares 25 principles that provide the basis for countless martial arts strategies. The strategies can be used not only in martial arts practice but also in business or personal life.

National Association of Professional Martial Artists: http://napma.com
> This website contains information designed to help martial arts school owners succeed, and it provides access to a magazine that covers topics ranging from leadership to martial arts principles.

REFERENCES

Dougherty, N. (2010, February 10). The importance of family involvement at the school [Web log post]. Retrieved from http://martialarts4u.wordpress.com/2010/02/10/the-importance-of-family-involvement-at-the-school/

Mason, A. (n.d.). *Martial arts belt systems and goal setting.* Retrieved from http://www.selfgrowth.com/articles/martial_arts_belt_systems_and_goal_setting

AUTHOR BIOGRAPHY

Anne Paonessa founded Yongin Martial Arts, in Naperville, Illinois, in 1995. Her family-centered martial arts school offers classes for ages 4 through adult. She currently holds the rank of fourth-degree Black Belt in Tae Kwon Do and second-degree Black Belt in Hap Ki Do, both Korean martial arts. Anne has experience as both a bilingual and English language teacher and she is now the ELL/bilingual facilitator for Lombard School District 44, in Illinois. She also designed and teaches a graduate-level course called Innovative Methods for ELL Teachers through the Illinois Resource Center. She can be seen in a "Someone You Should Know" segment from Chicago's ABC-7 at http://youtu.be/1j7iX4ooLlE.

CHAPTER 4

How Would a Role-Playing Game Master Engage Learners in the Quest for Knowledge?

Roger Dupuy

The Ashmouthe Tavern has seen better days. The war that tore this city in two has taken a toll on every establishment. There are days when the tavern has not enjoyed a working kitchen or healthy fire in its hearth. At least the ale flows freely. These are the thoughts of Hywin, a young warrior sitting at the end of one of the heavy wooden tables in the main chamber. His back is against the far wall, opposite the entrance, and his entire armored body is wrapped in a dark cloak from ankle to hood. The hood is pulled over his head, putting his face in shadow. He clasps one gloved hand around the battered tankard of ale, pulls the frothy beverage toward the shadow of where his mouth is, but doesn't drink. His attention is drawn to the front door, or more accurately, where the front door used to be.

The explosion that rendered the iron-shod doors into a fine cloud of splinters dissipates, revealing a large hulking figure, armed with a huge mattock.

"Hywin! You fool!" he exclaims in a low menacing voice. "I am here to repay my debt to you!"

"I've been waiting for you," answers Hywin. The two slowly approach each other. They stop within arm's length, and without pause, embrace. The young warrior's tankard of ale, still in his hand, splashes wet arcs on the wood-dusted floor.

"I miss you, my brother," confesses the larger of the two.

It's easy to be drawn into a scene like this. If you are a spectator, there's a sense of drama, of unexpected action. If you are one of the performers, you may have context and pre-established patterns that can guide your next move, but you are still not quite sure how the other player will react. Role-play is at the core of this encounter. It catalyzes language and communication.

I have been gaming all my life. *Gaming* in this chapter refers to the design of, refereeing of, and participation in role-playing games (RPGs). I am also an English language teacher. Certain game design elements of RPGs are reflected in my language teaching. Recently, the term *gamification* has been used to describe how certain game design elements can be incorporated into non-game contexts (Deterding, Dixon, Khaled, & Nacke, 2011). I draw from my own experience and familiarity with role-playing games to achieve this. This chapter addresses the question: How can elements of game design inform and improve certain aspects of language teaching?

What is a role-playing game? Tychsen (2006) offers the following general definition:

> All forms of role playing games . . . share a group of characteristics, which makes them identifiable from other types of games: storytelling with rules, control of fictional characters, a fictitious reality, usually the presence of a game master (or game engine), and at least one player. (p. 76)

An RPG is a socially engaging game, in which players and the game master often hold gaming sessions in intimate settings like a dining room or around a coffee table. Luke Crane (2011), creator and designer of the RPG "Burning Wheel," sounds like he could be describing RPGs in general as he introduces his game:

> In the game, players take on the roles of characters inspired by history and works of fantasy fiction. These characters have a list of abilities and skills rated with numbers and a list of player-determined priorities. The synergy of inspiration, imagination, numbers and priorities is the most fundamental element. . . . Expressing these numbers and priorities within situations presented by the game master (GM) is what the game is all about. (p. 9)

It is this synergy among the game players and the game master that makes it a rewarding experience for the participants. All participants work together to achieve their goals. This should not sound unfamiliar to anyone in the workplace. Crane could have been giving an inspirational talk about teamwork at the beginning of some high-level corporate meeting. He also could have been introducing the context for the galvanizing power of cooperative and participatory learning in language education.

At the very beginning of an RPG session, the participants agree on a genre and setting. Typical genres are fantasy and science fiction. The specific settings usually resemble ones from classic fantasy literature like J. R. R. Tolkien's *Lord of the Rings* trilogy, but other settings abound. After the genre and settings are established, the referee (or in RPG parlance, the game master) begins introducing various objectives for the game players. These objectives are commonly called quests. As RGP players develop strategies to fulfill these quests, they need to interact within the established setting, adhering to its laws and rules.

Often quests are the stuff of fairy tale stories we are all familiar with. The quest may require the heroes to travel great distances, defeat evil foes, and recover precious treasure. Other quests can involve unraveling mysterious plots or saving people from harm. There are as many possible quests as there are plot devices in stories, and all quests are filled with obstacles that the game players must overcome. Game players solve a series of increasingly difficult obstacles to finish the quest via planning, teamwork, risk-taking, and a little bit of luck. The quest allows for all the players and the game master to engage in this synergy.

AN RPG MASTER'S TIPS FOR THE LANGUAGE CLASSROOM

In the language classroom, the teacher reveals the "setting" through establishment of the syllabus and course plan. The students show their buy-in, or willingness to participate, by registering for and attending class. As the contents of the syllabus, the schedule, the text, and the curricular mandates of the institution are shared, the teacher also establishes the rules, plans, and expectations for how the students are to engage in the class. It is in this convergence of the setting, genre, and rules that the quest for language learning begins.

What all this means up to now is that we have a convenient parallel metaphor between what initially occurs in a role-playing game and what initially occurs in the language learning classroom. To move beyond a mere metaphor to more practical applications for language teaching requires subsequent analysis of what makes a successful RPG quest. This chapter looks at several RPG elements that are analogous to characteristics of language teaching: quest engagement, set-up, avatars, leveling-up and experience points, character sheet, and equipment inventory.

Tip 1: Engage learners in a quest.

Quest engagement is a good term for the game design element that provides context and motivation for players to invest their time, attention, and energy to play and finish the game. Participating in an RPG is interactive. Game players and the referee need to work together, engaging in a series of conversations interspersed with narrations, stories, and plot-moving events. It is this interplay that keeps the game moving. It holds the players' interest. It is motivating.

How can this dynamic inform language learning? The language teacher and language learners share a common responsibility. On the first day of class, the language teacher sets up the course and invites the language learners to join him or her on this quest. If there is no buy-in from the language learners, the established goals of the course will be much harder to achieve. Both parties are responsible. Both need to interact well to succeed.

The RPG referee spends a great deal of time preparing the various quests before the game session begins, thinking about the various strengths and weaknesses of the game players and determining which obstacles would provide the fairest challenges for them. The referee includes those elements but throws out others that are too difficult for the players. If a quest is so difficult as to almost guarantee the deaths of the heroes in the game, it is not an appropriate quest. Quests of this sort can demoralize and discourage players. Additionally, if the type of quest does not match the sensibilities of the game players, then they can lose interest or even choose not to do the quest at all. For example, if the group of players is only interested in fighting monsters and accumulating treasure, then a quest steeped in mystery, puzzle-solving, and political intrigue would not be interesting to the players. This is true even if the quest's level of difficulty is appropriate. The game players would still not be motivated to commit to the quest. Also, to motivate players' investment in the game, the skillful referee highlights the rewards if the players are successful in their quest.

Of course, these are the challenges of the language teacher. One goal is to create lessons, activities, and assessments that provide challenges that spur growth without demoralizing or discouraging learners. Another goal is to spark the learners' interests. The third goal is to highlight the rewards that the learners will receive upon successful completion of these lessons, activities, and assessments. When a language teacher, like the successful RPG referee, does these things, language learners become engaged and motivated to strive to overcome whatever challenges are put before them.

Tip 2: Begin with an engaging set-up, and promote teamwork.

There is more to quest engagement in an RPG. A significant amount of time and effort is required to introduce each quest, giving players a reason to have a personal stake and to work together. This is called the set-up. A quest is usually introduced in a very dramatic way in an RPG. The game master begins with a moving narrative that details the features and potential risks of the quest, perhaps using music and even realia to evoke the desired mood. For example,

> There is a growing sickness in a village, and there are rumors that the cause is a mysterious, unsettling fog that appears on the streets at night. Moreover, the fog has been seen emanating from a nearby forest that many of the villagers deem cursed. The heroes (the game players) hear of this as they pass through this village, picking up supplies. At first, the heroes decide not to pay heed to the villagers' needs, but then one of their own party is stricken with the same strange illness.

There is no more need for motivation for the players. The set-up is such that the heroes have a personal stake in this quest into the cursed forest.

For the language learning context, a language teacher can foster interdependence and teamwork through task-based lessons, activities, and assessments. The teacher could set up an appropriately challenging task, place students into groups, and supply each group with an integral piece of information needed to complete the task. The task cannot be completed individually. Students must work together to be successful. Penrod's (2002) *Touchy Situations* is a good resource; many of the chapters contain a scenario that provides a set-up for students to engage in and solve.

Tip 3: Use avatars.

Avatars in RPGs are fictitious personas that players take on to immerse themselves in the game. This persona, normally called a player character, can be a warrior, scientist, superhero, spy, animal, or almost any animate being. Hiding behind this persona allows game players to take on behaviors that are different from real-life, for instance, taking on a role of a character that is usually bigger and greater than themselves. The anonymity afforded by the avatar, and the license to act bigger than life, gives players the freedom and courage to defeat foes, do heroic acts, and fulfill quests. The fictional persona allows them to take greater risks and also explore and approach problems that they would not normally face.

For the language classroom, what if a language learner had the ability to hide behind an avatar? What would the associated benefits be? Would the language learner be willing to take more linguistic risks? If so, what degree of anonymity would be optimal? Would implementing avatars in the language classroom require complete anonymity or just an alter ego that other classmates know about?

In my experience with RPGs, game players know the real identities of the other players, but there still seems to be enough anonymity to be effective. I propose that language teachers use avatars in the same way. Role-play is a familiar feature of many language classrooms. Ladousse (1988) states that

> role-play helps many shy students by providing them with a mask. Some reticent members of a group may have a great deal of difficulty participating in conversations about themselves, and in other activities based on direct experience. These students are liberated by role-play as they no longer feel that their own personality is implicated. (p. 6)

Role-play helps language students take more risks, and as Brown (2000) says,

> Risk-taking is an important characteristic of successful learning of a second language. Learners have to be able to gamble a bit, to be willing to try out hunches about the language and take the risk of being wrong. (p. 149)

The more frequent the risks, the more of the learner's language fluency is exercised. The more frequently the language learner interacts in the target language, the more language is possibly learned. This seems to be a desired behavior for a language learner, a behavior that could be fostered through the use of avatars and role-play.

Sample Activity: My Hero

Other than standard role-plays, another way to incorporate the avatar element of RPGs in the classroom is to have language learners take on the persona of a superhero using the My Hero activity. The steps are as follows:

1. Show the opening clip from *The Incredibles* or a similar superhero movie.

2. Discuss the popularity of Pokemon, Yu-Gi-Oh!, Harry Potter, and Marvel/DC Comics movies with heroes (e.g., *The Avengers*, *X-Men*, and *Iron Man*). Ask students to think about their favorite superheroes.

3. Have students brainstorm about the characteristics of a hero. (Time permitting, the menu on the supplemental DVD of *The Incredibles* has a Top Secret section with a wonderful database of NSA [National Supers Agency] Files that outline in detail all the "Supers." It is worth looking through to get ideas for what to include in a superhero file.) Characteristics that students may choose to brainstorm include name; hometown; nickname (e.g., Batman); cover (e.g., when not acting like a superhero, Bruce Wayne is a billionaire philanthropist); physical description (with space provided for a sketch or picture); description of powers, including strengths and weaknesses (e.g., Superman's vulnerability to kryptonite); and origins/background story (how did they get their powers?).

4. The language learners flesh out the details of their superheroes by filling out a handout (see Figure 1), which resembles an NSA file.

5. After the file has been created, each language learner is paired up with a partner to perform a mock interview. One student poses as a superhero, and the other student as the interviewer. After a bit of practice at their seats, these interviews are then performed in front of all their classmates.

6. Follow-up activities may include using these heroes in other role-playing and conversation situations, writing stories and using storyboards to map out a simple narrative, and recording news reports regarding the actions of their hero in dramatic situations.

All these tasks are intended to thrust the language learner into the persona of the superhero. Students will often pick out superpowers they personally wished they had. Through this My Hero activity, it is possible that these superheroes become a faint, idealized version of themselves. Perhaps language learners using superhero personas will be willing to speak more freely and take more risks in speaking.

Tip 4: Use character sheets to keep track of experience points and help students level-up.

In RPGs, avatars eventually develop and improve in abilities and skills. Once they complete a quest, they are awarded *experience points*. An experience point is an abstract numerical representation of training and experience that translates into increased effectiveness or additional abilities. In RPG parlance, when player characters (avatars) increase their abilities through experience, it is called *leveling-up*.

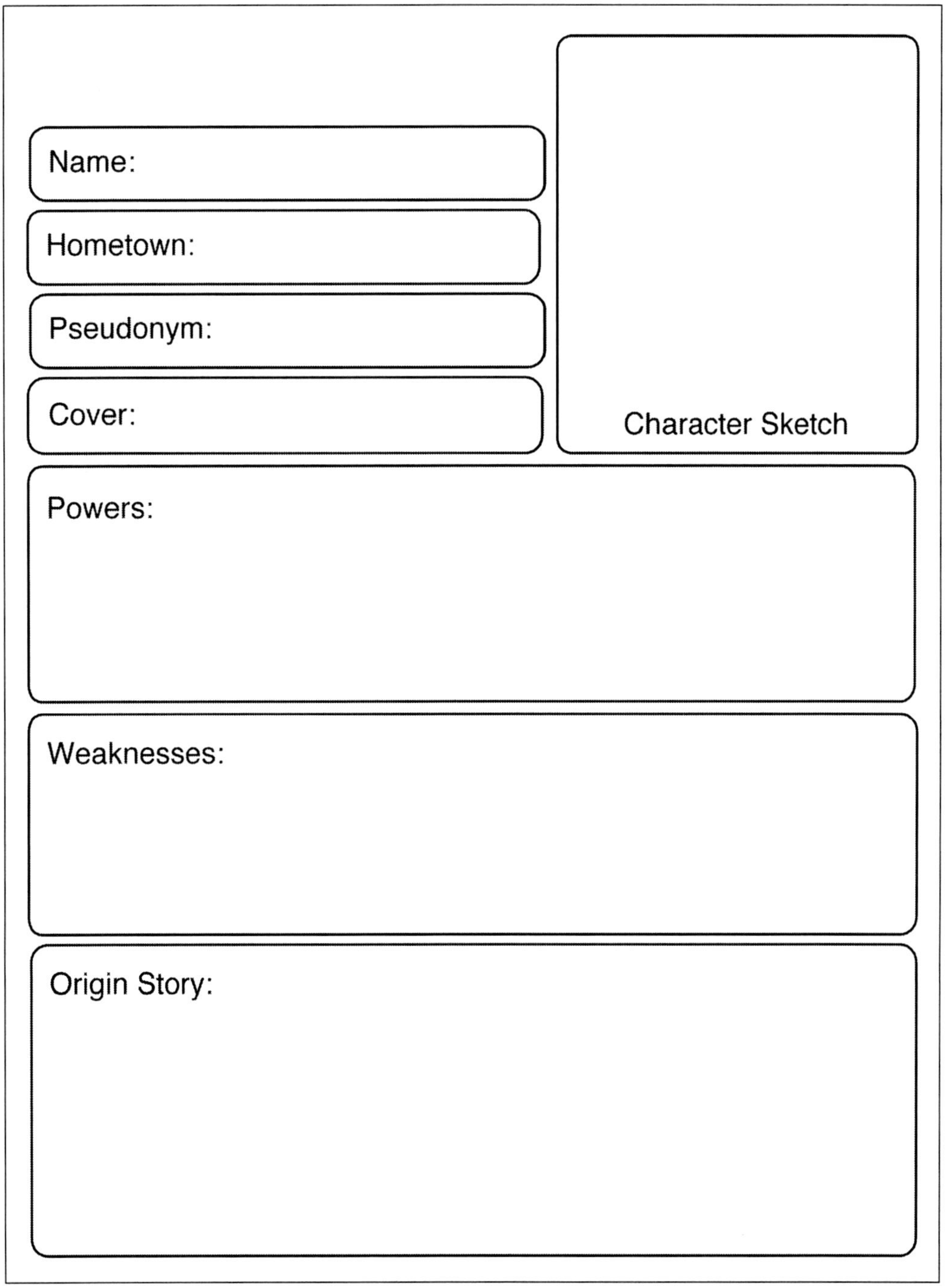

How Would an RPG Master Engage Learners in the Quest for Knowledge?

Name:	
Hometown:	
Pseudonym:	Character Sketch
Cover:	

Powers:

Weaknesses:

Origin Story:

Figure 1. My Hero Worksheet

Leveling-up involves the tracking of growth and progress of player characters. For example, beginner player characters typically start off relatively weak. However, as they level-up, they gain abilities and skills that help them survive and fight better (e.g., attack more effectively, dole out more devastating damage to opponents, withstand greater amounts of damage). These changes provide a clear, measurable, and motivating mechanism for the role-player to continue on in the struggle to complete the adventure. How could leveling-up be incorporated in language teaching pedagogy?

An RPG player maintains accurate knowledge of his or her strengths and weaknesses by utilizing character sheets to record the player's abilities and track the experience points that lead to leveling-up. These statistics can be quite detailed. They often represent very specific and discreet abilities. The character sheet shown in Figure 2 includes separate numerical statistics for power (physical strength), agility (reflexes), forte (stamina), perception, and so on. From the character sheet, game players know, for instance, how strong, agile, resilient, intelligent, and wise they are. With this awareness, they know which obstacles may be too strong for them to tackle. As the game progresses, those character sheets help game players track progress.

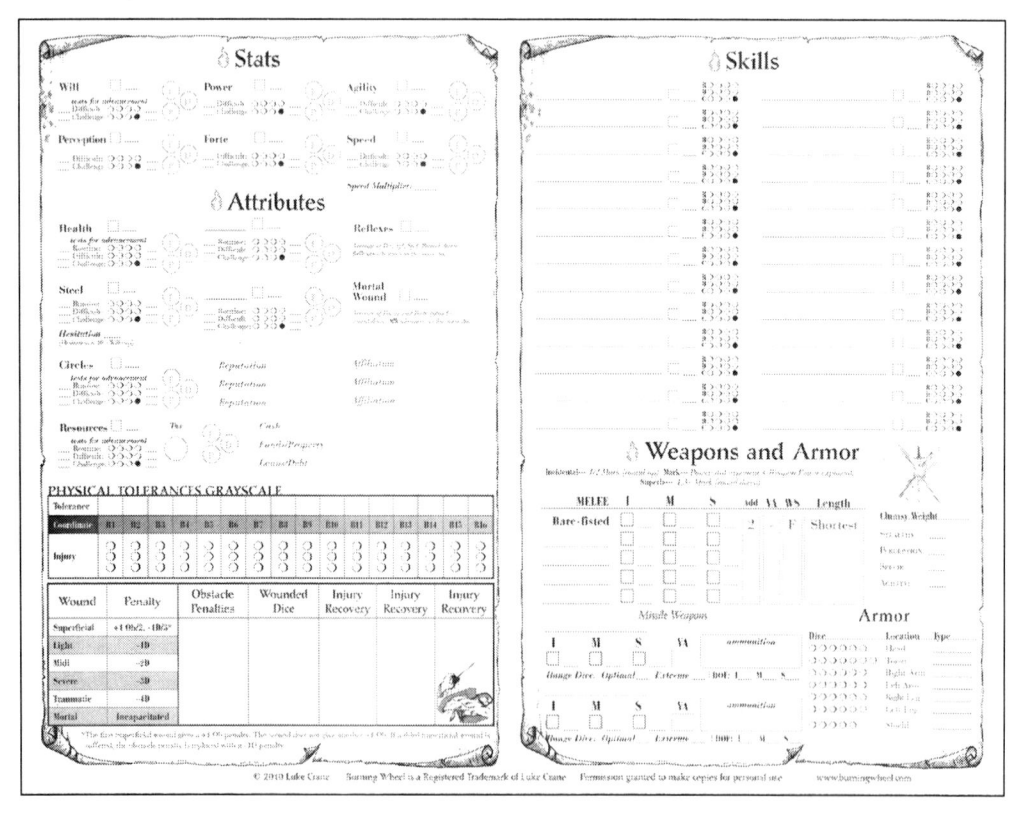

Figure 2. Character Sheet From Burning Wheel
Source: Crane (2011).

A low-level game player would be able to confront only those foes and obstacles that are easy to overcome. A high-level game player would be able to defeat more difficult foes and obstacles. For example, if a game player has a high statistic in physical strength, then his or her character is physically strong and is normally successful in completing tasks like lifting heavy objects and breaking down doors.

In Figure 3, we see that a character sheet may also include a section called Skill Being Learned. There is a place to write in a skill, a score (called *aptitude*), and a running checkbox that records the number of tests (instances) that need to be completed in order to level-up in this skill.

Perhaps language assessment could make use of such RPG elements. There are already many types of assessments, such as high-stakes exams (e.g., TOEFL, TOIEC, and IELTS) to measure language proficiency, placement tests to place students into a spread of language levels, and achievement tests to check for language mastery. But the key issue is actually hidden in the mind and heart of the language learner. Other than a number or a level, how do these measurements inform the language learner? Can a Level 4 (say, intermediate level for the sake of argument) language student infer what language skills he or she has now and, more important, what he or she needs to work on in order to improve? This student needs more effective indicators than just a number. Students need to know where they are and what they need to do in order to improve their language abilities. Language learners often complain that they do not notice that they are improving in English at all. Teachers should give learners a roadmap to help them strive for a better outcome. Such RPG elements as leveling-up, experience points, and character sheets can be incorporated to develop alternate markers that denote progress in language learning, with rubrics that are specific, simple, and clear.

A character sheet for the language classroom should include descriptions of two main elements: current language abilities and desired language abilities. Descriptions of current language abilities should be as specific, measurable, and discrete as possible. In addition, assigned to each description should be a numerical value that indicates how proficient the language learner is in that specific skill. For example, Figure 4 shows that one description for a presentation class could be "The speaker used repetition in an effective way to remind the audience of the main point." The numerical value could be expressed as a 2 out of a possible 5. According to the legend, a 2 means "needs improvement." The language learner would know that he or she is weak in this area and needs to improve.

How could the student improve without a roadmap? The Desired Language Abilities column of the character sheet addresses this question. It provides a list

Skill Being Learned:	Aptitude (out of 5):	Instances Needed:
__FENCING__	__2__	__25__

Figure 3. Leveling-Up

Current Language Abilities	Current Score	Desired Language Abilities
The speaker used repetition in an effective way to remind the audience of the main point.	2	To get a 3: Write the main idea on the board at the beginning of the presentation. To get a 4 or 5: Do the above, plus try repeating your main idea at the beginning of each section and once more at the end of the section.

Scoring Legend

5: Shows Mastery—The student did such a great job exhibiting this described behavior that the student could teach this behavior to others.

4: Good—The student did a good job exhibiting this described behavior. With careful practice and refinement, the student could become a master.

3: OK—The student did an adequate job exhibiting this described behavior. There are a few things that the student could do to be considered good at it.

2: Needs Improvement—The student did not do an adequate job exhibiting this described behavior. There are many things that the student could do to be better at it.

1: Didn't Do It at All—The student did not exhibit this described behavior at all.

Figure 4. A Language Learner's Character Sheet

of suggestions or desired behaviors that would help push the 2 score up to a 3, 4, or 5. These suggestions allow the language learner to use the character sheet like a roadmap to track and develop better linguistic outcomes. If formatted into a single document, the character sheet could be something that the language learner would always keep handy, for a constant reminder of where the student is and what he or she needs to do next. In addition, the teacher could support students' progress by focusing on these descriptions of current and desired language abilities as teaching points in lessons.

Tip 5: Keep an equipment inventory.

Another aspect of RPG design that could serve as a useful metaphor for language learning is the equipment inventory. Usually in adventure games a player acquires equipment such as weapons, armor, and special items that give the player a better chance to defeat foes and overcome other obstacles. When language learners employ notecards for study and review, we might similarly say that they are using physical equipment to help them in their quest for language proficiency. Textbooks, dictionaries, computers, televisions, and mobile phones are other physical examples of language learning equipment. There are also many nonphysical pieces of equipment, such as various learning strategies that increase the effectiveness of language learning (e.g., skimming and scanning strategies for reading). Any tool or strategy that is employed to help language learners in their quest to improve their language proficiency could be included in an inventory of language learning equipment, and learners could occasionally refer to this list to remind themselves of the resources they have. As Richards (2000) has noted, successful language learners are the ones with a large and effective set of language learning resources and strategies.

CONCLUSION

A number of useful parallels can be drawn between the worlds of role-playing games and language teaching. RPG elements of quest engagement and the set-up can be useful reminders to language teachers of the importance of crafting syllabi and lessons that are appropriate to language learners in terms of difficulty, relevance, and hope of rewards. The set-up reminds us how important it is to create a positive, synergistic, adventurously risk-taking mood for students. The use of avatars, through such activities as My Hero, may encourage more timid language learners to take more risks. To give language learners a more concrete roadmap to improvement, the elements of leveling-up, experience points, and character sheets may be options for language teachers. Incorporating and adapting these RPG elements through meaningful diagnostics and progress markers can encourage learners to get a better sense of their progress in a language. Finally, the equipment inventory is a convenient analogy for physical and cognitive tools that language learners can employ for maximum learning impact.

However, the use of these role-playing elements may pose challenges. For instance, employing all or some of these elements in your language teaching may draw resistance from legacy language learners, learners who are convinced that grammar translation, rote memorization, and similar mental disciplines are the best ways to learn a language. Also, the value of the avatar element may be lost on language learners who have no desire to "pretend." They might see this as wasteful play and might have a hard time reconciling language learning with taking on roles. Moreover, teachers should bear in mind that the creation of effective assessment is an ongoing quest. It can be difficult to capture, assess, and offer suggestions for improvement of language behavior. The character sheet would need to be simple enough for the students to use and understand and yet loaded with enough details to give adequate roadmaps for better linguistic behavior. These character sheets should be fashioned in such a way as not to be overly time-consuming for the language teacher to use regularly. Finally, creating an effective set-up also takes time and energy, but when one considers the potential motivating synergy among students that would result, it seems clear that it is time and energy well spent.

RESOURCES FOR FURTHER EXPLORATION

Kleon, A. (2012). *Steal like an artist: 10 things nobody told you about being creative.* New York, NY: Workman.

> This little book talks about the right ways to steal in order to do worthwhile and artful things. Page 39 has a wonderful two-column table comparing "Good Theft" and "Bad Theft"—brilliant. For instance, I "stole" from RPG game design to create new connections in teaching language.

Koster, R. (2005). *A theory of fun for game design.* Scottsdale, AZ: Paraglyph Press.

> With a page of art facing a page of text, Ralph Koster cleverly introduces and then dissects what makes a game fun, and relevant to not only gaming, but to life in general. A quick read.

RPG.net

> RPGnet is an independent website about tabletop role-playing games. This site is not centered on any specific game or game system, so you'll find discussion of many different role-playing games, including the more esoteric ones. RPG.net also includes discussions of other topics of interest to role-players, including computer games, miniatures, board games, comic books, movies, and television.

REFERENCES

Brown, H. D. (2007). *Principles of language learning and teaching.* White Plains, NY: Pearson Education.

Crane, L. (2011). *The Burning Wheel fantasy roleplaying system* (3rd ed.). New York, NY: Burning Wheel.

Deterding, S., Dixon, D., Khaled, R., & Nacke, L. (2011). From game design elements to gamefulness: Defining "gamification." In *Proceedings of the 15th International Academic MindTrek Conference: Envisioning Future Media Environments.* New York, NY: Association for Computing Machinery.

Ladousse, G. P. (1988). *Role play.* Oxford, England: Oxford University Press.

Penrod, G. A. (2002). *Touchy situations.* McHenry, IL: Delta.

Richards, J. C. (2000). *Reflective teaching in second language classrooms.* Cambridge, England: Cambridge University Press.

Tychsen, A. (2006). Role playing games: Comparative analysis across two media platforms. In *Proceedings of the 3rd Australasian conference on interactive entertainment* (pp. 75–82). Murdoch, Australia: Murdoch University. Retrieved from http://dl.acm.org/citation.cfm?id=1231906

AUTHOR BIOGRAPHY

For 18 years, Roger Dupuy (rdupuy@uci.edu) has taught English and trained language teachers in the United States, China, Taiwan, South Korea, and Kirghizstan. He has a passion for the arts, curriculum design, content delivery, and emerging technologies. He has been a regular presenter at teacher training conferences such as California TESOL and TESOL International Association for the past 14 years. He is a hopeless generalist, currently teaching in and responsible for curriculum design and coordination of all teacher training for International Programs at the University of California, Irvine.

Dealing With Challenges

CHAPTER 5

What Does It Mean to Be a Whitewater Language Teacher?

Karen Blinder

As the paddler approaches the river, she and her companions scout it well, looking for possible sources of difficulties and ways to circumnavigate where necessary. They look for places where the current may be used to advantage and ways to transition from one section of the rapid to the next. Having planned well, the paddlers embark upon the course. Slipping into the current, the paddler is filled with a sense of joy: It is a thrill to face the constantly shifting demands of the river. Reaching the first rapid, strong currents move her in an unexpected direction. She realizes a change of course will be necessary and deftly maneuvers to another channel. She smiles. That was fun! As the current shoots her into the next channel, her bow heads straight for a huge boulder. After an initial second of panic that makes her want to lean away from the rock to apparent safety, her training kicks in, and she does just the opposite. Leaning downstream, tipping the boat at a 45-degree angle, she leans directly toward the rock. But she doesn't hit it! Instead, the boat is lifted up over the rock, and she shoots down that rapid with a rush of adrenaline joy. But at the next rapid, as she works her way over a small ledge, she misjudges a twist in the current. Almost before she knows what happened, she is upside-down, bouncing through the rapids. However, this has happened before, and she doesn't panic. Instead, she remembers the skills she was taught. Capitalizing on the leverage of her long paddle, she rolls the boat and proceeds on her way. Her friends flash her grins and thumbs up signs as they see her quick recovery. At last, the boat comes to a quiet pool at the end of the rapids. It has been a wonderful run!

In many ways, paddling illustrates a microcosm of a teacher's life. In paddling, we face a constantly changing environment. Used to our advantage, this is a great part of the fun. It is a process involving incremental progress punctuated by periodic failures and occasional moments of joyous victory. Insights are often very pragmatic in nature: *Hold the paddle like this, not like that, for greater leverage.* Hardships are part of the package. Soreness, fatigue, and heat or cold must all be endured on occasion, and paddlers learn to face these aspects of their sport with good humor. We also learn the importance of recognizing realities: Few paddlers can oppose a very strong current. Instead, we use it; the best paddlers like to "play" in the current. Learning to read the currents is a critical skill. And in the end, when we learn to maneuver with the currents, and not against them, joy and confidence are our reward. We learn early on to lean on the group for education, moral support, and practical assistance. We also learn the philosophy of passing on to others what we learn. As we are taught, so we teach others, with no expectation of recompense. Finally, the sport by its nature encourages reflection. On quiet stretches, hours are spent in rhythmic paddling, keeping company with one's own thoughts. The rapids, on the other hand, test our skills and provide the excitement and challenge we need to grow.

Language teaching shares all of these characteristics with paddling: incremental progress, hardships, changing environment, and community spirit. Like paddling, teaching language successfully is the cumulative effect of many small victories, often the result of pragmatic insights on the part of the teacher as well as the students. Often I have found that I achieve a small breakthrough when I suddenly realize *exactly* what it is that a student is failing to understand. Another similarity is that each entails some hardships. (For teachers, long hours spent grading come to mind.) As for paddling, keeping good humor is easiest when the joys of the activity are also remembered. There are reasons that, overall, we enjoy what we do, and if we can recall those reasons, the hardships are not burdensome. Part of what I most enjoy about both teaching and paddling is the ever-changing nature of the challenge: the "current." As a teacher, the current I face consists of the strengths, weaknesses, and individual personalities of my students, my colleagues, my institution, and myself. If I maneuver through these currents with skill—using but not fighting the forces I face—the end result can be joyful, confident play. My ability to do so is enhanced greatly by drawing on the knowledge, support, and camaraderie of my colleagues. As I receive, so I give; I believe in the importance of teaching at all levels and in all directions. However, even when actively involved in a professional community and "traveling in a group," in some ways each person's voyage remains her own. Both quiet reflection and difficult challenges are necessary for a teacher to grow.

In the following section, I share a few tips that a whitewater paddler might give to a language teacher. These lessons were learned over the course of a number of years as I gradually acquired paddling skill under the guidance of other paddlers in the Washington, DC, area. These paddlers freely shared their time and expertise and taught me not only the technical skills, but a way of looking at the world.

A WHITEWATER PADDLER'S TIPS FOR LANGUAGE TEACHERS

Tip 1: Plan thoroughly.

Make use of all available resources to prepare a good syllabus, schedule, and lesson plan. The textbook and teacher's manual are only a place to start. They serve the same purpose as a map does for the paddler. However, paddlers also consult websites and talk to other paddlers about conditions on the river and best approaches to rapids. Additionally, paddlers study books and subscribe to outdoor magazines in which they read articles about the sport itself. Teaching is likewise greatly enriched if a teacher consults colleagues, does Internet-based research, subscribes to professional journals, and reads books about the teaching craft.

Tip 2: Paddle with others.

Make use of the collective knowledge and moral support of colleagues at work, in professional organizations, and at conferences.

Tip 3: Always carry a spare paddle and an emergency kit.

Sometimes things do not work out as planned. When this happens, it is helpful to have a spare paddle and an emergency kit. Some suggested items are given in Figure 1.

Tip 4: Read the water.

"Reading the water" refers to interpreting the pattern of the current to decide what is the best course, which paths are safe, and which are best for a challenging but fun ride. Good teachers read the water in a number of ways. The first is by doing a thorough needs assessment early in the course. Another is by constant reassessment throughout the course—judging students' moods, attentiveness, performance, and progress toward overall goals. Read the signals from students, and be flexible in response to these. Are the students tired? Confused? Frustrated? Any of these may require a change of plans.

Tip 5: Look where you want to go.

Paddlers sometimes become distracted by a rock they fear they might hit and are then, it seems, invariably drawn to the rock on which their gazes are fixed. Experienced paddlers learn to keep forward-focused—on the goals, not the obstacles. Teachers do well to do the same.

Tip 6: Keep loose.

A good teacher, like a good paddler, must be relaxed but alert. This is a skill (in both settings) that comes with time, experience, and a growing confidence. The maiden teaching voyage, like the maiden paddling voyage, may be characterized

> Need a sudden activity? Class energy dragging? Keep these on hand for emergencies. If you have your own classroom or desk, you will be able to keep all of these items on hand, but if you are itinerant, you will have to choose which to carry.
>
> 1. **A Spare Paddle**
>   Emergency lesson modules. Prepare several all-purpose 15- and 50-minute lesson modules in advance. Carry these with you to pull out if you should suddenly find that your lesson plan is not long enough for the class or if you should suddenly need a new plan for any other reason. Some of these lessons may be taken from your Emergency Kit's emergency reference book collection.
>
> 2. **Emergency Kit**
>   a. Emergency reference books. Keep these books on hand, and study them in your free time. They are most useful in an emergency if you are already fairly familiar with their contents.
>   i. *Fun With Grammar: Communicative Activities for the Azar Grammar Series*, by Suzanne Woodward (1997). This book contains many activities that require no preparation. The activities, clearly organized by grammatical topic, are very engaging and well received.
>   ii. *Zero Prep: Ready-to-Go Activities for the Language Classroom,* by Laurel Pollard and Natalie Hess (1997). The same publisher also has a version for beginners.
>   iii. Books from TESOL International Association's New Ways series, such as *New Ways of Teaching Writing* (White, 1995).
>   b. Communicative prompts
>   i. *Chat Pack: Fun Questions to Spark Conversations* (The Question Guys, 2007). This box of cards is available online for approximately $10. It contains hundreds of small cards, each with a question to be answered. The questions are most appropriate for intermediate- and advanced-level learners. For speaking and listening classes, the questions can be answered orally; for reading and writing classes, the students can write their answers and show them to their partners.
>   ii. Pictures. Keep on hand a collection of thought-provoking or funny pictures large enough for the whole class, or make a collection incorporated into a PowerPoint presentation. National Geographic online is one excellent site for photographs. These can be used as prompts for writing or speaking.
>
> *Continued on page 55*

by more than a little nervousness, and perhaps some outright fears. The unknown is the culprit, of course. As we face daily challenges, we learn where the "rapids" can be expected. We also gain skills in negotiating them. As this happens, we become more relaxed, and our minds can be freed from fear to exercise their more helpful function—that of being appropriately alert. In such a state, a paddler floats with his grip secure but loose on the paddle, his body posture ready but loose. Teachers, too, can learn to "float," keeping their hands at the ready on the "paddle" while never letting their gazes be distracted from the "currents." Their postures will be erect but relaxed. Their faces will show no signs of tension. In this alert, relaxed state, their senses will not miss any incoming signals from the class. They will keep control seemingly without effort.

> c. All-purpose game supplies
>   i. Beanbags. Students can toss these to one another to choose who is "it" to answer the next question. To work best, the questions should have short answers, so that the pace is rapid.
>   ii. Enough dice for the class. These can be used in a variety of ways. One way is to write different tasks on the board corresponding to each number on the dice (e.g., "1. Complete the following sentence: *I have often . . .* "). Students take turns rolling the dice, and complete the tasks according to the numbers. If desired, groups can be paired as opposing teams, and points can be given for correct answers.
>   iii. M&M candies. Tell students they can take one, two, or three M&M's, but cannot eat them until they answer a question (one question per M&M).
>   iv. Two flyswatters. These can be used for practice in distinguishing between minimal pair words, between two grammar features, or for any other paired discrimination. In minimal pair discrimination, write two words on the board that differ in one sound. Two teams of students are formed and line up. The first student in each team comes to the board and takes a flyswatter. Turn away from the two students (so that they cannot lip read), and say one of the two words. The students swat the word they hear, holding their flyswatter down on the word after they swat. The first to swat correctly gets a point for his or her team. The next two players then come forward, and new teams are formed. This game usually has the whole class laughing in a short time.

Figure 1. A Language Teacher's Spare Paddle and Emergency Kit

Tip 7: Use the current.

A great part of the joy of paddling is the dance paddlers do with the currents. They grab fast tongues of current adjacent to the channels they are in, and they are rewarded by sudden accelerations as their boats ride the new tongues of water. They turn their boats so that the stern ends are angled to the currents and cause the current to ferry them from one side of the river to the other, all without ever paddling across the river. What paddlers quickly learn, however, is that, regardless of how strong they may be, there are currents that are stronger. It is futile to fight these currents. Teachers can capitalize on sudden fortuitous currents just as paddlers can. Make use of the unexpected teachable moment. Also learn which currents are too strong to fight. Be ready to change lesson plans if called for.

Tip 8: Be willing to adjust course at a second's notice.

Truly, that is part of the fun! It allows you to exercise your skills and build confidence.

Tip 9: Use your paddle.

Never forget that you have skills and tools at your disposal. Novice paddlers, in a difficult moment, sometimes freeze with their paddles in the air, where the paddle is unable to assist them in any way. Veteran paddlers will grin and shout, "Put your paddle in the water! You can't paddle air!" Similarly, novice teachers, faced with an awkward moment (such as a behavioral problem or a section of the lesson plan that bombs) may suddenly feel an emotion akin to a rising panic. In such a situation, it is good to remember that any purposeful action is better than none. Retain authority (your grip on the paddle), and move on.

Tip 10: Lean downstream, *into* the rock you are afraid to hit.

This is one of the hardest skills for a paddler (or teacher) to learn. When the bow of the boat hits a submerged rock, the current tends to grab the stern and swing the boat sideways to the current. Beginning paddlers are told to lean downstream in such situations. But it is a hard thing for them to make themselves do, because it feels like that will lead to disaster. In fact, however, it is just the reverse that is true. If the paddler leans away from the rock (upstream), the current catches the deck, and the boat will capsize. On the other hand, if the paddler leans downstream, leaning into that scary rock and causing the boat to tip in a way that feels very precarious, the current will instead catch the hull and lift the boat safely off of the rock (Grant, 1997). So, too, a teacher sometimes tries to avoid risk by relying on what seems safe—following exactly the lesson plans outlined in books or hiding behind prepared PowerPoint lectures. Such "safe" behavior may lead to just the outcome the teacher fears: poor overall teaching performance. The best paddling runs come from trying some rapids that may seem a little scary at first. Similarly, some of the best teaching comes when we take a few judicious chances. Try sparking a lesson with communicative techniques such as skits, debates, and mock trials. Students love the drama of these, and there are always a few ham actors. Explore some new features of your learning management system, such as discussion boards, blogs, wikis, drop boxes, voice email, or video postings. Students live much of their lives connected, so having a good online presence is definitely worthwhile. Incorporate new audiovisual materials, such as videos and animated clips, into your lesson. There is a wealth of material available on the Internet, and using it makes for a great change of pace. Another activity worth considering is having a field trip. The library is one great place to try, and the librarians are always happy to oblige. Board games are also worth exploring. Games can be used to teach grammar, speaking, and listening, and even adult students usually enjoy them. The ideas are endless, limited only by your imagination. I set a goal for myself to try at least one new "rapid" each semester. This keeps me growing. It also makes my life as a teacher more fun.

Tip 11: Try a difficult rapid, but be sure there is a pool at the bottom.

Try a promising but risky lesson section, but have the foresight to plan a surefire, safe activity immediately after it.

Tip 12: Learn to roll.

Sometimes, the boat capsizes. When this happens, paddlers roll, and flip the boat upright once again. For teachers, there are lessons that don't go as planned, days when things seem not to go right. That is part of the rhythm of teaching. If a planned lesson segment proves unsuccessful, one of the tools from the Emergency Kit (Figure 1) may save the day. Stay calm and move on.

Tip 13: Enjoy the adventure!

Once paddlers develop good skills, they find they are able to "play" in rapids. So a teacher is able to take pleasure from confronting the daily challenges. With skill comes freedom of movement, and that allows both paddler and teacher to dance.

CONCLUSION

On the best days, teaching is every bit as exhilarating as whitewater. The adrenaline rush of a good class is hard to beat. But just as with sports, this kind of high comes as the result of disciplined development of skills and confidence. This development requires a teacher to be willing to stretch a little outside of his or her comfort zone—to take a few chances in order to grow. These chances, like rapids for the paddler, gradually increase a teacher's agility in the currents of teaching. The teacher becomes more skillful, more adaptable, and more adept. Teaching begins to feel like dancing. That is when the excitement and joy really kick in. So the parting recommendation is this: Challenge yourself to try new "rapids." Come on in! The water's fine!

REFERENCES

Grant, G. (1997). *Canoeing: A trailside guide*. New York, NY: W. W. Norton.

Pollard, L., & Hess, N. (1997). *Zero prep: Ready-to-go activities for the language classroom*. Provo, UT: Alta Book Center.

The Question Guys. (2007). *Chat pack: Fun questions to spark conversations*. Yankton, SD: Questmarc.

White, R. V. (Ed.). (1995). *New ways in teaching writing*. Alexandria, VA: TESOL.

Woodward, S. W. (1997). *Fun with grammar: Communicative activities for the Azar grammar series*. Upper Saddle River, NJ: Prentice Hall Regents.

AUTHOR BIOGRAPHY

Karen Blinder has taught ESL to adults for 5 years. She is currently teaching at the English Language Institute at the University of Maryland Baltimore County, and at Prince George's Community College. As a young woman, she spent many hours paddling whitewater canoe (C-1 and open tandem canoe) on the rivers in the Washington, DC, area. She now paddles tandem canoe with her husband. Hours spent on the water have allowed her time to reflect and develop a personal philosophy related to canoeing, a philosophy that is reflected in this chapter.

CHAPTER 6

How Would a Zen Master Bring Compassion, Equanimity, and Choiceless Awareness to the Language Classroom?

John Spiri

"Never let them see you sweat" was a famous advertising catch phrase by the Gillette Company in the 1980s. Language teachers know well the value of maintaining composure in the face of confusion. A Zen master, taking this one step further, might teach by the motto "Never sweat." The inner world is of utmost importance because all actions will flow from it.

A language teacher can impeccably plan *what* to do in a class, but another crucial ingredient is *how*. A teacher's calmness and kindness will certainly have a positive effect on students.

A Zen master, after doing various practices and austerities as a Buddhist monk, attains a state of equanimity and compassion, and the training the Master offers flows from this state. Our imagined Zen master will have keen powers of observation, will not be disturbed by ego, will have transcended emotions such as anger and fear, and will feel great compassion for individuals and act accordingly.

In regard to terminology, this chapter equates *equanimity* (a common adjective in the Buddhist canon) with calmness, patience, and focus, and equates *compassion* with kindness, concern, and unselfishness. The demeanor of a Zen master should not be confused with being "nice." Mainly, this chapter addresses the inner world of the Zen master and teacher, rather than his or her outward actions. Thus, while maintaining compassion and genuine concern for students, a Zen master might be strict or even severe when the situation dictates.

I have experienced the sharp pain of the *keisaku*, the flat wooden stick that monks use to whack practitioners on the back. With lay practitioners, at least, this is only used when requested, which I did, hoping to interrupt extreme fatigue. The vast majority of my time spent meditating at Zen temples, at home, or at a 10-day Buddhist retreat in Thailand was spent battling mundane demons: fatigue, boredom, and uninvited thoughts of every variety. In addition to insights gained on the meditation cushion, the teachings of J. Krishnamurti, Buddhism, and the four yogas (Raja [meditation], Bhakti [devotion], Jnana [knowledge], and Karma [service]), in particular, have guided and inspired me throughout my adult life.

At least as important as compassion, Zen masters teach mindfulness. The Buddhist term *mindfulness* is akin to keen awareness, the ability to notice and sense what is happening. Mindfulness is the state we seek, or demand, in students when we say, "Pay attention." Being in a state of keen awareness is surely beneficial to teachers. The phrase *choiceless awareness* includes that sense of mindfulness while addressing the issues of choice and will. Attaining choiceless awareness would mean directly observing and perceiving, without the corruption of judgments, assumptions, and expectations. Achieving such a state—or at least assuming such an attitude—has, like mindfulness, relevance to teachers.

Finally, it should be noted that I use the term *Zen* broadly and include quotes and ideas from Eastern spirituality that capture the spirit of Zen, even if they are not explicitly part of the Zen canon. Such Zen ideas invite practitioners to gain psychological understanding and are in no way sectarian. Any individuals, including atheists and the devoutly religious, are invited to consider the value of the practices contained in this chapter and the ways they might lead to improved teaching.

A ZEN MASTER'S TIPS FOR LANGUAGE TEACHERS

Tip 1: Act out of a space of genuine concern and compassion for students.

A teacher's inner state will not only guide the teacher's conduct but also affect the class atmosphere and student performance. Even if the teacher says the "right" things and attempts to implement appropriate activities, learners will be less likely to respond in a positive, constructive manner if the teacher is upset or confused. This is especially true for second language learners who feel anxiety and might be struggling to understand verbal messages. A teacher who is focused and projects calmness will naturally be more likely to connect with learners and make them feel at ease. Such a teacher will provide a model for students that goes beyond the acquisition of language: Students may look to, and emulate, the teacher as a human being.

It is not always easy for a teacher to see students with fresh eyes over the course of a semester or school year. A teacher may acquire subtle judgments that a student is lazy or not intelligent. But the Zen master exhorts us to "just observe."

The removal of clutter in the mind—which includes judgments, comparisons, insecurity, fear, and other negative emotions—allows compassion to flourish. The Zen master's teaching is that compassion is not something to acquire; rather, it is simply allowed to shine once the barriers are removed.

Tip 2: Practice choiceless awareness in the class.

Choiceless awareness, originally articulated by the Indian philosopher and educator J. Krishnamurti (1989), refers to a state of total awareness devoid of choice, control, and ultimately, devoid of self: "Don't let your prejudices cloud your observation of things as they are, just observe, and you will discover that out of this simple observation . . . something happens to you inside" (pp. 77–78). Krishnamurti maintains that we don't truly know other people. Rather, we create an image of others, and that is what we relate to. This is because our awareness is clouded by choices, driven by ego.

Choiceless awareness takes William Glasser's choice theory one step further, in at least one regard. Glasser (1999) emphasizes that the only person whose behavior we can control is our own, and we should thus yield control in the classroom. A teacher's understanding of Glasser's principle leads to offering students greater autonomy and reduces both inner and outer conflict that arises when teachers attempt to force students to think or act in a certain way. Meanwhile, choiceless awareness refers to a state where no choice exists, including self-control. In that state or attitude, a teacher is fully present and acts without pretension or contrivance.

> If you condemn a child or identify yourself with him, then you cease to understand him. So, being aware of a thought or a feeling as it arises, without condemning it or identifying with it, you will find that it unfolds ever more widely and deeply, and thereby discover the whole content of *what is*. To understand the process of *what is* there must be choiceless awareness, a freedom from condemnation, justification, and identification. (Krishnamurti, 1992, p. 143)

Hence, choice is seen as an expression of ego, a way to acquire "likes" and avoid "dislikes." Although the fuller ramifications of a state of choiceless awareness—enlightenment—are outside the scope of this chapter, the point here is to explore how such a state, or at least such an attitude, might be beneficial to a language teacher in the classroom.

Tip 3: To cultivate greater compassion and genuine concern for students, and practice choiceless awareness in the classroom, do a short meditation before class.

Lewitt (1986) notes that the Zen teaching method utilizes meditation. Whereas Lewitt describes traditional Zen meditation, *zazen*, the discussion here focuses on adapting *zazen* as a short preteaching practice. After making sure that your class planning is thoroughly complete, you are ready to begin. Sit with your back erect in a straight chair or meditation cushion. The goals of *zazen* and this preteaching practice are alike in that both are to cultivate calmness and clarity. However, while the fundamental goal of *zazen* is to ultimately gain enlightenment, the fundamental goal of this preteaching practice is to mentally prepare for a class. The typical Zen meditation technique is to simply count each inhalation and exhalation (breathe in and out and count 1, breathe in and out and count 2, etc.) up to 10. This cycle of counting pairs of inhalation-exhalation up to 10 is repeated over and over. In this pre-class meditation we may begin by using this counting technique, but we welcome any class-related thoughts that arise. There is no need to put our attention back on our breath when distracting thoughts arise, as a Zen practitioner would. Instead, we watch thoughts and our reaction to them: Is there anxiety about a problem student or situation? Tibetan Buddhist teacher Kongtrul (2005) notes, "Emotions can only overtake us when we're unaware of them. Then it's like the tail wagging the dog" (p. 55). Thus, welcome the thoughts and emotions as they arise, without getting lost in them. Similarly, watch feelings. Are we tired? Cranky? Pleased? Simply observe without judgment, censure, or anxiety. Kongtrul explains,

> The focus (of meditation) is on letting our state of mind reveal itself. If anxious, we may pay particular attention to our breath, breathing deeply to find greater calm. When disturbing thoughts and emotions arise, your only choice is to let them unfold naturally. Don't try to control or indulge them. Giving them importance only makes them more "real." Instead, shift your attitude a bit. (p. 7)

Teachers/practitioners may remind themselves of their intent: to be the best teachers they can be regarding both specific language instruction and the way they present themselves in front of students. The way, per Zen principles, should be calm and compassionate (which includes being firm when necessary). Thus, the pre-class meditation is focused on achieving calm and removing choice driven by ego and a desire to control.

The pre-class meditation may also include visualization of the upcoming class activities. Teacher trainer Hopkins (2011) notes, "The Zen here is 'conceptualizing' the lesson" (p. 19). Later, in a chapter subtitled "Meditating the Plan," Hopkins writes, "*Visualizing* what the teacher and the students will do in the lesson accurately is the art of lesson planning" (p. 121). The pre-class meditation is the best time to envision how the lesson might unfold, taking the opportunity to "see" how we as teachers might react to challenging situations.

Throughout the day, especially while at work, a teacher's thoughts may race, so subsequent brief moments of quietude, to reestablish a focus on calm and the importance of inner balance, may be practiced. Buddhist teacher Hardin (2011) suggests, "Take just a few minutes each day to be with yourself in a simple way, without busyness, distractions, or entertainment. Just sit down and be" (p. 24). Hopkins (2011) recommends focusing on the breath as a means to slow down:

"Breathe—bringing respiration to the conscious level is a trick used in everything from yoga to tennis to focus and slow down the pace" (p. 89).

Educators are, understandably perhaps, reluctant to talk about cultivating love in the context of teaching. However, love as a state of compassion that is not aimed at a particular individual can enrich the classroom and be an objective of the pre-class meditation. "Without the arising of love in your heart, life has very little meaning; and that is why it is so important that the educator should be educated to help [students] understand the significance of all these things" (Krishnamurti, 1989, p. 78). In the language learning classroom, love need not be discussed or mentioned overtly, but rather demonstrated by the way the teacher conducts the class.

One purpose of the pre-class meditation is to practice embracing, rather than struggling with, pre-class mental states, from trepidation and nervousness to fear and resentment, in an environment that does not include the challenges of human interaction. Teachers who share a common space before class will want to find a chair in the corner of the room where they can shut their eyes and not feel distracted by the noises of an office. Meanwhile, teachers who have consecutive classes may only be able to do the pre-class meditation once, early in the day.

Thus, the pre-class meditation is a 5- to 20-minute practice that teachers do before class. This practice, especially when done regularly, builds a reservoir of patience, compassion, and focus that will make the teacher better able to handle the challenges of teaching a class.

Tip 4: Understand the challenges to achieving choiceless awareness.

Krishnamurti, who first articulated choiceless awareness, maintained that any method to achieve it was doomed to failure and part of the same corruption of mind. Efforts to remove choice are just, paradoxically, further choices and expressions of a person's will.

However, many Buddhists, who essentially have the same aim, offer various suggestions regarding cultivating such awareness. Buddhist teacher Smith (2010) explains:

> Do not move by reframing, correcting, or altering whatever the mind is doing in this moment. When every state is fully embraced, we find awareness opening around and through states of mind. We surrender the mind to be just what it is, and with the absence of resistance to the mind, awareness is all-pervasive. (p. 127)

This is our practice as "Zen teachers." The removal of judgment, efforts to control, and ultimately, ego will make energy available to guide students to have an optimal classroom experience. Hopkins (2011) explains, "If there is one thing to be learned from many years of teaching and teacher training, it's that the ego gets in the way" (p. 27). There are many ways a teacher's ego can negatively impact a lesson. A teacher may get locked into a battle of wills with a recalcitrant student, a teacher may struggle with disappointment over an underwhelming reaction by students, or a teacher may simply try too hard to be funny or clever or dynamic. These expressions of ego manifest in choices that a teacher makes.

It is easy to conceive the benefits of greater calm and choiceless awareness in specific classroom situations such as those fraught with tension. If students are chattering excessively and not cooperating, for example, a teacher might feel annoyed or even angry. Removing judgment and ego allows a teacher to handle the situation from a state that is inherently more stable and authoritative. Such a teacher may sternly and loudly clap his or her hands to get attention, wait patiently, or deflect the chattering with a joke. The point is, there is no set way. Each unique individual teacher, in a unique situation, will be better able to take a suitable course of action when practicing choiceless awareness. The teacher will be poised, attentive, and sensitive to the needs of the students and can proceed accordingly.

CONCLUSION

This discussion of a Zen teacher is not meant to be prescriptive. It does not suggest that teachers should behave in a particular way. Teachers of varied temperaments, backgrounds, and personalities will naturally react to situations in distinct ways. A strict response may work better than a lenient one, or vice versa, depending on the individual teacher and situation. Thus, rather than suggesting *what* a teacher should do, this chapter suggests *how*. The Zen teacher teaches from a non-egotistical space of understanding that is sensitive to the needs of all members of the class.

A spirit of nonjudgment can permeate a teacher's in-class demeanor, but assessment remains an integral aspect of teaching. How does the Zen teacher reconcile this? Assessments, based on predetermined criteria, whether tests, reports, or some other measure, must still be handled in a responsible manner. Although it is outside the scope of this chapter to delineate specifically how a Zen master might handle end-of-term grades, in general, the approach would avoid norm-referenced grading because it is based on comparison. Ideally, the grading would be pass/fail. Teachers typically do not have that option, but they can at least include an element of self-assessment. The Zen teacher is, after all, striving to overcome the tendency to judge a student as "good" or "bad," which inevitably includes corresponding reactions of attraction and aversion. Personal judgments and reactions that a teacher might feel about a student or situation, whether it be for perceived laziness, disinterest, rudeness, or other behavior, should be put aside. Ideally, the teacher sees and perceives students directly, without any labels or baggage.

The practice of choiceless awareness, however, does not preclude the ability to discern quality, including the quality of a student's classwork. The point of choiceless awareness is to be fully present, without likes or dislikes, without expectations, without demands, and, to the extent possible, without ego. Formal assessment, such as the assignment of grades at the end of a term, is often required, and when required, should be doled out to each student in accordance with the syllabus.

Considering all the research topics that are addressed in education communities, as well as in informal discussions by teachers, we might find little attention paid to the cultivation of equanimity and compassion in the classroom. Perhaps such discussions seem inappropriate or unscientific, or would involve actual classroom discussions about love or peace, which might very well be inappropriate in some teaching contexts. The Zen teacher, however, need not make changes to course content. Instead, the point is for teachers to explore their inner world and the way they project themselves. The Zen teacher not only excels at his or her official duties, including teaching, research, advising, and the like, but also practices to cultivate awareness and compassion. The beauty of teaching is that the only way we can truly perfect our craft is to perfect ourselves—a monumental challenge.

Carl Jung notes, "Where love rules, there is no will to power; and where power predominates, there love is lacking. The one is the shadow of the other" (quoted in Salzberg, 2002, p. 48). Too often, teaching involves an expression of power over students. Teachers can seek to move toward the cultivation of love rather than power by practicing choiceless awareness, which is simply a kind of mindfulness that focuses in particular on our tendency to judge, seek pleasure, and avoid pain. Zen practice for teachers leads to greater equanimity and compassion, which in turn, has a positive effect on students and classroom interactions.

RESOURCES FOR FURTHER EXPLORATION

Krishnamurti, J. (1981). *Education and the significance of life*. New York, NY: HarperOne.
> Although the Krishnamurti classic *Think on These Things* (1989) was my introduction to Eastern philosophy and continues to provide the foundation for my world view, I recommend *Education and the Significance of Life* for educators. As with all Krishnamurti teachings, the discussion is general, focusing on fundamental issues. You will not find any prescriptive suggestions for solving educational or human problems. Stridently anti-authoritarian, Krishnamurti's only aim was to "set men absolutely, unconditionally free."

Smith, R. (2010). *Stepping out of self-deception*. Boston, MA: Shambhala.
> There are plenty of good dharma books for individuals with an interest in Eastern spirituality. Tibetan masters, for example, have many excellent books on the subject. But Smith offers unique insights as well as inspiration. He takes what may be called dharma clichés such as "let go of ego" one step further, providing insights into the nature of the problem. For example, he notes, "The effort (that should be made) is toward allowing all things to be what they are and relaxing more deeply within them" (p. 100).

REFERENCES

Glasser, W. (1999). *Choice theory.* New York, NY: Harper Perennial.

Hardin, M. (2011). *A little book of love.* Boston, MA: Shambhala.

Hopkins, D. (2011). *ZEN TESOL: The mental game of teaching English to speakers of other languages.* Self-published: Author.

Kongtrul, D. (2005). *It's up to you: The practice of self-reflection on the Buddhist path.* Boston, MA: Shambhala.

Krishnamurti, J. (1989). *Think on these things.* New York, NY: HarperOne.

Krishnamurti, J. (1992). *Choiceless awareness.* Ojai, CA: Krishnamurti Publications of America.

Lewitt, P. (1986, November). *Zen and the art of composition: A comparison of teaching methods.* Paper presented at the Japan Association of Language Teachers' International Conference on Language Teaching and Learning, Seirei Gakuen, Hamamatsu, Japan.

Salzberg, S. (2002). *Loving kindness.* Boston, MA: Shambhala.

Smith, R. (2010). *Stepping out of self-deception.* Boston, MA: Shambhala.

AUTHOR BIOGRAPHY

In addition to teaching EFL for 1 year in Taiwan, composition for 5 years at colleges in Vermont, and EFL for 15 years at universities in Japan, John Spiri has been a regular Zen practitioner for more than 20 years. He has lived at the Mandala Buddhist Center in Vermont, done numerous zazen-kai *Zen meditations in Japan, and done a 10-day retreat at Suan Mok Monastery in Thailand. He presently teaches in the Education Department at Gifu Shotoku Gakuen University, a Buddhist university in Japan.*

Teaching the Four Skills

CHAPTER 7

How Would a Restaurant Reviewer Critique Student Writing?

Sylvia Whitman

Many practitioners have observed parallels between writing and cooking. Both are creative acts, elevated to art by the gifted but also practiced widely as craft by the average Joe. Both reinforce human connection and communication (Reichl, 2005). Unless someone is a raw foodie, cooking is an essential part of everyday life, as is writing. A good paper, like a good meal, starts with high-quality ingredients, which the writer-cook transforms through a complex and recursive process into a satisfying product.

That's the ideal. In practice, pots boil over, entrées burn, and sauces break, and part of the process involves sipping from the spoon and correcting the seasonings—or starting over, if necessary. To achieve consistently appetizing results, student writers and cooks must practice, and sometimes fail. Teachers can help, but they need patience and a digestive system that can handle half-baked ideas and overdone metaphors (like this one).

In class, a teacher often serves as a master chef instructing apprentices on cooking basics. Organization follows from *mise en place*, the assembling and prepping of ingredients. Ideas need to simmer. Instructors may provide recipes for certain genres so that novice writers learn traditional pairings and common substitutions, but as students progress, teachers challenge them to move beyond cookie-cutter papers. By reading/eating, students develop a more sophisticated palate, gaining confidence to experiment. (For a more abstract exploration of the cooking-in-writing metaphor, see Elbow, 1973.)

In a sense, all writing is only due, never done. But at some point in the semester, students have to put their papers on the table. Then an instructor takes on another role: restaurant reviewer.

As with so much of my life, I backed into restaurant reviewing. I had been contributing freelance articles to glossy *Central Florida Magazine* when the editor asked if I would take on the critic's job—$150 (if I remember correctly) for a roundup of three restaurants, plus expenses, which meant three fully reimbursed three-course meals every month, for two, so I could taste a broad swath of the menu. (Yes, my husband and my friends rejoiced.) That I had no experience mattered less than that I could construct a sentence.

I took the responsibility seriously. The reviewer consumes and evaluates, awarding anywhere from five stars to none. This reductive grading satisfies a broad public. The food's good, or bad, or just not worth the money. But for the long-term development of the chef, the review's thick description matters more. A term popularized by anthropologist Clifford Geertz, *thick description* implies an ethnological encounter with prose, a willingness to look at context as well as text. What did the chef bring to the dish? What did the reviewer experience? What worked well? What was confusing or disappointing? What did the reviewer surmise about the writer's intent?

A RESTAURANT CRITIC'S TIPS FOR LANGUAGE TEACHERS

Tip 1: Wield your power judiciously.

Just as a harsh review can close a restaurant, scathing (or simply overwhelming) teacher comments can shut down a writer for the rest of the class—and sometimes for life.

Jonathan Gold, who won a Pulitzer Prize for criticism in 2006 (the first for a restaurant reviewer), made his name poking around out-of-the-way ethnic restaurants in Los Angeles, sampling authentic dishes that he and many of his *LA Weekly* readers had never heard of. In a National Public Radio interview, Gold explained that he can make a hard-working restaurateur "a little more successful," but he dislikes the flip side, that he can put the same sort of person out of business (Raz, 2010). With the reviewer's power comes great responsibility—especially because Gold often crosses cultural boundaries. Here he describes his encounter with unfamiliar Taiwanese food in a mall:

> There was a dish with what's often translated as stinky tofu, which is this fermented tofu that can often be delicious but smells like garbage left festering outside for the entire month of August.
>
> And as I was eating this food and hating every single bite of it, I was looking around and I realized the fault was not with the chef, who was doing what he did with great skill. The problem was with me and my cultural relativism. And I went back to the restaurant, and I went back and I went back, and I went back so many times that the waitresses were practically trying to set me up with their daughters.

> And I think when I ended up writing up about it, I had been 17 times. And I'm not sure I liked it any better, but I understood it and I understood the way it could be. And I thought I was able to write about the restaurant in a reasonable manner. (Raz, 2010)

When teachers put the critic's napkin in their lap, they have a duty first to consider a language student's context. What is the student attempting? Only after understanding a student's aim and appreciating what works well can an instructor fairly evaluate a composition.

Even the humblest paper offers some nourishment to the reader. Give thanks for it. Aren't instructors lucky, after all, to be sitting at the table supping rather than, say, disposing of toxic nuclear waste? As writing center luminary Brad Hughes (2011) has argued, praise—deserved praise—can launch revision even more effectively than a laundry list of shortcomings. Great critics are generous as well as judicious. They savor the job.

Tip 2: Never visit the work just once.

As Gold suggests, repeated "readings" yield a deeper appreciation for the creative effort. Writing instructors have a luxury that food critics don't: They can sample a work in progress. Once a chef plates an entrée and hands it off to a waiter, there's nothing to do but stand back and wait for the reviewer's verdict. But if the reviewer tastes what's in the pan, feedback can take the form of dialogue about possible interventions. In fact, responding to chunks of a paper (a thesis, an annotated bibliography, an introduction, an outline, the rebuttal section, an early draft) allows a teacher to head off problems. There's nothing more painful than reading a competent paper that simply fails to address the assignment.

Although writing is not a lockstep process, papers do evolve in stages. In the early stage, writers are marshaling sources and sorting out ideas. As they organize these thoughts, they form paragraphs and make connections between and within them. Once writers have fleshed out their texts, they can focus on polishing the prose—balancing quoting and paraphrasing, varying sentence types, and improving word choices.

By dipping into a student's paper at each of these points, instructors—supplemented by well-directed peer reviewers—can meet writers where they are and help them see opportunities for improvement. Targeted, timely feedback by a teacher or peer embodies Lev Vygotsky's notion of scaffolding, of experienced guidance in a zone of proximal development (Yuanying, 2011). Frequent but limited commenting allows a writer to understand and deal with problems in manageable doses. Portioning feedback also makes a more efficient grader. Why point out comma splices in an early draft when the writer likely will toss out many of those sentences along the way?

A teacher thinking like a restaurant reviewer might visit students' work on a schedule like the one laid out in Table 1.

Table 1. Stages of Reviewing Student Work

Draft stage	What the Student Might Produce	What the Teacher Might Address
Early (ingredients, *mise en place*)	Journal about the assignment	Does the writer understand the task?
	List of sources/annotated bibliography	Is the writer gathering appropriate evidence?
	Thesis/research question	Is the thesis arguable? Does the question have a suitable scope?
	Concept map (with verbs connecting bubbles)	What ideas is the writer putting into play? How are they connected?
Middle (cooking)	List of topic sentences/outline	How is the writer mapping out the essay?
	Sticky notes for each paragraph—main idea or rhetorical purpose (to introduce X, to rebut Y, etc.)	How might these paragraphs be rearranged for the best logical flow or rhetorical punch? Are there ideas in each paragraph that belong elsewhere? How is the writer making transitions?
	Introductory paragraph(s)	Does the writer hook the reader and give a roadmap? Does the thesis launch the discussion?
	Section of paper where student feels bogged down	What is the writer thinking? How might the writer clarify on paper what's clear in his or her head?
	Conclusion	Where is the paper headed?
Late (saucing/seasoning)	Sample page	Is there a pattern of grammatical errors? Identify a few patterns and model how to fix mistakes before launching the writer on a seek-and-correct mission.
		Are citations correctly formatted? Model fixes.
		Could the writer improve the reader's experience through sentence variety (in length or clauses) or expansion of vocabulary?
		Is the formatting as assigned and reader friendly?

There is an exception to this multi-visit rule. A teacher should not write more than the student did. Just as a food critic would not waste ink on frozen fish sticks popped in the oven, a teacher should not invest more time commenting than a student spent composing.

Tip 3: Emphasize thick description rather than stars.

When Jonathan Gold moved to the *Los Angeles Times* in 2012, the newspaper announced that it was dropping stars from its restaurant reviews. The traditional rating system seemed inadequate to address Southern California's diverse dining options. "Furthermore, the stars have never been popular with critics because they reduce a thoughtful and nuanced critique to a simple score" (Parson, 2012). Instead of stars, the *Times* will provide review summaries.

Summary, it turns out, is one of the most effective forms of writing feedback (Nelson & Schunn, 2007). Every writer needs to know if the reader understands a paper's key points. Informing writers about what they have communicated—as well as pointing out inconsistencies or murky spots—underscores the author's responsibility in creating meaning and conveying it to the reader. A teacher channeling a restaurant reviewer spends the bulk of his or her time reporting rather than correcting, describing rather than evaluating, commenting rather than grading. Although the school system requires the bare grade, the rich feedback on the paper makes the A, B, C, or D self-evident, almost an afterthought.

CONCLUSION

Research from the huge Harvard and Stanford longitudinal studies of student writing underscores the importance of teacher feedback in writer development (Rogers, 2008; Walk, 2000). According to Nancy Sommers, Harvard freshmen who received feedback "early and often" grew the most as academic writers (Walk, 2000, p. 2; Sommers & Saltz, 2004). Analyzing the Stanford data, Paul Rogers found that "students valued feedback at all stages of the writing process, but especially early on in the process when feedback clarified teacher expectations, and clearly connected to writing and revision processes" (Stanford Study of Writing, 2008).

Far from the Ivy League, two community college instructors (Calhoon-Dillahunt & Forest, 2007) conducted a much smaller study and found that their basic writers also appreciated feedback more than correction, particularly end comments with suggestions for improving papers. However, many of these students did not make the changes advised, perhaps because they did not understand how to perform these academic tasks. In a language classroom, teachers may need to supply a glossary of feedback terms and very specific examples of how a writer analyzes, synthesizes, or elaborates.

Imagine sitting down to a banquet of student papers as a restaurant reviewer. How are you going to distill the experience of each meal in a couple of paragraphs?

The reviewer notes first impressions and then digs in, considering ingredients. Are the ideas fresh? Are they well sourced? The reviewer represents the intended audience. Is the cook serving pizza to a fine diner expecting beef Wellington? Is the evidence appropriate and the argument well prepared?

A reviewer considers the meal as a whole. The appetizer paragraphs should whet a reader's appetite; the main course should satisfy hunger; the dessert should leave a sweet taste in the mouth. In each paragraph and in the paper overall, food items should complement each other in taste, color, and form, distinct and yet connected. A diner should finish with the feeling that the meal is greater than the sum of individual courses.

Although presentation generally carries less weight than taste, a pleasing physical aspect to the meal predisposes the diner/reader to a favorable experience. Like a sauce, style can enhance or detract. A skillful writer adjusts to the rhetorical situation, adheres to formatting guidelines, and cleans up grammatical errors, which in large numbers buzz like flies in a soup.

Like a restaurant reviewer, a writing teacher reflects on the experience of reading the text. Using full sentences, he or she starts with praise, considers strengths and weaknesses across the meal, and encourages the writer with two or three concrete suggestions. As Anton Ego, the archcritic in Disney's *Ratatouille* (Bird, 2007), concludes after his comeuppance, negative criticism "is fun to write and to read"—except for the cook, who has put heart, soul, and sweat on the line. But criticism isn't worth much, Ego continues, except when it discovers and defends the new. "The world is often unkind to new talent, new creations; the new needs friends." So the teacher-critic must build up rather than break down, not slicing and dicing student writers but championing their creative effort.

RESOURCES FOR FURTHER EXPLORATION

Bean, J. (2011). *Engaging ideas: The professor's guide to integrating writing, critical thinking, and active learning in the classroom* (2nd ed.). San Francisco, CA: Jossey-Bass.

> An English professor at Seattle University, John Bean has written several texts about reading and writing. In this nuts-and-bolts book for instructors, Bean discusses the process of teaching writing across the curriculum, from designing problem-based assignments to coaching writers through reading difficult texts to responding to student work effectively and efficiently.

Gottschalk, K., & Hjortshoj, K. (2004). *The elements of teaching writing: A resource for instructors in all disciplines.* Boston, MA: Bedford/St. Martin's.

> Cornell University colleagues Katherine Gottschalk, who directs the first-year writing seminars, and anthropologist Keith Hjortshoj, who directs writing in the majors, collaborated on this brief, practical guide. Topics include "An Approach to Avoid: Reading Student Writing With Grading as a Goal," "In-Class Work on Revision," and "Responding to Sentence-Level Problems of ESL Students."

Hinds, J. (2007). Gather 'round the table: Writing on food, feasting on words. *Teachers & Writers Magazine, 39*(1), 27. Retrieved from http://www.twc.org/resources/lessons/writing-on-food-feasting-on-words/

> Writer and Bard High School Early College library director Jess deCourcy Hinds shares a food writing assignment that animated her City University of New York writing class, which had a mostly Latino mix of native and nonnative speakers with a range of abilities. Students described their favorite foods and passed out samples while giving oral presentations to the class. "Even students who usually resisted writing anything personal warmed up to the idea of writing about food and the role it played in their lives," Hinds reports.

REFERENCES

Bird, B. (Screenwriter and Co-director). (2007). *Ratatouille* [Motion picture]. Burbank, CA: Walt Disney Home Entertainment.

Calhoon-Dillahunt, C., & Forest, D. (2007). *Conversing in marginal spaces: Basic writers' responses to teacher comments.* Retrieved from http://www.mhhe.com/socscience/english/tbw/nov.html

Elbow, P. (1973). *Writing without teachers.* New York, NY: Oxford University Press.

Hughes, B. (2011). *General principles for responding and evaluating.* Retrieved from http://vanhise.lss.wisc.edu/wac/?q=taxonomy/term/121/all

Nelson, M., & Schunn, C. (2007, August). *The nature of feedback: Investigating how different types of feedback affect writing performance.* Paper presented at the 29th Annual Conference of the Cognitive Science Society, Nashville, TN. Retrieved from http://csjarchive.cogsci.rpi.edu/proceedings/2007/docs/p1823.pdf

Parson, R. (2012, March 8). Stars are out, at least for restaurant reviews. *The Los Angeles Times.* Retrieved from http://www.latimes.com/news/blogs/

Raz, G. (Host). (2010, March 27). Pulitzer Prize–winning writer will try anything [Radio New Program]. *All Things Considered.* Washington, DC: National Public Radio. Retrieved from http://www.npr.org/templates/story/story.php?storyId=125260607.

Reichl, R. (2005). *Why food matters.* Retrieved from http://tannerlectures.utah.edu/lectures/documents/Reichl_2007.pdf

Rogers, P. M. (2008). The development of writers and writing abilities: A longitudinal study across and beyond the college-span. *Dissertation Abstracts International: Section A, 69*(7).

Sommers, N., & Saltz, L. (2004). The novice as expert: Writing the freshman year. *College Composition and Communication, 56*(1), 124–149.

Stanford Study of Writing. (2008). *What is student writing development?* Retrieved from http://ssw.stanford.edu/research/paul_rogers.php

Walk, K. (2000). Study underscores the importance of feedback. *Harvard Writing Project Bulletin.* Retrieved from http://www.usfca.edu/uploadedFiles/Destinations/Office_and_Services/Academic_Support/Learning_and_Writing_Center/HWP.responding.pdf

Yuanying, W. (2011). College English writing on scaffolding. *Studies in Literature and Language, 3,* 46–48. doi:10.3968/j.sll.1923156320110303.210

AUTHOR BIOGRAPHY

For more than 3 years, Sylvia Whitman reviewed restaurants for Central Florida/Orlando Magazine *and citysearch.com—part of a blissful, underpaid life as a freelance writer. Since then she has worked in and around academia, most recently as a writing specialist at Marymount University. She still writes, although she struggles to find the time. Sylvia's latest project—besides this chapter—is a young adult novel,* The Milk of Birds *(Atheneum, 2013). She has taught college writing through culinary writing and found food a universal language. Although students often hesitate to enter Academic Conversations with Scholars about Big Ideas, experience at the table gives them confidence in their own expertise to talk and write about cooking, eating, and culture.*

CHAPTER 8

What Can We Learn From Certified Ski Instructors About Teaching Academic Speaking Skills?

Li-Shih Huang

I had my first skiing lesson at the age of 32. Most people would consider a person of that age too old to pick up the sport, and I distinctly recall that I fell 30 times on my first day of skiing. Thinking about a contribution to this volume prompted me to recall how I became a certified ski instructor a few years later through the lessons I received and how some of the principles and lessons from my ski training overlap with and permeate my practice as a language teaching professional. Reflecting on those experiences led me to write this chapter, which brings together my passion for language teaching and skiing.

A certified, professional ski instructor's daily challenge is to seek ways that will help learners with different learning preferences acquire the confidence they need to face intimidating slopes and put what they have learned into practice in an experiential way as they progress through what ski instructors call "steps." Ski instructors are trained to remember the need to explore ways to build a solid foundation of the techniques that are critical at each step, while simultaneously creating the right conditions for each skier to experiment with and succeed in what he or she is learning.

The tips featured in this chapter are derived from my teaching of academic speaking skills, my own research, and my skiing instructional experience, but the tips are also applicable to the teaching of speaking for general purposes. Before I present the seven tips, it is useful to explore some of the key theoretical bases the two professions (i.e., ski instructor and language instructor) share—namely, the principles of experiential learning and task-based instruction, Vygotsky's zone of proximal development, and Rogers's (1983) humanistic approach to learning.

THEORETICAL BASIS

A key, underlying theoretical basis that both ski and language instructors share is *experiential learning*, which postulates that "learning is the process whereby knowledge is created through the transformation of experience" (Kolb, 1984, p. 38). Experiential learning remains an influential theory in education, as well as in the field of TESOL, and it has generated a rich body of literature in both fields for decades. As illustrated in Figure 1, the theory involves cyclical stages of learning, which include concrete experience, reflective observation, abstract conceptualization, and active experimentation.

In skiing terms, a trainee has a *concrete experience* when he or she actively experiences an exercise. *Reflective observation* occurs when the trainee consciously reflects on the experiences of doing and observing. *Abstract conceptualization* ensues when the trainee conceptualizes the theory behind a specific technique or

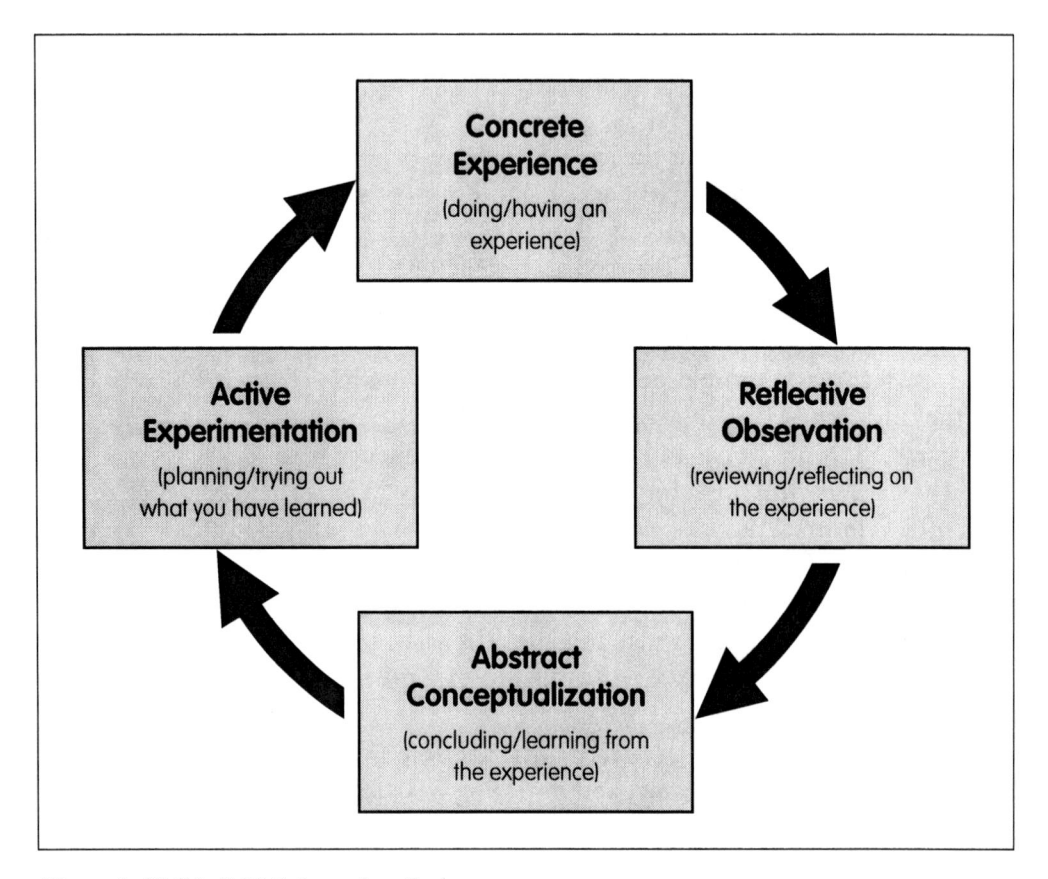

Figure 1. Kolb's (1984) Learning Cycle

hypothesizes a solution. *Active experimentation* takes place when the trainee tests the hypothesis. In both skiing and language learning, through reflection, experience is translated into concepts, which in turn, are used to guide active experimentation.

Another concept that is pertinent to the tips presented in this chapter is Vygotsky's (1978) *zone of proximal development* (ZPD). The ZPD is a theoretical concept in sociocultural theory that depicts the difference between a learner's actual and potential levels of development (Lantolf, 2001). Vygotsky maintains that when a learner is working within the ZPD for a particular task, appropriate assistance (i.e., scaffolding) will enable the learner to accomplish the task. Once he or she masters the task, the scaffolding can be removed so that the learner can complete the task independently. As Vygotsky (1987) states, "instruction is only useful when it . . . impels or wakens a whole series of functions that are in a stage of maturation lying in the ZPD" (p. 212). ZPD is thus an important pedagogical concept, serving as the foundation for exploring technical skill development in skiing or speaking development in a second language. Rogers's (2001) *humanistic approach to learning*, which emphasizes learners' affective development, as well as the importance of both providing a learner-centered environment and helping learners learn *how to learn* (Brown, 2007), is also fundamental to teaching in both professions and is highly applicable to the tips presented here.

Some other key principles, particularly those essential to task-based instruction (i.e., learner-centeredness, task dependency, recycling, and active learning; Nunan, 2004), are also essential and applicable in teaching both skiing and academic speaking skills. First, much like a ski lesson, language teaching typically consists of a series of tasks that learners engage in, given an appropriate setting, in order to achieve a specific outcome. Second, in both language and skiing teaching terms, the *learner-centeredness* approach emphasizes taking individual learners' experiences, perspectives, capacities, and needs into account in order to maximize learning outcomes. Third, *task dependency* is characterized by the way pedagogical tasks must grow out of and build on the ones that have already been completed. Fourth, the principle of *recycling* entails creating opportunities for learning about language use or skiing techniques in different contexts. Finally, *active learning* involves making sure that learners get to use and experiment with the techniques that they are learning.

Having explained the theoretical basis and principles that are central to the tips featured in this chapter, we can now move on to the next section, which presents the seven tips that demonstrate the intersections between the two professions and their approaches to learning.

A SKI INSTRUCTOR'S TIPS FOR LANGUAGE TEACHERS

Tip 1: Understand learners' needs.

Before conducting a lesson, a certified ski instructor will always take trainees out on a slope or a run for a free ski to determine each learner's level and to prioritize what to teach during the time allotted to the training session. In the field of language instruction, although the importance of learners' needs assessment is well recognized, the exploration of learners' language learning needs is often circumvented when teachers are busy creating and implementing tasks or lessons.

Plenty of research has highlighted the mismatch between learners' and instructors' views about areas where learners need help (see Huang, 2010b). Whether learners' perceived needs accurately represent their realities, few instructors would argue against the idea that learners' perceived needs represent their versions of reality and are sound starting points for instruction (the principle of learner-centeredness), because what learners believe about what they need to learn strongly influences their receptiveness to learning (Huang, 2010b). Furthermore, because learners' needs are context specific, it is important for instructors to conduct their own learner needs analysis, which will help them prioritize and focus their teaching.

In a manner similar to the way a ski instructor would gauge each skier's ability and approach each lesson in a learner-centered way, a language instructor may choose to assess learners' needs by having learners perform speaking tasks that they would normally have to do in their daily lives or have learners reflect on their own speaking challenges in academic settings (Huang, 2011a).

Tip 2: Provide guided practice.

In a ski lesson, a ski instructor typically uses several interconnected exercises that operate much like the task dependency principle in task-based language instruction (Nunan, 2004); these exercises are designed to develop a skier's technique and confidence at each step/level. Each exercise builds on the ones that have already been completed, and each has a clear goal and outcome that the ski instructor clarifies with students before they begin. By clarifying the goals and outcomes in language that learners can understand (often using various everyday activities, ideas, or metaphors that different students can relate to) and by providing guidance that is within learners' zones of proximal development about how to accomplish each technique, the instructor provides learners with the support they need to succeed.

Tip 3: Recycle in different contexts.

The cyclical nature of experiential learning mirrors the idea of this tip. In a ski lesson, trainees are often required to apply the same technique on different terrains through a process of concrete experience, reflective observation, abstract conceptualization, and active experimentation. The basic goal for a specific technique remains the same, but given the variations in skiing conditions, learners have multiple opportunities to solidify their new skills. In a similar vein, language instructors can create opportunities for learners to learn about specific aspects of language use in different contexts (e.g., interpersonal communication, small-group discussions, seminar meetings, class/departmental presentations). Growing evidence indicates that even performing the same task in different contexts can be productive for learners at different levels (e.g., Lynch & Maclean, 2000; Nunan, 2004). Vocabulary learning is another example where word associations, collocations, formality, and connotations are often context dependent and can best be learned through multiple exposures to words in a variety of contexts (Schmitt & Schmitt, 2011).

Tip 4: Help learners to visualize succeeding.

A technique that top athletes often mention is to vividly visualize themselves at the top of their games. As a skier facing intimidating terrain or doing alpine racing, I was taught to use a visualization technique that connects the current reality (i.e., how I would navigate present challenges and obstacles) and the desired future (i.e., how I would tackle the terrain and make it down the hill with speed, style, and grace). I often use this analogy and technique in language teaching by encouraging learners to see themselves as fluent and confident speakers and to visualize ways that they can successfully overcome challenges and deliver their ideas, with cheers from listeners. Supported by empirical research in social and educational psychology, the act of visualizing both relevant obstacles of present realities and the desired future can trigger strategic or creative solutions, leading to positive changes in a wide range of professional, academic, and life pursuits (see Oettingen, 2012). It is a transferable self-regulatory strategy that can energize language learners to successfully attain goals that are within their ZPDs.

Tip 5: Warm up the gears.

Before a ski lesson, a ski instructor will lead the students in some exercises to warm up the "gears." Much like a warm-up that one would do before exercising or playing a sports game, before speaking, encourage learners to do warm-up exercises in order to optimize their speaking performance. Some of the exercises that require students to access their sense of adventure and humor by stepping outside of their comfort zones to do some unusual physical movements have the added benefit of lowering speaking-related anxiety.

Many of the stretches and flexibility exercises used in skiing instruction can be effectively modified and integrated in a language classroom. To provide an example, the exercise of saying the phrase "Jack and Jill went up the hill" while extending and swinging our arms from the right to the left, or the exercise of swinging each leg from front to back and from left to right, will help learners loosen muscular tension (see, e.g., http://youtu.be/HW9rqrCUYRQ).

The physiological aspect of teaching speaking is often neglected in the TESOL field. Showing the intersections between skiing and speaking instruction adds a fun twist to speaking, a skill that language learners often find challenging and, in some cases, paralyzing, especially when the stakes are high.

Tip 6: Provide individualized feedback.

The provision of individualized feedback is an ongoing and integral part of a ski lesson. Throughout a lesson, learners receive this feedback from ski instructors after each technical exercise (related to Tip 2, *provide guided practice*), and again at the end of each lesson to provide learners with a clear idea of what stage they are at in the skier development progression (see, e.g., http://goo.gl/3nvxd) and what areas to focus on in order to progress to the next step/stage. Applicable to both ski and language instruction, the feedback should be delivered according to the principle that information should be offered in a way that is *timely* (right after each exercise when learning from the experience can best be maximized), *specific* (in relation to the goal of the exercise or the specific aspect of the lesson), *personal* (in an encouraging and supportive tone), *relevant* (in terms of the level that is appropriate to a learner's developmental stage and relevant to the intended outcome of the exercise), and *manageable* (with concrete, thoughtful comments about what the learner has done well and about one important area for further work) (Huang, 2011b).

Tip 7: Facilitate learner reflection.

When I was training to become a certified ski instructor, my trainers often videotaped each trainee to facilitate the provision of individualized feedback. For us learners, nothing was more impactful and effective than seeing ourselves from an outsider's perspective and checking our perception of what we thought we did versus what we actually did. I often use the same videotaping technique in teaching academic speaking skills, along with some guiding questions (which I elaborate on in the Sample Activities section) that help learners reflect on different aspects of their oral production and learn how to learn. As Rogers (2001) articulates, the goal of reflection is to "integrate the understanding gained into one's experience in order to enable better choices or actions in the future as well as enhance one's overall effectiveness" (p. 41). Facilitating reflection is vital in helping learners critically observe and think back on what they have experienced and engage in purposeful thinking directed toward future actions.

SAMPLE ACTIVITIES

In this section, I provide some sample field-tested activities that are designed to give learners opportunities to practice their speaking skills in different contexts. The first activity is what I call a *Poster Tour* (Huang, 2005) or what Lynch and MacLean (2001) call a *poster carousel task* that illustrates the principle of recycling (Tip 3). Next, I present a "black diamond run" task called *Research Talks* (Huang, 2010a) that integrates many of the tips presented in this chapter. Finally, I elaborate on how to incorporate videotaping learners' talks to facilitate reflection through guided questions and further feedback.

Poster Tour

A great in-class language task that involves the principle of *recycling* is a Poster Tour, which requires learners to prepare a poster presentation based on their areas of research. There are many possible variations in the way the task can be implemented. For example, distribute a flip chart or poster paper to each student, and provide some preparation time for learners to jot down key ideas in point form or as figures on the paper. Have learners operate in pairs, and ask them to run through their ideas before their poster presentations using the poster papers with each other. For a speaking class of 20, randomly divide the class into two groups, and ask those assigned the number 1 to be the first group to pin the sheets to the wall around the classroom and the first group to do poster presentations. Those assigned the number 2 will circulate around the room and ask questions. After Group 2 members have viewed all the posters, the roles are switched, and the task is repeated, with members of Group 2 taking the role of presenters. The members of Group 1, who act now as visitors, cycle through and ask questions. For a speaking class larger than 20, divide the class into more than two groups, and repeat the task until everyone has had a chance to be a presenter.

Aside from the physical movement involved in touring posters and the lively atmosphere the activity creates, because learners are required to repeat the synopses of their posters to visitors, explain, and answer similar questions, this task provides a substantial opportunity for "retrial" (Lynch & MacLean, 2001, p. 159), which promotes fluency, complexity, and accuracy. Given that several people will visit the poster and that the various individual developmental paths may be quite different from one another, learners' language production may be influenced by their interlocutors because of the nature of conversation, as co-constructed between or among speakers. This observation is supported by Larsen-Freeman's (2006) repeated-task design study, through which she suggests that

> the emergence of complexity, fluency, and accuracy can be seen, not as the unfolding of some prearranged plan, but rather as the system adapting to a changing context, in which the language resources of each individual are uniquely transformed through use. (p. 590)

Research Talks

In an academic speaking class, learners can be asked to deliver 1-, 3-, 5-, and 10-minute talks, focusing on each length at a different stage of the course. This exercise in a way mirrors the practice of having learners try out the same skiing technique on different runs with various difficulty levels and lengths (related to Tip 3, *recycle in different contexts*). Each talk should be a description of the learner's research, expertise, or study. Instructions such as the following can be provided to learners:

1. Prepare to give a **10-minute talk** aimed at a nonspecialized audience. This is applicable to research talks or job talks that ask you to make your research and expertise accessible and interesting to faculty and students alike. Carefully consider the need to provide more context for the information and to not assume any specialized knowledge.

2. Prepare to give a **5-minute talk** aimed at an audience with mixed levels of background knowledge. This is the scenario typically encountered when you speak at conferences and in all situations in which time is a constraint. Consider what background information must be provided and what details should be eliminated.

3. Prepare to give a **3-minute talk** aimed at a specialized audience. Be very precise and succinct in your description, without neglecting any essential background information needed for listeners to understand the nature and significance of your research.

4. Prepare to give a **1-minute talk** aimed at generalists. This is highly applicable to various formal and informal speaking settings. Focus on modifying your language and contextual information to make your talk accessible and concise, and provide an account of the practical significance of your work. Ask yourself: What do I want listeners to think about when they leave?

Practicing talks of different lengths simulates real-world activities, such as thesis defenses, conference presentations, job talks, and interviews, which require students to speak about their research and expertise at different levels of formality. The ability to zoom in and out in the communication of complex ideas in a way that makes them accessible to the intended audience is an important communication skill to develop. This exercise is designed to enhance the clarity of language and context that is essential in communicating with people who have a wide range of areas of expertise.

Prior to each talk, provide learners with adequate preparation time to experiment with Tips 4 and 5, visualizing success and warming up. Remind learners to never expect any new technique to work magically the first time they try it. It takes a few rounds of experimentation for learners to discover for themselves the visualization and warm-up routine that works best.

Videotaping and Reflection

To facilitate reflection and/or feedback on their speech, I usually videotape students' talks and upload the clips to a private YouTube channel made available only to individual viewers or to the group, depending on the consent received from students and their comfort with receiving feedback from their peers. Some guiding questions for self-reflection include the following:

- What surprised you as you watched your clip?

- What did you notice about your nonverbal language? What aspect of your nonverbal language would you like to improve?

- What did you notice about the vocal qualities (e.g., speed, volume, pitch, pause, tone) of your talk? What aspect of your vocal image would you like to improve?

- What did you notice about the use of language in your talk? What aspect would you like to improve?

- What did you notice about the content and structure of your talk? What would you like to improve?

Learners' responses to these questions provide insight into how they perceive their skills and needs (related to Tip 1, *understand learners' needs*), which can then serve as the basis for further feedback and information about what practice and guidance are needed (related to Tip 2, *provide guided practice*). Drawing on Rogers's (1983) humanistic approach to learning, it is important to acknowledge learners' strengths or to encourage learners to identify strengths they have noticed while watching the clips. Much like the way ski instructors focus on a specific aspect of a technical skill in offering feedback, language instructors should also keep in mind that it is neither possible nor productive to examine all aspects of speaking in a single viewing or feedback session. Instead, they should choose different aspects of speaking to focus on with each viewing.

CONCLUSION

Using the tips and field-tested pedagogical tasks in this chapter, language instructors can help language learners build successes. Minimizing the intimidation experienced by trainees looking down at a challenging or unfamiliar slope and hesitating about taking that first step for fear of doing a "yard sale" (i.e., a spectacular fall at the bottom of a run where many skiers are usually gathered and skis, poles, gloves, and goggles are scattered as if at a yard sale) is much like helping language learners muster enough courage to utter an opinion even when they fear failure or negative judgment. With proper needs assessment, guided retrials, purposeful practices, psychological techniques, and physiological exercises, language learners can also experience the exhilarating feeling of conquering a run and looking back at the slope in order to gain perspective about what they have just accomplished, to develop a renewed sense of confidence, and to feel excited about hopping on the lift to do it all over again.

REFERENCES

Brown, H. D. (2007). *Principles of language learning and teaching* (5th ed.). White Plains, NY: Pearson.

Huang, L.-S. (2005). Fine-tuning the craft of teaching by discussion. *Business Communication Quarterly, 68*(4), 88–95.

Huang, L.-S. (2010a). *Academic communication skills: Conversation strategies for international graduate students.* Lanham, MD: Rowman and Littlefield.

Huang, L.-S. (2010b). Seeing eye to eye? The academic writing needs of graduate and undergraduate students from students' and instructors' perspectives. *Language Teaching Research, 14,* 517–539.

Huang, L.-S. (2011a, Winter). Key concepts and theories in TEAL: Language-learning needs assessment. *TEAL News,* pp. 15–19.

Huang, L.-S. (2011b, Fall). Key concepts and theories in TEAL: Reflective learning. *TEAL News,* pp. 9–13.

Kolb, D. (1984). *Experiential learning: Experience as the source of learning and development.* Englewood Cliffs, NJ: Prentice Hall.

Lantolf, J. (2001). *Sociocultural theory and second language learning.* Oxford, England: Oxford University Press.

Larsen-Freeman, D. (2006). The emergence of complexity, fluency, and accuracy in the oral and written production of five Chinese learners of English. *Applied Linguistics, 27,* 590–619.

Lynch, T., & Maclean, J. (2000). Exploring the benefits of task repetition and recycling for classroom language learning. *Language Teaching Research, 4,* 221–250.

Lynch, T., & Maclean, J. (2001). A case of exercising: Effects of immediate task repetition on learners' performance. In M. Bygate, P. Skehan, & M. Swain (Eds.), *Researching pedagogic tasks second language learning, teaching and testing* (pp. 141–162). Harlow, England: Pearson Education.

Nunan, D. (2004). *Task-based language teaching.* Cambridge, England: Cambridge University Press.

Oettingen, G. (2012). Future thought and behaviour change. *European Review of Social Psychology, 23,* 1–63.

Rogers, C. R. (1983). *Freedom to learn for the eighties.* Columbus, OH: Charles E. Merrill Publishing Company.

Rogers, R. R. (2001). Reflection in higher education: A concept analysis. *Innovative Higher Education, 26*(1), 37–57.

Schmitt, D., & Schmitt, N. (2011). *Principles for effective vocabulary teaching* [Pearson Longman ELT Series webinar; no longer available]

Vygotsky, L. (1978). *Mind in society.* Cambridge, MA: MIT Press.

Vygotsky, L. (1987). *The collected works of L. S. Vygotsky* (R. W. Rieber & A. S. Carton, Trans.). New York, NY: Plenum Press.

AUTHOR BIOGRAPHY

Li-Shih Huang is associate professor of applied linguistics in the Department of Linguistics and the Learning and Teaching Centre Scholar-in-Residence at the University of Victoria. Her training includes degrees in organizational psychology, international business and marketing, education, and applied linguistics, culminating in a PhD in applied linguistics from the University of Toronto, Canada. Since her first language teaching job in 1992, Li-Shih has garnered extensive instructional and curriculum design experience in Canada and overseas. Her creativity in developing pedagogical materials has been recognized by the TESOL International Association. Li-Shih is also a Canadian Ski Instructors' Alliance–certified ski instructor/pro. Twitter: @AppLingProf.

CHAPTER 9

How Would an Actor Teach Language Learners to Improvise and Fluently Speak the Speech?

Christopher Stillwell

"Now I'm really angry," I said, searching for my line. For all of my young life, I had dreamed of performing in a school play, and now here I was in the spotlight. But after months of practice and learning my lines forward and backward, my deepest fear became reality. I looked out at the audience for the briefest of moments, when my mind suddenly went blank. My fellow actors looked back at me, waiting, expecting me to continue yelling at my would-be girlfriend over the nails and broken glass her brothers had put in the street for me to drive over. For that moment, the auditorium was as silent as a graveyard, and it felt like my funeral. I searched for the words. I found nothing. At a complete loss, I finished the sentence: "I can't remember my next line!"

My appreciation for the value of an actor's skills in the language classroom comes from my own frustrated attempt to make it big on Broadway. As I kept a day job in the classroom, I came to realize that, whether they can remember their lines or not, actors are naturally suited to language teaching. Their dramatic instincts can bring the dullest of lessons to life, and their ability to communicate meaning and emotion can be engaged to vividly address every lexical, pragmatic, or cultural question a student might have. Their training in clear speech is transferable to conducting pronunciation exercises, and because a crucial aspect of acting is *reacting* to one's fellow actors, many actors in the classroom are naturals at listening and responding to students' needs. Although we all suffer the classroom equivalent of stage fright from time to time, actors are meant to have facility with taking on roles and should be able to "assume a virtue, if you have it not," and this should enable them to project confidence even when besieged by jitters.

Actors also cultivate an ability to improvise. Anything can go wrong on the stage—an actor might forget a line, a prop might go missing, or a costume might tear. When such things happen, there is no opportunity to call "time out" and do it over; the only option is to find a way to keep the scene on track through improvisation. Actors develop this ability during rehearsals, through games that require them to step into scenes and create something from nothing. Many actors who thrive in this area will take an interest in improvisational comedy, or improv, in which whole shows are created before a full theater (or "house") from nothing more than a few suggestions provided by the audience. The skills required to survive such performances, if shared with language learners, could be of great use in facilitating development of fluency in oral communication, helping learners survive and thrive in conversation.

AN ACTOR'S TIPS FOR LANGUAGE TEACHERS

In this chapter I share tips for helping students develop fluency in their second or foreign language. These tips are presented in broader terms of how an actor might teach language, through such specific means as applying the first rule of improv to practice exercises, using story contexts to dramatize lessons, creating scenarios that facilitate exploration and discovery rather than simply providing answers, and maintaining interest through mystery.

Tip 1: Ask, "What's my objective?"

As actors prepare for performances in plays, they will often look at the actions and language that the script prescribes for their character, and they will ask, "What's my objective?" They will want to know *why* their character says and does the things they do. Knowing the objective provides a fuller understanding of the scene as a whole, giving the actor a vivid context within which to realize appropriate ways of fulfilling the instructions of the script.

With every lesson that they teach, particularly as they move from textbook lesson to textbook lesson, teachers also should ask, "What's my objective?" As Stanford University's William Damon (2009) suggests, "Every part of the curriculum should be taught with the 'why' question squarely in the foreground. . . . Why do people study math and science? Why is it important to read and write? To spell words correctly?" As we will see in this chapter, if a teacher determines that the objective of a speaking activity is not to develop accuracy but rather fluency, that teacher may then have the clarity of purpose to realize that framing the activity within the context of improv will help the students learn to make the most of their practice time.

Tip 2: Identify parallels between the first rule of improvisation and fluency development.

Imagine, if you will, that you are an actor performing in an improv show. You are on stage in front of a full house of patrons. Because this is improv, you have no costumes, sets, or props. Most crucially, you have no script. No prepared speech of any sort. Your scene partner addresses the audience:

"Okay, everybody, for this next scene we need your help. We need you to tell us who we are, and where we are. Ready? Me first. Who am I?"

Audience members shout a number of ideas. One is the loudest: "Brad Pitt!" Your scene partner responds, "Brad Pitt! Okay!" You step forward and ask who the audience wants you to be in the next scene, and the first, loudest answer is clear: "An elephant!"

"I'm going to be an elephant—guess I better pack my trunk. And where are we?"

"McDonald's!" shouts an audience member.

"McDonald's, great," you agree. "OK, so he's Brad Pitt, I'm an elephant, and we're at McDonald's? Got it. Here we go!"

You look to your partner, Brad Pitt, and he begins:

"Hi, elephant! Thanks for meeting me for a midnight snack. I told you this is a really great McDonald's. You won't be disappointed. Do you want to get a milkshake?"

It is your turn to speak. Because this is a comedy show, the audience expects you to be funny, but you have no script, no memorized lines, nothing prepared. Two ideas come to mind:

1. "Milkshake?! I'm an elephant!"

2. "Sounds great! I wonder if they have peanut flavor."

Which do you say?

As part of an effort to help students discover rules of improvisation and fluency development, I have shared this scenario in many of my classes. I ask the students to write their choices in their notebooks, then to exchange ideas with a partner. Next I have everyone vote for #1 or #2 by raising one or two fingers. Typically, there is a nearly even split between the two answers. I ask the 1s to share a rationale for their answers, and then I give the 2s a turn. It may seem like this is really a matter of opinion, that it depends on which answer you happen to think is funnier. Then I share that almost all improv comedians would agree that one of the answers is the best.

Which one is it? Why?

By this point, I can usually identify at least one person who has figured it out, and I call on that student to explain why the second answer is best. From there, it's time to look at the rules of improv. Many improv coaches and comedians have shared their own rules of improv, I say, and each list has its distinctions. Still, they tend to have one rule in common, and it tends to be first: "Say 'Yes, and . . .'"

Much like language students engaging in a conversation activity in class, both actors are attempting to create something from nothing, to make a new story in the moment. Brad Pitt probably suggested getting milkshakes as an idea for continuing the scene. If the elephant says, "Milkshake?! I'm an elephant!" the elephant creates a bit of a crisis for his scene partner by blocking his partner's idea. Instead of maintaining and building a sense of momentum, the two actors must now find a way around a self-imposed obstacle.

In the arts, the value of improvisation is not limited to comedy performance. As just one example, it can be essential for musicians in a band. As the musicians take turns performing featured solos, they each must jump in and create something from nothing, and accidents may happen. During a guitar solo, the guitarist may play notes that were not intended. This musician might use the idea of "Say 'Yes, and . . .'" in an internal dialogue. The guitarist will not stop playing and wait for a good idea to come, but will instead continue playing, and perhaps even find a way to build from the mistake by using it as a springboard to explore musical territory that might never have been considered otherwise. Similarly, when language students write and speak, they may need to "Say 'Yes, and . . .'" to themselves, instead of getting hung up on self-correcting or trying to find the perfect words. If the goal is to practice the use of language, it is usually best to continue the scene, building momentum and thus developing fluency while producing a large amount of language in a limited period of time.

Of course, in improv comedy and in conversation practice it is at times necessary to disagree with a scene partner, to "Say 'No.'" What happens then? The partner who disagrees should recognize the impact disagreement has on the flow of the activity. This partner should take the extra responsibility of finding a way around the obstacle, suggesting an alternative avenue for continuing the conversation.

Students are not improv comedians, of course, and will need to experience this rule for themselves in order to fully appreciate the idea and its applicability to their language practice. A good story can provide an ideal context for such experience. In the next three tips, we further explore the value of story and experiential learning.

Tip 3: Place your message or lesson within an appropriate story.

Actors are storytellers. They know that messages conveyed through story are naturally interesting and powerful. In addition, they know how to enhance the drama, through such techniques as "raising the stakes," or enhancing the importance of events by increasing the potential of loss or gain. Neuroscientists would add that dramatic stories can be especially brain-friendly, because they can appeal to the senses, they can provide contexts that stimulate interest and provoke exploration of ideas, and they can tap into our desire to see whether our predictions about outcomes are correct (Medina, 2008).

To enliven a lesson about a specific language point, find the story. Instead of presenting passive and active voice as two ways of conveying the same information, provide a story in which the difference between the two could save the teacher from getting fired, as in the case of the new teacher who accidentally broke a chair in class and had to coach the students on whether to tell the principal that "the teacher broke the chair" or "the chair got broken." When teaching students to make the most of fluency exercises and participate actively in class, let them explore principles of improvisation through segments from *Alice in Wonderland* (see Tip 4), and then share the story of Brad Pitt and the elephant. And when it comes to the grammar of storytelling (e.g., use of indirect vs. direct speech), be sure to have the students develop their skills by sharing exciting stories of their own.

Tip 4: Let the audience draw conclusions from their own observations.

Actors who have spent a great deal of time analyzing texts and creating scenes through improvisation know a basic principle of storytelling that can be useful in teaching: Show, don't tell. The idea is that audiences will be more absorbed if they have the opportunity to draw their own conclusions from characters' actions rather than simply hearing characters verbalize their inner feelings. In an improvised scene, an actor playing Heartsick Harry might state, "I am in love with Susan," but the performance will be much more engaging if he instead communicates this information through his character's nervousness when in Susan's presence, his intense interest in her whereabouts, his extended gazes in her direction, and his efforts to be caring, amusing, and agreeable toward her at all times.

This idea of letting audience members draw conclusions from their own observations can be applied to a wide range of lessons in the classroom. For instance, virtually any grammar point can be taught inductively by providing students with examples taken from a corpus and letting them work out the patterns and rules for themselves. When helping learners develop fluency, instead of simply telling students to "Say 'Yes, and . . . ,'" a teacher can give the students the opportunity to experience the impact of saying *yes* firsthand. A lesson placed in the context of Lewis Carroll's *Alice in Wonderland* can provide just such an opportunity.

First, a bit of review of the story of Alice and the Red Queen is in order. Students might be assigned the excerpt in which Alice happens upon a trio of playing cards furiously painting the roses red. This passage could be read for homework, or the teacher might use the image from the book or screen captures from the Disney movie as prompts for students to retell the story from memory with their partners. The key line is "This here ought to have been a *RED* rose-tree, and we put a white one in by mistake; and if the Queen was to find it out, we should all have our heads cut off, you know."

Once the class is familiar with the story, it is time for the experience to begin. The teacher says:

> The Queen is going to be your teacher today, and she wants you to write a paragraph. You can't make any mistakes. **If the Queen was to find out, you might have your head cut off, you know!** (Any topic is fine. If you cannot think of an idea, you can write about "Making Mistakes.")
>
> As soon as it is clear that the students understand the instructions and have their blank papers and pens ready, the teacher can give the class 2 minutes to write. When the time is up, the students can set aside what they have written and read aloud another part of Alice's adventures:

> "Would you tell me, please, which way I ought to go from here?" asked Alice.
> "That depends a good deal on where you want to get to," said the Cat.
> "I don't much care where—" said Alice.
> "Then it doesn't matter which way you go," said the Cat.
> "—so long as I get SOMEWHERE," Alice added as an explanation.
> "Oh, you're sure to do that," said the Cat, "if you only walk long enough."

Now the students should be ready for a new guest instructor and a distinct task:

> The Cheshire Cat wants you to write a paragraph. It doesn't matter which way you go, if you only write long enough. Keep writing, and don't stop. Don't worry about mistakes, and don't worry about repeating yourself. If you run out of ideas, you can write: "I don't know what to write now, but I'll keep writing, writing, writing, until I get an idea, I'll just keep writing . . . ." (Any topic is fine. If you cannot think of an idea, you can write about "Creativity.")

Again, the students have 2 minutes to write, and when the time is finished, they should put their pens down, even if they are in midsentence. The students can then reflect on the experience, first in individual journal writing and then in small-group discussions. Four questions guide their thinking and discussion:

1. In which writing task did you do better, writing for the Queen or writing for the Cheshire Cat?

2. In which writing task did you write more?

3. Which writing task was better for language practice? Why?

4. Did you think in your first or second language for the Queen? For the Cat?

A few notes about these four questions: The first question is deliberately ambiguous, inviting students to use their own criteria to determine what it means to "do better" on this task. The second question provides a more concrete measure, but makes a distinction between writing more and doing better. (Some students will see Questions 1 and 2 as the same, whereas others will have interesting ideas about how they are distinct.) The third question's focus on *language practice* is also open to interpretation; some students will answer this question in terms of the accuracy of their writing, whereas others will consider the development of their fluency. The fourth question is a bit of a departure from the rest, intended to provoke thought and discussion on a fascinating topic that students may not have previously considered.

Tip 5: Remember: Unsolved mysteries maintain interest better than freely provided answers.

As the teacher goes over students' answers to the questions, it can be useful to maintain an air of mystery. Rather than sharing general observations and providing the main point for students, the teacher can put a blank table on the board and have students share their responses to each question by raising one finger to vote for the Queen or two fingers to vote for the Cat (see Table 1). The teacher can then elicit explanations of various responses from the students. The more the teacher can remain neutral and draw complete responses from students, the more a sense of exploration and discovery can be used to motivate students' interest. As the numbers appear on the board, students can draw their own conclusions

Table 1. Sample Student Responses

	Red Queen	Cheshire Cat
1. I made greater progress with . . .	5	**19**
2. I wrote more for . . .	0	**24**
3. I got better language practice from . . .	4	**16***
4. I thought in English more for . . .	1	**18****

*Four students voted "neither"; it depends on the objective.
**Five students voted "neither"; they thought in the same fashion both times.

and slowly but surely find out if their predictions regarding how their classmates found the experience are correct.

The idea of maintaining a sense of mystery is related to another storytelling principle familiar to actors and playwrights: Always end a scene with a question, or a bit of ambiguity in need of resolution. Doing so produces a knowledge gap that creates in the audience a desire to learn more. Screenwriter and director J. J. Abrams, co-creator of television programs such as *Lost* and director of *Mission Impossible 3* and *Super 8*, has much to say about the importance of withholding answers in storytelling. He likens unanswered questions to sealed boxes with unknown contents, which he calls mystery boxes:

> What are stories, but mystery boxes? . . . What's a bigger mystery box than a movie theater? You go to the theater, you're just so excited to see anything—the moment the lights go down is often the best part. [Kept closed, a mystery box] represents infinite possibility. . . . It represents hope. It represents potential. (Abrams, 2007)

But once the box is open, the fascination is over.

This principle is at work in the classroom discussion of Brad Pitt and the elephant described earlier. Instead of simply telling students that the elephant's second response to Brad Pitt's suggestion was the better answer, the teacher gives students time to think about it, to explore both possibilities, and to build feelings of anticipation and interest in finding out the answer. Spending time hearing from students in support of both answers, and being careful not to express an opinion of his or her own until the very end, helps the teacher maintain the mystery and keep students hooked on finding out what happens next.

Teachers wanting to stimulate interest in an upcoming lesson might similarly pose questions in the preceding class, questions that will only be answered the next day. For instance, in the class before the *Alice in Wonderland* fluency exercises, the teacher might ask, "How would the Red Queen teach a writing class? What about the Cheshire Cat? We'll find out tomorrow!"

Tip 6: Maintain curiosity, then provide resolution when the time is right.

Like it or not, a teacher is viewed as the class authority. Students will often want to hear the teacher's opinion about which answers were "correct" in discussions such as the one regarding the Queen and the Cat. This is clearly a legitimate desire, particularly if the students would otherwise be left wondering, "What was the objective?"

Though most of the students will have stated that the Cat was the better teacher for them overall, there will be those who prefer the Queen. Perhaps they feel that writing for the Queen made them mindful of their language, so they could better concentrate on avoiding mistakes. This is of course a perfectly good answer, particularly if the goal of the writing activity is to improve accuracy. However, if the goal is to develop fluency, the case can be made that the Cat's approach is better, because it leads to the most language production. In my classes, I have typically saved the Brad Pitt and the elephant discussion to follow the Queen and the Cat, so that I can use it to draw a connection between developing fluency in language production and developing the ability to improvise. To show the universality of these ideas, I also like to have students think about brainstorming, because brainstorming could be considered another form of fluency—fluency of idea generation. A typical set of brainstorming rules would include the following:

1. Emphasize quantity over quality.
2. Don't make judgments. Just get ideas out there.
3. It is okay to repeat ideas.
4. It is okay to repeat ideas.
5. It is okay to build on other ideas, even ideas that are not originally your own.

If these rules sound familiar, perhaps it is because they all say essentially the same thing as the first rule of improvisation did in three words: "Say 'Yes, and . . .'"!

CONCLUSION

Different classes will respond differently to the tasks described in this chapter. Although many may enjoy undertaking the writing challenges and imagining themselves in a performer's shoes, some may have difficulty saying yes to relatively offbeat activities. An actor turned fluency teacher might reflect on these differences between "audiences" through the lens of his or her previous experience with live performance.

Both acting and teaching involve repeated performance of the same content. Actors perform their shows on multiple nights, and teachers often repeat the same course for different classes of students. In both cases, every audience will be different and will therefore respond differently to what they experience. If you have ever gone to see the same film more than once, you may have noticed a similar phenomenon. Though the film remained exactly the same, the opening night audience may have been energetic and responsive, while the matinee audience may have been perfectly silent.

For the live performances of teaching and acting, the presentation of the content itself is also ever changing, at some times only subtly distinct and other times more overtly different. Actors sometimes fall into a trap of expecting to get the same reaction from each audience. When a line that got a big laugh on Friday is met with dead silence on Saturday, actors may infer that either their performance is weak or the audience is bad. Teachers may similarly expect students to find the same aspects of the course interesting or challenging every time, and may be confused or frustrated when this does not turn out to be the case.

It can be useful to remember that just as performances and audience reactions are "live" and never the same, learners' individual needs and differences must be addressed in their own distinct fashion every time. Much like actors, teachers need to be limber and ready to listen, react, and improvise in response to each new situation. Although the content may not be received with the same enthusiasm by one class as it was in another, the class should not be labeled "bad" any more than one audience should be considered bad for not laughing at the same jokes as other audiences.

Finally, just as no two classes are the same, each teacher is unique. From time to time, it is important to reflect and get back in touch with what makes us special to students, and how we might better develop our talents in order to best satisfy this audience. For development as professionals, we can ask ourselves a deeper version of "What's my objective?" as in "What's my purpose in being a teacher?" Answering such questions can make work meaningful and can help us align our purpose with our talents and actions. Damon (2009) suggests that we should even address this question in front of students, because it "helps students better understand the purpose of schooling [and] exposes them to a respected adult's own quest for purpose." Just as actors are accustomed to taking on roles, teachers should remember that the most important part they play may be that of role model. By demonstrating enthusiasm for learning and exploration (saying "Yes"), keeping a focus on useful objectives, and sharing inspiring stories of our own, we can motivate students to develop language fluency and seek the thrill of discovery through learning.

REFERENCES

Abrams, J. J. (2007). *The Mystery Box*. Retrieved from http://www.ted.com/talks/j_j_abrams_mystery_box.html

Damon, W. (2009). The why question: Teachers can instill a sense of purpose. *Education Next, 9*(3). Retrieved from http://educationnext.org/journal/

Medina, J. (2008). *Brain rules: 12 Principles for surviving and thriving at work, home, and school*. Seattle, WA: Pear Press.

AUTHOR BIOGRAPHY

Christopher Stillwell's undergraduate studies consisted of a double major in psychology and theatre arts at the University of Pennsylvania. He is thankful for the lessons he learned from his former professors and the casts he has had the opportunity to act with and direct at that time and since. Time and again he has found that this training has suited him particularly well for one occupation above all others: language teaching. He has taught in Spain and Japan, as well as in his native United States, with an MA from Teachers College, Columbia University. As a PhD student at the University of California Irvine's School of Education, his present research interests involve teacher development. (StillwellC@aol.com)

CHAPTER 10

How Would an Architect Such as Frank Gehry Design Language Learning Tasks?

Tim Stewart

Imagine that you are sitting in a teachers' room pressed for time and feeling stressed. Class is about to begin, but you need a teaching activity. Frustrated, you crumple up your brainstormed notes and toss the paper on the floor. As you move to pick it up and drop it into the trash, something catches your eye. You stop, stand back, and take a longer look. "That's it!" you exclaim and rush off to class with another brilliant teaching idea in hand.

Could it happen? Faithful viewers of *The Simpsons* might recognize this scene. That popular animated TV series paid homage in 2005 to Frank Gehry, the most famous architect of our time (Odenkirk & Nastuk, 2005). Gehry is known as a designer of spectacular buildings that twist, fold, and bend in gleaming geometric shapes. In this episode of *The Simpsons*, Marge Simpson convinces the town of Springfield to hire Gehry to design a new concert hall. Gehry proceeds to crumple up a piece of paper in frustration and toss it, only to discover that the crumpled paper is the design he wants for the new concert hall. Picking up the paper, he exclaims, "Frank Gehry, you are a genius!" If only it were that easy.

ARCHITECTURE AND HOW IT SPEAKS TO LANGUAGE TEACHING

This chapter takes me back more than 20 years, when I taught at a small design college in Vancouver, British Columbia. During my 4-plus years there, I regularly worked with professional architects, interior designers, and builders. I learned a lot about house design and the creative process while working with those colleagues. In reflection, the more I think about how architecture and language teaching intersect, the more links I see.

At the outset we should establish that design, like teaching, is an art. This is art as professional practice. All art is based on some principles of practice that professionals in a given field agree upon as being fundamental in some way. Architecture in practice is a process of discovery, not unlike teaching, wherein practitioners ask themselves questions in the search for unique solutions. Teaching professionals also constantly puzzle over ways to improve their practice. In this chapter I broadly focus on the theme of the opening vignette, that is, the creative process and professional practice, as they relate to some principles of design.

Design sense is something that emerges from our individual sensitivity. Living in built environments, we are immersed in architecture from the start of our lives. Architecture is ingrained in our cultural experience and can be likened to language in the sense that it structures our world. Architectural knowledge, however, is normally not put to use in the way language is, so scholars like Zumthor (2002) believe that it is necessary for architects to activate their background knowledge through a process of consciously exploring their biography. For instance, what was it about certain spaces or materials we encountered in the past that made us feel some sensation/emotion?

This point about design as a cultural and personal construct is a key link connecting architecture and language education. Designing structures for human use is not an abstract exercise. Architecture is always about something concrete and real. There is a plan drawn on paper/screen, but this is not architecture any more than music is notes written on a page. The plan must be executed. All of these principles will be familiar to language teachers. Lessons have to be planned around objectives, and materials need to be created or adapted to particular circumstances. But it is the execution of the plan, that is, the interaction between teacher, students, and materials, that forms the learning opportunity or lesson.

Meeting client needs is central to the work of architects. They are hired to design structures that people live, work, play, study, shop, commute, and relax in. During my years working with architects, I learned about the care that good architects take to understand the client's desires and their efforts, sometimes, to try to educate clients about the real possibilities that a building site offers. In this mix are needs (of the client), potential (of the site), skill (of the architect), materials (for the building), resources (of the client), and communication (between architect and client). Out of this mix, a design emerges. Design is about patterns. An appropriate pattern has to be discovered, and the design sense of that pattern must be communicated to the client. Simplicity often is at the heart of good design, just as with effective language teaching. Communicating complex ideas with elegant simplicity is not easy.

Architects straddle the border between aesthetics and function. A well-designed space is pleasant to inhabit and is easy to go about your business in.

But, like all art, at times it can inspire. As language teachers, we seek to motivate and inspire learners. Cookie-cutter methods do not go very far in this regard. Materials must be created for classroom presentation, and lesson plans must be executed. Material and presentation/execution combine to communicate the intent of the lesson. The following activities are representations of this cycle.

LANGUAGE TEACHING TIPS INSPIRED BY ARCHITECTS

Language teachers do not simply focus on content themes such as customs, holidays, greetings, shopping, and hobbies. Most teachers will want students to explore deeper social issues. The pedagogical challenge then becomes how to integrate conceptually difficult material into language lessons. In this regard, principles of design can be applied to the development of language teaching materials, as well as lesson design in general. In this section I present four teaching tips that are influenced by concepts familiar to architects. Comprehensible communication of sophisticated ideas is the focus of the tasks outlined in these tips. The tips emphasize improving comprehension through the visual presentation of information.

I have consistently worked in programs in which I needed to create original teaching materials. Because I am not gifted at drawing, I had shied away from the use of visuals in my teaching until I more fully appreciated the power of visual information while team teaching with designer colleagues. I imagine that my hesitation regarding creating visual materials might be shared by other language teachers. The root of my unwillingness to create visuals for lessons was simply a misunderstanding about the nature of visuals for teaching.

The first three tips focus on key visuals (also called graphic organizers), which are representations of concepts or knowledge structure. Teachers of reading skills in particular will be familiar with the range of visual aids such as tables, tree diagrams, graphs, flow charts, timelines, and action strips, among others. For teachers and students, visuals have at least three major applications: (1) generative—to promote language production, (2) explanatory—to increase content understanding, and (3) evaluative—to assess content and language understanding.

How might an architect introduce conceptually difficult information into classes for language learners? Starting on a design, architects build a foundation that forms a basic plan. Next, they work with their design by exploring the possibilities for the structure. Finally, after the design is clear, the ideas can be explained in a "big picture" summary. Here is one example of how these three steps can be applied in the profession of second language teaching.

Tip 1: Build a foundation with key visuals.

Most likely an architect would first need to activate a client's relevant background knowledge. This is something that teachers are highly skilled at. More than this, an architect would look for patterns when designing a space and would use those patterns to reveal the underlying principles and ultimate theme of the design to the client.

Language educators also look for patterns, and making these patterns as transparent as possible is a key pedagogical goal. As one simple example, Figure 1 is a basic tree diagram that teachers can create to help students comprehend complex texts and/or concepts. Teachers should recognize the following from Figure 1:

- Information has structure that can be represented visually.
- Clearly designed visuals can reduce linguistic and cognitive burdens for students when introducing difficult concepts.
- Simple visuals can be used in a variety of learning activities.
- Many visual structures are universal and so are familiar to students.
- Visuals are not difficult for teachers or students to create once they understand the structure.

Figure 1 can be introduced in a number of ways: (1) a short lecture or reading where students fill in gaps in the visual, (2) a partially finished visual that is completed through individual or whole-class brainstorming, (3) an information-gap activity where students exchange information to complete the visual. The aim is to have students understand the basic concept so that they can then go on to higher processing of information and deeper understanding.

Tip 2: Explore structure.

Design and language both have internal structure that determines them. In addition, the achievable possibilities for language and design are often learned through play. Play is vital to all learning, and through playing with a visual plan,

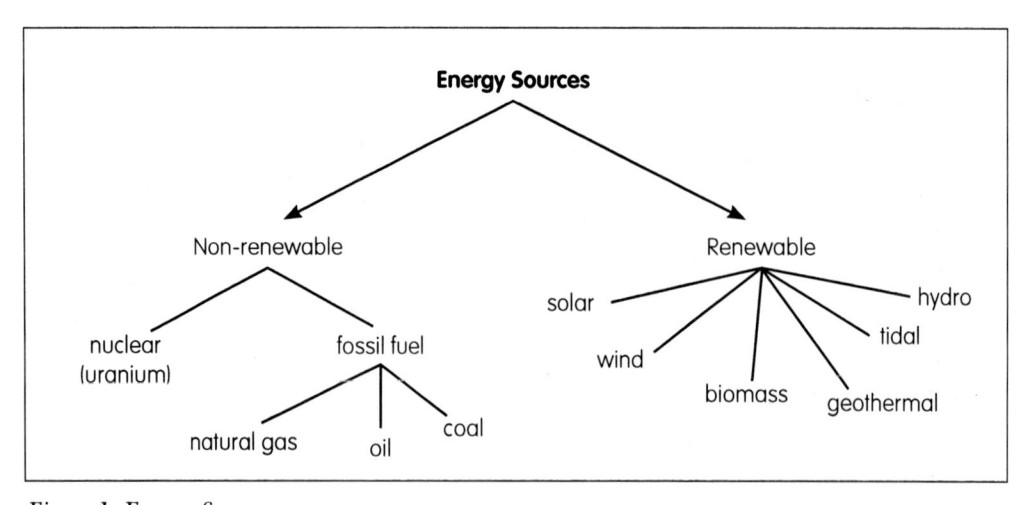

Figure 1. Energy Sources

> - Into how many main groups/categories can energy sources be divided?
> - What are the groups/categories called?
> - What is the difference between the two groups/categories?
> - What are some examples of (non)renewable energy sources?
> - How many types of nonrenewable energy sources are there?
> - What are these types called?
> - Which energy sources are in the fossil fuel group?
> - Is biomass a renewable energy source?
> - What type of energy source is nuclear power?

Figure 2. Guiding Questions

architects can stretch the boundaries of a design concept. Initially, teachers should demonstrate to students the language necessary to talk about categories in English through questions such as those in Figure 2. Teachers can use these questions to introduce the syntax and lexicon of categories to learners. However, once students understand the basics, they should be allowed space to explore the possibilities for explaining a visual by writing/asking their own questions. Language play is fun. Key visuals open up many possibilities for creativity.

Tip 3: Communicate the big picture.

Of course, after planning and reworking ideas, professionals ultimately need to grasp and explain the big picture, that is, convey the meaning of abstract ideas. For architects, this would involve convincing the client of the appropriateness of the finished design, which means making the design make sense to others. Similarly, students need to explain their thoughts using writing, discussion, and presentation formats. Figure 3 illustrates how students can demonstrate the depth of their understanding as well as the sophistication of their writing. The key visual structure (Figure 1) provides students with visual hooks on which they can hang the language of categorization, for instance. Students learn how to read visual aids just as architects do with designs, and this allows them to make sense of complex information.

The step represented in Figure 3 is simply a detailed reading and description of Figure 1. This writing step can naturally be followed up by introducing readings or lectures on the topic prior to having students express their opinion. The goal should be to encourage students to express an informed opinion supported by research and/or a deeper level of thought.

Once students are familiar with the rhetorical structure of information, can create their own visuals, and are able to talk about the information, they can

> Write a paragraph about energy sources using the tree diagram.
>
> Energy sources can be divided into two groups, renewable and nonrenewable. The former group has a number of sources, while the latter has two sources. The two types of nonrenewable energy sources are . . .

Figure 3. Writing Exercise Sample

begin to deal with complex ideas in second language classes. Simply put, the visual representation of information empowers students through a rational structure that facilitates communication by making the organization of information transparent to language learners. The scaffold built by visual representations of knowledge lays a foundation that can wean language learners from overreliance on reading scripts. This is the focus of Tip 4.

Tip 4: Design poster presentations for language learners.

We all try to have students do various types of presentations in our classes. One of the main problems with second language presentations is the stress of talking in a foreign language in front of peers. This fear naturally encourages many students to write out their full text and then proceed to read it. The result is typically a nonstop stream of information read in a monotone voice at a rapid pace with limited or no eye contact. So for language learners, the goal of the presentation is simply to finish reading their prepared text. Although this may be acceptable in some cultural contexts, it makes for an uninspiring presentation because audience comprehension is largely ignored.

How do architects present their designs to clients in order to make the needed sale? This is a valuable question for teachers to consider because a good deal of classroom instruction is presentation. Architects engage an audience by combining clear visuals and focused explanations. Good presenters know their point, and they get to it in an entertaining manner without getting bogged down in details. This skill can be taught and learned. But how do teachers start this learning process with students who have low English proficiency?

As stressed in Tip 3, visual representations of information should be a major part of most presentations. The challenges are to get students to be intelligently selective of the information they choose to present and to help them create attractive visuals that they can talk about during presentations to wean them from the use of scripts. In a design presentation, architects walk clients through the design—this is the pedagogical goal of the poster presentation explained here.

Once a presentation topic has been defined, the first thing students need is information. Readings could be provided as handouts, the teacher could give a lecture, and/or students could be asked to search for information on their own.

1. Create groups of between two and five students (depending on the size of your class).
2. Select a general topic and subtopics for investigation.
3. Have each group choose a subtopic to research. These students will become the "expert" students on this topic.
4. Provide appropriate readings to each group member. Each group member should have a different reading on the same subtopic.
5. Each group member reads his or her article and creates a summary of main ideas and important supporting details.
6. Each group member shares the summary of his or her article with other members, who take notes and ask questions so that all members can become experts on all aspects of their group's subtopic.
7. Monitor each group to ensure that the most important points have been identified and understood.
8. Each group draws up a draft poster and discusses it with the teacher. Posters should include only images and key words.
9. Once poster designs have been finalized, provide each group with paper and markers. Posters are created.
10. Give students time to practice talking about their poster. The point is that students use the key words on the poster as prompts, not detailed scripted notes. Standing next to the poster and pointing out the information sequence is the preferred presentation style. In other words, students should talk about their poster and draw listeners' attention to it (i.e., walk them through).
11. Create new groups called "jigsaw" groups. Each jigsaw group contains at least one member from every expert group.
12. Display posters at various locations around the classroom.
13. The jigsaw groups go to different posters. Whoever in the group represents that particular poster is the presenter. The audience listens, takes notes, and asks questions. The information collected can be used for an essay, a short writing, or a test later.
14. The groups rotate around the room from poster to poster until everyone has presented.
15. If time permits, remix the jigsaw groups and do a second round of presentations.

Figure 4. Group Poster Carousel

Next, students must identify the main ideas and key details in the information sources. Following this, the summarized information should be verified by the instructor. Afterward, key words and images need to be decided upon and a poster created. Then the presentation needs to be practiced, and finally the poster will be presented. Obviously, all of this activity can proceed in a number of ways (see Li-Shih Huang's alternative version of a poster carousel in Chapter 8). For speakers at beginning and low-intermediate proficiency levels, I recommend the sequence detailed in Figure 4.

The strength of this approach is that students work in teams and share information on their subtopic. This group-oriented approach to learning mimics the work culture of architectural firms. As a group, students select the theme and design of a visual and create it. Next, they work together on refining their presentation skills with a focus on walking listeners through their poster. I have done this with very low-level English speakers and have witnessed their confidence swell by the end of the process. The carousel style keeps all students occupied taking notes and asking questions because presentations take place simultaneously in small groups. In addition, unlike class-fronted presentations, students do not present as a group, which means that every student will present all of the information related to the topic. (Further information on the advantages of poster presentations can be found in Stewart, 2009a; see also Brandt, 2009; Carduner & Rilling, 2009; Stewart, 2009b).

CONCLUSION

Visuals reshape text and reinforce key concepts through design simplicity. A well-designed visual displays textual information clearly so that students can move through it like they would in a well-designed architectural space. For student presentations technology may help, but it requires a high degree of communicative and design sophistication to control effectively. For instance, some people are highly critical of how PowerPoint encourages overly presenter-focused events (see Byrne, 2003; Patty, 2007; Reynolds, 2005). There are architects who agree with this criticism. In 2003, two young architects channeled their PowerPoint critique into a passion for improving presentations. Their idea was to simplify the presentations made by designers through connecting visual representations of concepts with key words. Klein and Dytham (see Pink, 2007) created timed PowerPoint presentations and called them PechaKucha (also known as 20x20 presentations). The objective of this format is to force designers to present information concisely using exactly 20 slides that are shown for exactly 20 seconds each (see www.pechakucha.org). TESOL practitioners Christianson and Payne (2011) have adapted this idea in a presentation course for students based on the 20x20 format. The obvious goal is to simplify the matter of dealing with complex ideas and vocabulary through a communication style emphasized in architecture that is based on the power of visual information. This style of communication aims to help presenters avoid losing listeners by including too much detail. In short, it aims to teach students the golden rule of public speaking: Respect your audience. Basically, this means that presentations should be created for the audience (audience-centered) rather than for the presenter.

Returning to my chapter opening, I wish to stress the creativity of teaching. Language teachers are not simply technicians grinding out lesson after lesson at the chalk face. As educators we seek inspiration in our work in order to develop the art of teaching into something potentially inspiring for students. So how do architects or educators create greatness out of thin air? They don't. Teachers can learn much from architects like Frank Gehry, but the most valuable lesson from that field has to be that creativity is not an isolated activity achieved by lone heroes. In reality, creativity is socially constructed through reinterpretation of existing ideas, inspiration that comes from collaboration with others, and determination to see a project through to completion. The lesson here for teachers simply reinforces the importance of working with colleagues and students to explore and create on your own scale. These interactions are the stuff that makes teaching worthwhile. We cannot all become Frank Gehry, but by constantly looking for alternatives, seeking improvement, and developing our own creativity, we can all deliver the best possible lessons to learners. Our struggles with these small steps of discovery combine over time to create the architecture that makes the unique genius of professional practice possible.

ACKNOWLEDGMENTS

Thanks to Vancouver architects Roger Willoughby-Price and Rob Salikan for introducing me to a new world of design 20 years ago, and to Nathan Rehorick for all-around coolness. I also need to shout out Aloha to a great teacher-mentor, Karen Wilson, now roughing it on the big island of Hawai'i!

REFERENCES

Brandt, C. (2009). PowerPoint or posters for EAP students' presentation skills development. In T. Stewart (Ed.), *Insights on teaching speaking in TESOL* (pp. 153–168). Alexandria, VA: TESOL.

Byrne, D. (2003). Learning to love PowerPoint. *Wired, 11*(9). Retrieved from http://www.wired.com

Carduner, J., & Rilling, S. (2009). Data and donuts: Preparing graduate students in language education to speak at conferences. In T. Stewart (Ed.), *Insights on teaching speaking in TESOL* (pp. 123–137). Alexandria, VA: TESOL.

Christianson, M., & Payne, S. (2011). Helping students develop skills for better presentations: Using the 20x20 format for presentation training. *Language Research Bulletin of International Christian University, 26.* Retrieved from http://web.icu.ac.jp/lrb/2011/12/02/docs/Christianson%20LRB%20V26.pdf

Odenkirk, B. (Writer), & Nastuk, M. (Director). (2005, April 3). The seven-beer snitch [Television series episode]. In M. Groening & J. L. Brooks (Producers), *The Simpsons*. Los Angeles, CA: Fox Broadcasting.

Patty, A. (2007, April 4). Research points the finger at PowerPoint. *The Sydney Morning Herald.* Retrieved from http://www.smh.com.au

Pink, D. H. (2007). Pecha Kucha: Get to the PowerPoint in 20 slides then sit the hell down. *Wired, 15*(9). Retrieved from http://www.wired.com

Reynolds, G. (2005). *Top ten slide tips*. Retrieved from http://www.garrreynolds.com/Presentation/slides.html

Stewart, T. (Ed.). (2009a). *Insights on teaching speaking in TESOL*. Alexandria, VA: TESOL.

Stewart, T. (2009b). (Re)Cycling speaking tasks on the road to pedagogical renewal: Drama in the ESOL classroom. In T. Stewart (Ed.), *Insights on teaching speaking in TESOL* (pp. 107–119). Alexandria, VA: TESOL.

Zumthor, P. (2002). *Thinking architecture* (2nd ed.). Berlin, Germany: Birkhausen Architecture.

AUTHOR BIOGRAPHY

Tim Stewart is hopeless as a designer and builder of things, but is lucky to have many former colleagues who happen to be designers, builders, and tinkerers. Tim sticks to teaching, editing, and encouraging novice writers. He created and edits the TESOL Journal *section Communities of Participation in TESOL and encourages you to submit a manuscript. Tim teaches at Kyoto University, in Japan's ancient capital.*

CHAPTER 11

How Would a Basketball Coach Get a Team to Talk the Talk?

Sylvia Whitman

If you've ever played basketball, you've probably heard the coach's lament from the sidelines: "Talk to each other, guys!"

How might you carry that challenge into a TESOL classroom? By teaching students some conversation plays, of course.

With a court-centered lesson, you're likely to engage the sports fans in class. Appealing to varied learning styles, you can draw the plays or stage them so that people get up and move around. And whatever the vocabulary or language form you want students to master, along the way they're likely to pick up a few basketball terms handy for social conversations. Talk about the **shot clock** when you set time limits, award extra credit for **free throws**, or tell the class you want everyone to speak, not just the **ball hogs**. (For definitions of bold terms, see the glossary in this chapter's Appendix.) With a basketball theme, you can also draw in all sorts of film clips, from the cotton-candy song-and-dance numbers of *High School Musical* to the true-to-life civil rights struggles in *Remember the Titans*.

I belong to the Title IX generation of female athletes. Passed in 1972, Title IX required any educational institution receiving federal funds to offer equal opportunities to men and women—in sports as well as academics (The Margaret Fund of the National Women's Law Center, 2013). Long excluded, girls and young women began to get in the game at many levels. In the late 1970s, I played basketball on a middle school team dubbed the "Knickettes" in honor of the nearby New York City franchise, the Knicks. Although I switched to squash in high school and college, my son's and daughter's love of basketball has brought me back onto the court with a group of senior women athletes interested in serious play. They outshoot, outpass, and outdribble me, but they welcome all comers.

Coaches run practices every day; the good ones can teach instructors a thing or two about how to structure a lesson (Pennington, 2009). "Always be prepared," says basketball coach Tim Sayles (2013), who suggests scaffolding drills so that players' skills advance in small increments from where they are to where you want them to be. His advice: "Keep them moving. . . . Make everything competitive. . . . Don't do any one thing too long."

Outstanding coaches build confidence as well as skill. Drilling mind and body, they use pace and challenge to improve motivation, essential for success. The winningest coach in Division I college basketball, Mike Krzyzewski, of Duke University and the U.S. Olympic team, has inspired generations of players with a sense that he cares about them as people as well as athletes. "Coach K only knows one way to go about his business, and that's with passion and with energy and with discipline," Houston Rockets forward Shane Battier told a reporter. "But at the same time, you always have a good time. . . . . He gets people to play hard and play together" (DuPree, 2006). Like great coaches, great teachers empower students as lifelong learners.

A BASKETBALL COACH'S TIPS FOR LANGUAGE TEACHERS

Communication is key in basketball, but it's usually short and fast. These lesson tips focus on speed, deft handoffs, and practice, practice, practice.

Need another voice to reiterate that message? Check out Johnson's (n.d.) 1-minute video on basketball fundamentals.

Tip 1: Emphasize the physical, as well as verbal, components of communication.

Good basketball and good conversation start with body language and spatial awareness. In a game, players communicate through eye contact, gestures, and positioning on the court. You might show videos of **fast breaks** and point out wordless "talk." For instance, in this clip from a 2010 National Basketball Association (NBA) game, Miami Heat teammates Eddie House and LeBron James keep their eyes both on the ball and on each other: www.youtube.com/watch?v=7dmJoqqqSDk. In this clip, without a word, several Brooklyn Nets combine choreography and conversation: www.youtube.com/watch?v=E_FNaDu1z8A. How do these players use their faces and their arms to signal their readiness to receive the ball?

Drill: Over the Top

- In small groups students brainstorm body language "rules" that can improve conversation. dxpham (2008) lists 18, including nod, smile, and lean in. Students may come up with many other suggestions. They may also compare different cultural norms for conversation.

- Scribes from each group take turns writing their rules on the board. For a laugh, you can violate or overdo each action as students report it. For instance, to illustrate the elasticity of personal space for different types of conversations, you might stand in the doorway and shout, "I love you" to someone in the far corner of the room, or stand nose to nose with a student and whisper, "I want to discuss this contract."

- Divide the class into groups of three, and assign one student as observer. Give the conversation pairs a simple topic (e.g., *tell us about your name*), and challenge them to practice either good or inappropriate body language—slightly exaggerated for the sake of the observer. After a minute, the observer reports. Students then switch roles.

Drill: Triple Threat

When a player receives a pass, she or he must decide what to do with the ball. Coaches advise players to **pivot** to face the basket so that they pose a **triple threat**—ready to shoot, pass, or **dribble** (see Figure 1).

In conversation, a speaker also has options. You can help students get into triple threat position to respond to a question.

- With a ball in hand, demonstrate the triple threat move. You pass the student a question: "What is the office dress code on casual Friday?" The student pivots. Now she or he can do one of the following:

    a. Shoot. This is the best move if the student knows the answer. "Women can wear pants, and men can skip the jacket and tie."

    b. Pass the ball. The student might pass back the question. "Could you repeat that?" Or "Please explain what you mean by dress code." She or he might also pass the question to a teammate, but must do so with a transition. "Paul is better prepared to answer because he's worked here longer than I have." Or "Paul, what do people wear on casual Friday?"

    c. Dribble. The player moves the ball, buying time to shoot or pass. "Casual means less formal. But in our office we still see clients on Friday. I'm guessing that we have to be clean and neat, but we don't have to wear a full suit."

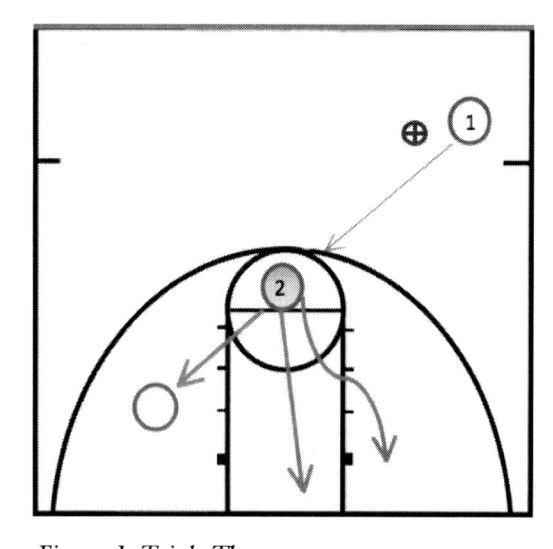

Figure 1. Triple Threat

Language Teaching Insights From Other Fields: Sports, Arts, Design, and More

- Divide the class into groups of three or four, and give each a stack of questions. In each group, Student 1 (the starter) passes a question to Student 2 (the receiver), who decides to shoot (answer), pass (call on a teammate), or dribble (think aloud before passing or answering). Once a shot has been made, a referee decides if the speaker has made a **bucket** with a good answer. Students rotate through the roles: starter, receiver, teammate(s).

Tip 2: Develop your own playbook of language drills.

Good game play is the sum of many small moves. Teach these skills to students, first walking them through the drills and gradually picking up the pace. Practice repeatedly until students can make these moves without thinking. For inspiration, check out basketball drills from The Coach's Clipboard (Gels, 2001–2013). Start with simple, stationary drills and then advance to plays that put several students in action together. Allow students to call **timeouts** when they need to ask questions.

If you want students to visualize the basketball metaphors, use a Nerf basketball if your class space can't accommodate a real ball. Set a metronome, tap a ruler, or use any other rhythmic sound to encourage speed. The following are some sample plays.

Drill: Stack

Player 1 holds the ball, prepared to throw it in from the sidelines. Players 2–5 line up. When Player 1 slaps the ball, the others scatter in all directions, ready to receive a pass (see Figure 2).

You could make this a vocabulary drill. Player 1 throws out a word, and all the other players have to come up with an example or a synonym. For instance:

> Pierre (#1, throw in): Fruit!
> Nan: Banana!
> Giselle: Apple!
> Paolo: Mango!

Drill: Fake

Player 1 (offense) moves in one direction, then backtracks to shake off a defender.

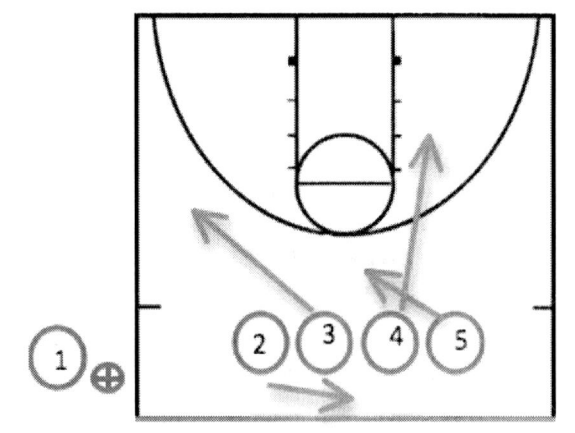

Figure 2. Stack

You could present this as a rhetorical move. Divide the class into pairs. Give the offense a list of "change of direction" words, such as *but, however, although, on the contrary,* and *on the other hand.*

> Linda (offense): I love cars.
> Jose (defense): You love cars.
> Linda: I love cars, but I hate trucks.

Drill: Layups

The most basic and reliable shot in basketball, a close-in bounce off the backboard, the **layup** requires arm-leg coordination. Coaches often set up two lines for a steady chain of practice (see Figure 3). Player 1 passes to the lead player in the shooting line (#2), who goes in for the shot. Player 1 **rebounds**, passes the ball back to the new lead of the rebounding line (#3), and circles into the shooting line while the shooter crosses to join the rebounding line.

Collocations, words that commonly go together in English, also imply coordination. Although the thesaurus often suggests a multitude of words with similar meanings, certain combinations sound right or wrong to the native speaker's ear. Mastering collocations gives language students an easy layup in English.

Have the class make two lines. Line 1 you prime with half a collocation. If you're interested in verb-object collocations, for instance, you give each player in Line 1 a card with a verb: *do, make, take, keep,* and so on. The lead player in Line 1 calls out the verb, and the lead player in Line 2 has to complete the collocation to score. If the Line 2 player misses, the Line 1 player can rebound and correct the collocation. Both players then switch lines.

> Ahmed (in Line 1): Pay!
> Layla (in Line 2): Attention!
> Coach: Score!
> Sammy (in Line 1): Do!
> Warda (in Line 2): A mess!
> Coach: Miss! Rebound, Sammy?
> Sammy: Do business!
> Coach: Score!

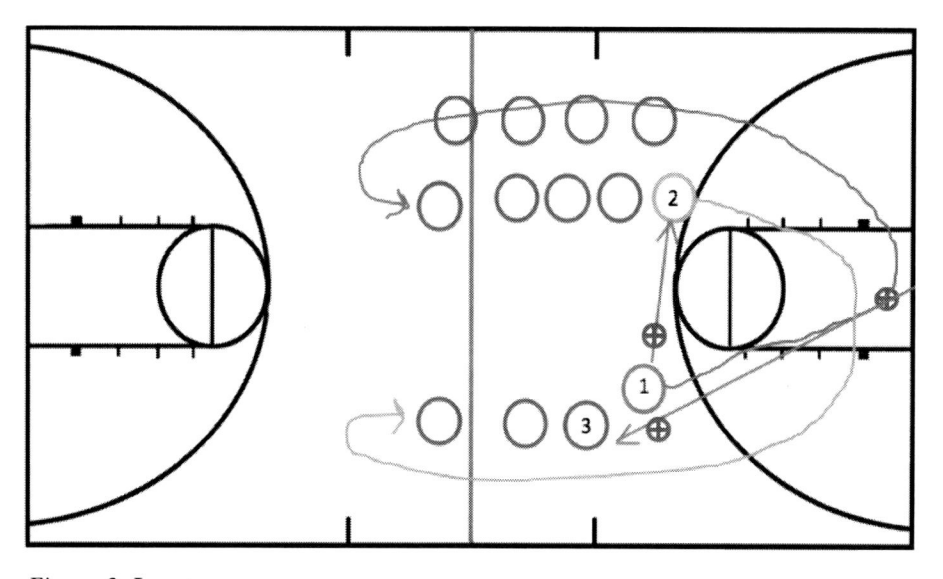

Figure 3. Layup

You can run the drill both ways, starting with the verb or the object. Other collocations include phrasal verbs (*put on a sweater*), adjective-noun combos (*busy bee*), noun-noun combos (*round of applause*), and so on. You can have students make collocation cards as they read texts for class or tap one of the many collocation lists on the Internet (EnglishClub, 1997–2013).

Drill: Rebound

Teams score many, many points off missed baskets that a player rebounds and shoots again. You can make rebounding a verb tense game, for instance.

Divide the class into groups. Each appoints a **point guard**, in charge of two stacks of notecards, one with verbs and another with tenses.

At the start of play, the point guard draws a card from each stack (e.g., *jump/future tense*), and the chosen shooter must make a sentence (e.g., *I will jump for joy tomorrow*). If the point guard feels the sentence is incorrect, she or he calls "Rebound!," and the next player must try for a correct sentence.

After students have practiced in groups, bring the class together for a team shootout. Appoint a referee, who will take on point guard responsibilities, and a scorekeeper. Teams line up so that everyone gets a turn. The referee announces the verb and the tense. The shooters at the head of each line race to articulate a sentence. The first one, if correct, earns two points. If it's incorrect, the referee calls "Rebound!," and anyone on either team can make a correction and score. Set a time or point limit for the game.

Drill: Give and Go

In this basketball standby, Player 1 passes to Player 2, Player 1 moves, and Player 2 passes it back (see Figure 4). Demonstrate with the ball.

Let's say you want students to practice the simple past tense in statements and questions. Divide the class in half, and then have students in each group line up across from each other and take turns.

Player 1 starts with the ball, asking the question. Player 2 answers and generates a new question. Player 1 fields the new question and answers.

> Chen: What did you do last night, Ahmed?
> Ahmed: I went to the movies. What did you do, Chen?
> Chen: I played basketball.

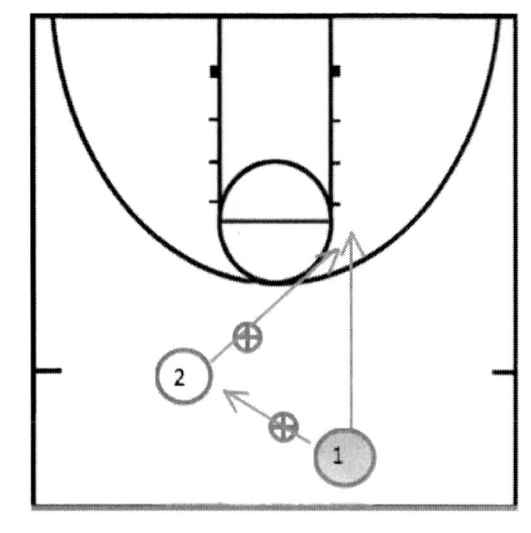

Figure 4. Give and Go

Drill: Page From the Playbook

Once you have a playbook, consider sharing a hard copy or online copy with the students. They will have a visual aid as you refer to plays by name. You might also invite students to design new plays to practice new material.

To change up the pace in the middle of class, for instance, you might call out, "Stack!," and review vocabulary for a few minutes. Or you might announce familiar plays as students converse and require them to implement those moves. You can have conversation scrimmages, fielding teams from the class and tracking **fouls** (errors) and buckets (perfect sentences/rhetorical moves).

Tip 3: Motivate your team.

In his *Ultimate Guide to Motivating Players,* Jeff Haefner (2013) emphasizes the importance of frequent, positive, specific feedback. Reward students—with words, a high five, recognition in front of the group, or time off for a game or favorite activity. Does a student speak a sentence without an error? Call out **"Swish!"** for a perfect shot. Instead of counting individual errors, you might track team "fouls." Make sure to name the **MVP** of the day, and give a reason for that honor. Pointing out what students do well, both in private and in public, encourages them to build on strengths. As the legendary UCLA basketball coach John Wooden remarked, "Youngsters . . . need models more than they need critics" (ESPN, 2001). Wooden was speaking about the coach's conduct, but helping students recognize their own fortes and find exemplars among their peers gives them many models to emulate.

Drill: Coach the Coach

If your constructive criticism rarely takes the form of praise, Haefner (2013) passes along a trick for improving your positive/negative comment ratio. Start with a handful of paper clips in your right pocket and a marble in your left. Whenever you compliment a student, move one paper clip to your left pocket. Whenever you critique a student, move the marble right. However, you may move the marble only when you've emptied the right pocket of all its paperclips. Repeat as necessary.

Drill: Head in the Game

As a listening or reading lesson, introduce students to inspirational sports quotes. As they parse the meaning and master the vocabulary, they may also internalize the message. You might start with these (Pumerantz, 2012):

- "An athlete cannot run with money in his pockets. He must run with hope in his heart and dreams in his head." Emil Zapotek, Czech long-distance runner who won three gold medals at the 1952 Helsinki Olympics

- "Champions keep playing until they get it right." Billie Jean King, U.S. women's tennis pro who won 12 Grand Slam titles

- "If you fail to prepare, you're prepared to fail." Mark Spitz, swimmer who won seven gold medals at the 1972 Munich Olympics

- "The more difficult the victory, the greater the happiness in winning." Pele, Brazilian soccer star

This lesson can expand in many directions; for instance, you can ask students to research the person quoted and present a short oral or written biography.

Drill: Diss This

Masters of disrespect, basketball players are famous for their trash talk. Although no one wants to spawn a class of braggarts, creative boasting may help shy and humble students break out of their shells. After giving some examples of disses (e.g., *I'm so good, your mama cheers for me*), divide the class into teams and give them a few minutes to come up with disses for the other group. The sassiest wins. To prime this activity for a lower level class, you can prompt the first half of the insult (e.g., *I'm so fast/You're so slow, I'm so good/you're so bad*). A tamer version of this game: Charge each team to come up with motivational quotes, along the lines of *Hustle and heart set us apart* or *Stand tall, talk small, and play ball*.

CONCLUSION

What makes a great coach? When the NBA surveyed hundreds of young visitors to its website, they said they wanted tough but fair mentors who balanced humor with straight talk. What should a coach care about most? Teaching new skills, replied 45% of respondents. But an almost equal number weighed in that a coach should give everyone a chance to play (Lyness, 2010). At the end of each class, ask yourself: Did everyone on your roster come off the bench and handle the ball? Drilling kinetically instead of asking questions and waiting for raised hands can draw in shy or underprepared students, especially when their classmates cheer them on. Team spirit can help every learner succeed.

Although a dynamic playbook will enliven a class, outstanding coaches bring more than technical knowledge and practice drills to the game. They have a vision. John Wooden pictured a "pyramid of success," a model he popularized not just for basketball but for business—and life. In 1973, his pyramid made the cover of *The New York Times Magazine* (see Figure 5 for an adaptation). When the legendary coach died in 2010, the flood of obituaries cited not just his winning record but his winning philosophy (Schudel, 2010).

What's your big picture?

Many academic institutions require instructors to lay out course objectives on their syllabi. The list may inform students and assessment committees, but it's

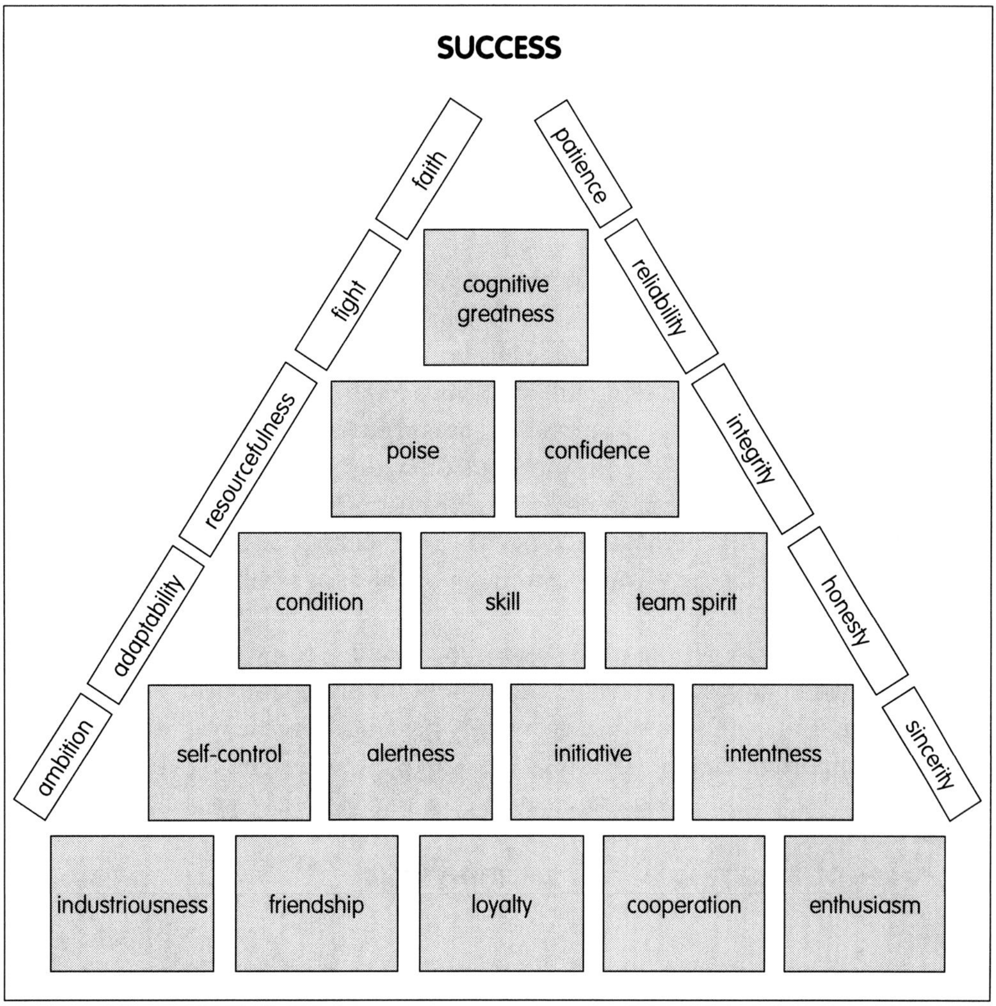
SUCCESS
faith
patience
fight
cognitive greatness
reliability
resourcefulness
poise
confidence
integrity
adaptability
condition
skill
team spirit
honesty
ambition
self-control
alertness
initiative
intentness
sincerity
industriousness
friendship
loyalty
cooperation
enthusiasm

Figure 5. Wooden's Pyramid of Success

often a numbing read: ***students will identify count and noncount nouns; correctly employ modal auxiliaries; receive, interpret correctly, and respond accurately to basic verbal messages and other cues that are commonly heard in college classroom settings as measured by completion and accuracy of individual and group tasks that are graded by teacher-generated rubrics and student self-evaluation***, and so on. Of course, a teacher needs to set measurable and achievable language goals for the semester. But on Wooden's pyramid, note that ***skill*** is not the pinnacle; it rests on a foundation of industriousness and enthusiasm and underpins poise and confidence. What do you dream for students, and what do you do as a teacher to incorporate that into your lessons?

Articulating your philosophy can transform your teaching and inspire both your peers and students. Coaching websites often provide models for reflection

(Fryer, 2012; Hanson, 2007–2013), as do faculty development sites (University of Minnesota, n.d.). If the word *philosophy* sounds intimidating, Gabriela Montell (2003) offers down-to-earth advice about tone and content. Get started by freewriting on questions like *What do you believe about teaching? About learning? What do you dislike in other classrooms? What's your style?* Ground every buzzword (*student-centered lesson, collaboration*) with an example of how you bring that about.

Although teaching has long been the sidecar to research in U.S. higher education, it is gaining importance, thanks in no small part to Pace University emeritus professor of management Peter Seldin. His books (Seldin & Miller, 2008; Seldin, Miller, & Seldin, 2010) and crusading as a consultant have prompted many colleges and universities to rethink assessment and urge instructors to build teaching portfolios, either for hiring and promotion (summative) or for improving their classroom practice (formative; Ohio State University, 2013). With a playbook, a teaching statement, and perhaps excerpts from student and institutional evaluations, you are well on the way to creating a portfolio for self-improvement or job hunting.

Doing all this work off the court allows you to come to practice with a game plan for students' success. As college coach Bobby Knight famously remarked, "The key is not the will to win . . . everybody has that. It is the will to prepare to win that is important" (BrainyQuote, 2001–2013). Understanding yourself, your students, and your lesson, you can create a class that is both purposeful and fun.

RESOURCES FOR FURTHER EXPLORATION

Hoops U
> Free printable court diagrams are widely available online, including at this *Hoops U* website: http://www.hoopsu.com/basketball-court-diagrams

Ming, Y., & Bucher, R. (2004). *Yao: A life in two worlds.* New York, NY: Miramax.
> International readers may take a particular interest in the journey of basketball phenomenon Yao Ming from the Shanghai Sharks to the Houston Rockets. In this clear and direct autobiography, the towering Ming (7 feet 6 inches) compares his native China to the United States and discusses the culture shock of being the NBA's first foreign #1 draft pick.

Nater, S., & Gallimore, R. (2005). *You haven't taught until they have learned: John Wooden's teaching principles and practices.* Morgantown, WV: Fitness Info Tech.
> Distinguished UCLA psychology professor emeritus Ronald Gallimore and player and literacy coach Swen Nater team up to highlight best practices that cross from coaching into teaching. Nater played basketball under Wooden at UCLA, and Nater and his former coach published a book on the offense.

REFERENCES

BrainyQuote. (2001–2013). *Bobby Knight quotes.* Retrieved from http://www.brainyquote.com/quotes/authors/b/bobby_knight.html

DuPree, D. (2006, August 2). It's all about the team for Krzyzewski. *USATODAY.com.* Retrieved from http://usatoday30.usatoday.com/sports/basketball/2006-08-02-krzyzewski-cover_x.htm

dxpham. (2008, February 3). Body language—Great tips for conversation [Web log post]. Retrieved from http://englishstudyforvms.wordpress.com/2008/02/03/body-language-great-tips-to-improve-our-conversation/

EnglishClub. (1997–2013). *Sample collocations.* Retrieved from http://www.englishclub.com/vocabulary/collocations-samples.htm

ESPN. (2001). *10 burning questions for John Wooden.* Retrieved from http://espn.go.com/page2/s/questions/wooden.html

Fryer, T. (2012). *5 keys to being a great basketball coach.* Retrieved from http://www.ihoops.com/training-room/coaches/5-Keys-to-Being-a-Great-Basketball-Coach.htm

Gels, J. A. (2001–2013). *Basketball drills, selecting and using drills.* Retrieved from http://www.coachesclipboard.net/BasketballDrills.html

Johnson, D. (n.d.). *Basketball fundamentals.* Retrieved from http://www.ehow.com/video_2285874_basketball-fundamentals.html

Haefner, J. (2013). *The ultimate guide to motivating players: 36 ways to keep your players focused and working hard ALL season long!* Retrieved from http://www.breakthroughbasketball.com/mental/motivate-players.html

Hanson, L. (Ed.). (2007–2013). *Example coaching philosophies from sports coaches.* Retrieved from http://www.athleteassessments.com/articles/coaching_philosophy_examples.html

Lyness, D. (2010). *What makes a good coach?* Retrieved from http://www.nba.com/nbafit/teen/nutrition_fitness_center/sports/41602_what_makes_a_good_coach.html

The Margaret Fund of the National Women's Law Center. (2013). *History of Title IX.* Retrieved from http://www.titleix.info/History/History-Overview.aspx

Montell, G. (2003, March 27). How to write a statement of teaching philosophy. *Chronicle of Higher Education.* Retrieved from http://chronicle.com/

Ohio State University, University Center for the Advancement of Teaching. (2013). *Teaching portfolio.* Retrieved from http://ucat.osu.edu/read/teaching-portfolio

Pennington, M. (2009, December 30). Ten tips for coaching basketball and writing [Web log post]. Retrieved from http://penningtonpublishing.com/blog/grammar_mechanics/ten-tips-for-coaching-basketball-and-writing/

Pumerantz, Z. (2012). *The 50 most inspirational sports quotes in history.* Retrieved from http://bleacherreport.com/articles/1156558-the-50-most-inspirational-sports-quotes-in-history/

Sayles, T. (2013). *7 tips for running a great basketball practice.* Retrieved from http://www.signupgenius.com/sports/basketball-practice-tips.cfm

Schudel, M. (2010, June 4). Legendary UCLA basketball coach John Wooden, winner of 10 national titles, dies at 99. *The Washington Post.* Retrieved from http://www.washingtonpost.com/

Seldin, P., & Miller, J. E. (2008). *The academic portfolio: A practical guide to documenting teaching research and service.* San Francisco, CA: Jossey-Bass.

Seldin, P., Miller, J. E., & Seldin, C. (2010). *The teaching portfolio: A practical guide to improved performance and promotion/tenure decisions.* San Francisco, CA: Jossey-Bass.

University of Minnesota Center for Teaching and Learning. (n.d.). *Background and contexts for teaching philosophies.* Retrieved from http://www1.umn.edu/ohr/teachlearn/tutorials/philosophy/background/index.html

AUTHOR BIOGRAPHY

Sylvia Whitman is no pro, having ended her scholastic basketball career in ninth grade as a Knickette. As a basketball mom, however, she watches a lot of games and has started playing again in an Arlington County, Virginia, intramural league for women over 50. She works as a writing specialist at Marymount University, supervising peer writing consultants and supporting faculty across the curriculum who assign writing. Off court, she writes books for kids. Her first novel for young adults, The Milk of Birds, *was published by Atheneum in spring 2013.*

APPENDIX: GLOSSARY

You can find basketball glossaries all over the web, including these:

    http://www.basketball.org/glossary/

    http://www.firstbasesports.com/basketball_glossary.html

    http://hoopedia.nba.com/index.php?title=Common_Basketball_Terms

Ball hog: Player who keeps the ball to himself or herself.

Bucket: Basket, as in *make a bucket.*

Dribble: Rhythmic move of bouncing the ball on the floor.

Fake: Move that fools an opponent into thinking you're moving in another direction.

Fast break: Quick offensive play after a change of possession with a long pass down the court.

Foul: Illegal action.

Free throw: Unchallenged shot taken after a foul.

Give and go: Quick play in which a player passes a ball and moves before receiving it back.

Layup: Near-basket shot bounced off the backboard.

MVP: Most valuable player.

Pivot: Move in which a player twirls on a toe to improve his or her position.

Point guard: The team's best ball handler, who leads the offense.

Rebound: Grab for the ball after an attempted basket.

Shot clock: Clock tracking the time limit (24 seconds in the NBA) for the offense to make a shot.

Swish: Basket made when the ball glides through the net without hitting the rim.

Timeout: Short suspension in play, during which players get advice from the coach.

Triple threat: Position from which a player may shoot, pass, or dribble.

CHAPTER 12

How Would a Social Activist Promote Critical Literacy in the Language Classroom?

Rawia Hayik

Dear Farmer Brown,
The barn is very cold at night.
We'd like some electric blankets.
Sincerely,
The Cows

(Cronin, 2000)

In Doreen Cronin's (2000) Caldecott-winning picture book *Click, Clack, Moo: Cows That Type*, the cows in Farmer Brown's barn have always suffered from cold nights. At last, they decide to take action and demand improvement to their work conditions, writing a letter of complaint to their boss. Unfortunately, true stories of social injustice are abundant in reality, constituting a considerable challenge for educators around the world, including language teachers. In many cases, such injustices can necessitate an urgent need for teachers to transcend the mere teaching of language skills and address social issues in the language classroom, teaching like social activists. Social justice picture books such as the ones suggested in this chapter have the potential to provide an effective tool for teachers to promote critical awareness, as does participatory documentary photography, further detailed here as well.

My personal and teaching reality have been packed with cases of social injustices that challenged me as an English language teacher to take some action. Being part of a Christian Arab minority among a Muslim Arab majority in Israel and the Middle East, a member of an Arab minority in a Jewish country, and a female in a male-dominated Middle Eastern society, I have encountered numerous incidents of injustice. Such problems surface in my Israeli-Arab elementary and junior high public school and pose a problematic scenario in which students usually befriend only those of the same faith, follow societal norms that restrict females' personal development, and are exposed to local media that alienates them and highlights their inferior status as a minority group in their own country. After years of silently noting the injustice but doing nothing to change reality, I decided to start critiquing unfair incidents that I encountered. I found local media to be an effective avenue for me to make my voice heard and often published short accounts of critique. Realizing the power of writing for an audience, I started addressing problematic issues in my English classroom through incorporating similar methods. I was committed to make justice my project (Edelsky, 1999): to begin teaching like a social activist.

Social activism starts in raising the public's awareness to imperfections in reality and develops into taking action for social justice. As a social activist who fought for the rights of farm workers in the United States, César Chávez started his quest by making the invisible visible. His first steps in social activism were opening the workers' eyes to their rights while simultaneously familiarizing the public with the difficult work conditions farm workers struggle with. In 1962, he managed to organize a union that could stand and face exploiting growers and succeeded in recruiting financial and moral support for his campaign. Using speeches, writings, and other forms of expression, he conducted a rhetorical campaign to educate his audience of workers and potential supporters of the power of unions (Jensen & Hammerback, 2002). His social activism culminated in powerful published letters and protests that helped to enact better work conditions in farms in his piece of the world.

Similar to the work of social activists in society like César Chávez, teaching like a social activist involves exploiting the power of the word to effect some change. Literacy can indeed serve as a powerful tool for social change. In a global reality fraught with injustices and the multiple challenges of life in multicultural societies, it becomes essential to connect the classroom, including the language classroom, to students' lives and communities. After all, "good teaching is ultimately a moral act" (Gee, 2008, p. 114). Teachers should have a moral commitment to educating students to social justice issues in addition to a responsibility for teaching them content matter. As Kohl (1998) proposes, we as educators "need to root our struggles for social justice in the work we do on an everyday level in a particular community with a particular group of students" (p. 286).

Materials that address social justice issues can, and in my view should, be incorporated into the fabric of everyday teaching practices. In this chapter, I bring examples of techniques language teachers might use to apply the general principles of social activism to contribute to enhancing students' awareness of social injustices and encourage them to act upon the world (Freire, 1970) while enriching their learning and developing their language skills.

A SOCIAL ACTIVIST'S TIPS FOR LANGUAGE TEACHERS

The language classroom can provide a stage for students to freely express (orally and in writing) their criticism while nurturing in them a desire to seek social justice. Such an attitude to teaching is grounded in critical literacy theory, which views education as transformative. Critical literacy challenges the culture of silence and promotes students' active participation in the learning process, aiming to educate socially aware citizens who can act to transform their reality into a better one (Freire, 1970). "A humane educator's fundamental objective," Freire (1970) states, "is to fight alongside the people for the recovery of the people's humanity" (p. 84). Rather than just a matter of skill acquisition or knowledge transmission, literacy education should "enhance . . . peoples' agency over their life trajectories" (Luke & Freebody, 2000, "Drawing on People's Agency," para. 5). A teacher who takes a critical stance is one who consciously engages in teaching and responding to events, entertains alternative ways of being, takes responsibility to inquire, and is reflexive (Lewison, Leland, & Harste, 2008). Such a teacher encourages students to take action for social change, thus contributing to potential empowerment through "bringing new voices and previously untold stories into conversations on topics about which these voices provide invaluable witness, critique, and alternative narrative" (Maynes, Pierce, & Laslett, 2008, p. 7).

As a social activist, a language teacher can take the invitation to act upon the world in an attempt to make it a better place (Freire, 1970) through providing literacy engagements that encourage students to question stereotypes, critique social injustices, and take action. The literacy engagements suggested in this chapter connect the language classroom to students' lives and community and provide a stage for them to express their critique and make their voices heard while writing and expressing themselves in English meaningfully and for a genuine purpose. Vygotsky (1978) discusses the significance of teaching writing in natural, meaningful ways. He stresses that writing should be "relevant to life . . . incorporated into a task that is necessary and relevant for life" (pp. 118–119). Hudelson (1989) also stresses that, similar to native language writing, ESL writing should also be meaningful, purposeful, and relevant to students' lives.

Tip 1: Use relevant picture books as a springboard for students' critical oral and written responses.

A picture book such as the one cited in the beginning of this chapter (Cronin, 2000) is a good example of a story that might lend itself to activities that inspire critical insights and actions. Scaffolded by the teacher's critical questions, it can raise students' awareness of improper work conditions and initiate an eye-opening inquiry into the issue. Students can end up writing projects on the issue and presenting them to an audience. Additionally, the nonviolent forms of social activism that the book suggests (writing a letter to the boss requesting some change and going on a strike if such a letter fails to bear the intended outcomes) can potentially empower students to act upon injustices they might encounter in their own lives.

The following subsections describe a unit that uses picture books as a springboard for students' critical oral and written responses. This particular unit aims to raise students' awareness of biased gender representations in traditional stories through reading English language children's literature and discussing messages that the texts convey, rewriting the stories to make them more emancipatory, writing letters to the author, and debating the issue of conventional role distribution.

Introductory Activities for Raising Awareness

Seemingly neutral texts sometimes hide biased messages with regard to gender issues. Take the traditional fairy tale of *Cinderella*, for example. It portrays the perfectly beautiful female protagonist as powerless, awaiting supernatural powers to change her reality. Such a children's book can serve as a catalyst for opening students' eyes to biased positioning of certain characters in literature and society in general.

A teacher as a social activist could start by inviting students to brainstorm descriptions of Cinderella and writing a character web for Cinderella on the board. A next step would be to encourage students to conduct a survey with at least three adults from their homes and/or neighborhoods with the question: What three words describe any/each of these characters: Cinderella, Snow White, and Sleeping Beauty? Their family members and/or neighbors can answer in their native language, but the students need to translate their answers into English and document the results to the teacher, who assembles all the results in one chart.

Asking Critical Questions

The survey results would usually align with Cinderella's character web. While displaying both together on the board or screen, the teacher can ask critical questions, such as the following, to raise students' awareness of the problematic portrayal of females in literature and media.

- How is Cinderella portrayed in the story? How is the prince portrayed?
- What was Cinderella's dream? What did she do to achieve her dream?
- What is this book saying about females? Is this true about all females? If yes, why are they this way?
- Who benefits from such stories being told/written like this?
- What if Cinderella was a male? How would you view him?

Such questions may encourage students to start viewing the traditionally admired story through a critical lens. They may begin to consider the disempowering messages of which they were previously oblivious. In addition, such topics as the commercial benefits companies gain through having girls preoccupied with their appearance can also be discussed.

Letter of Critique

After discussing these problematic issues concerning gender, the teacher can invite students to take some action to change such a reality. One possible way of taking action is writing a letter-of-critique to the author of the traditional Cinderella story (I used a simplified version of the story, called *A Dream for a Princess* [Lagonegro, 2005]). The teacher should first familiarize students with letter-writing conventions (e.g., that it should include the date, names of sender and receiver, and a proper beginning and ending). After getting acquainted with the conventions of writing a letter to the author, students are told that the content of their letters may include their impressions of the book and questions and/or comments they would like to communicate to the author. With the students' permission, the teacher can then locate the author's postal or email address online and forward the letters, making it possible for students' voices to affect future publications.

Alternative Endings

The unit can be complemented with alternative books with strong female characters who challenge the sexist portrayal of females and take action to change their gloomy life realities. Two especially inspiring books that provide an antithesis to the traditional Cinderella story are *Piggybook* (Browne, 1986) and *Cinder Edna* (Jackson, 1994). These thought-provoking picture books are manageable in terms of length and language complexity while addressing social justice issues suitable for older language students. *Cinder Edna* is a picture book that presents an alternative version to the traditional Cinderella story. It portrays passive Cinderella who waits for supernatural powers to change her reality alongside Cinder Edna, her powerful neighbor, who lives in similarly harsh circumstances but uses her creativity, talents, and determination to improve her life reality. For instance, she buys a dress for the ball on layaway using the little money she has earned from mowing the neighbors' grass in the limited free time she had after finishing her household chores and laboriously serving her stepmother and stepsisters. She also takes the bus to the ball instead of waiting for a fairy to magically turn a pumpkin into a carriage to transport her to the palace. Cinder Edna is more practical and controls her reality as much as she can under the injustices involved in life with her wicked stepmother and stepsisters. Despite her unattractive appearance, Cinder Edna eventually marries the interesting brother of Cinderella's handsome but shallow prince. The story ends with the question "Guess who lives happily ever after?" emphasizing that beauty does not necessarily bring happiness.

After reading *Cinder Edna*, the teacher can facilitate a discussion on the changes the author made to the original story. Students are encouraged to ponder the following questions:

- Why do you think the author wrote this book?
- What does the book tell you about her views?
- What is her underlying message?

Students prepare a compare-and-contrast chart of Cinderella and Cinder Edna in groups of four or five, and analyze the effects of the changes in the emancipatory version using a triple-entry journal table (Lewison et al., 2008, p. 174), which is a table with columns labeled "Event in the original fairy tale," "Changes the author made in the new version," and "How this change affected the meaning of the story." They then report their analyses to the whole class. Such activity encourages students to critically consider the author's decisions. After becoming aware of how making some critical changes in the text can change the messages it conveys, students are invited to rewrite traditional stories they are familiar with to make them more emancipatory. They can change some facts and events in the original text to empower the female protagonist and enable her to enhance her reality by her own (realistic) powers. The teacher can guide students' writing through providing different mini-lessons on writing powerful leads, using descriptive language, and crafting dramatic endings. Students' stories can later be shared with classmates, parents, and students in younger grades in order to provide empowering alternatives to the traditional stories.

Stories of Empowerment

Piggybook (Browne, 1986) also introduces a female who takes action to change her reality. A critical picture book, it portrays an overburdened wife and mother, Mrs. Piggott, doing all the household chores and constantly serving her lazy husband and two sons at the beginning of the story. At a certain point in the story, she takes action and decides to rebel against the traditional role of a female. She leaves the house inadvertently, an action that forces them to start taking care of themselves and eventually become more independent. Upon her return at the end, the lethargic males become more helpful and the entire role distribution in the house changes.

This story is timely and extremely relevant for a male-dominated society such as mine. Because it portrays a suffering female who takes action to change her reality, it not only would cause male students to question their practices toward their mothers and older sisters, but also might empower female students through encouraging them to change the status quo regarding conservative gender expectations.

Asking Questions at the Turning Point

After reading aloud the first part of the story, the teacher can stop before the turning point when the mother leaves, and ask students to share their feelings. Next, they are encouraged to write a short reflection starting with "If I were Mrs. Piggott, I would . . . ." After students share their responses, the teacher can finish reading the story. Students are encouraged to compare what they wrote with what the character actually did. Discussing Mrs. Piggott's action and the ending of the story is an additional activity. Was the action that Mrs. Piggott took satisfactory? Why or why not? Can you suggest an alternative action/ending? Students can brainstorm possible solutions other than running away.

The teacher can challenge students to further view the situation from different perspectives and seek social justice for all those involved in a situation by asking questions such as these:

- Is it OK if the father does all these chores?

- Why is it any worse for a mother to do that than a father?

- Does the situation change if the woman doesn't have a job? Is it fair then for the man to come home after a long day at work and start helping at home? Would it be fair for him to do two "jobs" while the wife does one?

Debate

A powerful follow-up activity would be a debate around equal role distribution in the house. Students are divided into two groups: one that advocates a traditional situation in which the woman is responsible for household chores and another that argues that each of the sexes should take equal domestic responsibilities. Members of each group team up to first write down a list of points supporting their views. They then choose representatives who stand in the front of the classroom facing representatives from the opposing team. The debate starts with each team making a statement and the other team responding in an attempt to repudiate their opponents' claim. It is essential here to highlight the significance of listening to the other group's views. The teacher should set and discuss with the students clear rules that urge students to respect opposing views even if they disagree with them and wait till their "opponents" finish talking before beginning to speak, rather than interrupting. After the debate ends, students reflect on the activity: How did they feel? Did it affect their views? How?

Throughout this unit, students are exposed to and use English in various ways. They get acquainted with authentic English language stories, answer critical questions, write letters and stories, and engage in a debate on the issue. Their oral and written use of the language is coupled with emerging awareness of a problematic issue in society and results in taking action to change reality through literacy. The next section includes an additional avenue in which students develop their language skills while trying to affect some change.

Tip 2: Give students opportunities to act as documentary photographers.

Through a social activist perspective, the teacher can encourage students to take photographs of things they suffer from or view as requiring improvement in their immediate environment, write a caption and short commentary underneath their photos, and later share them in a public exhibition. This approach to documentary photography is inspired by such activist photographers as Ewald (2001) and Hubbard (1994). It has been used by several researchers and educators (e.g., Kroeger et al., 2004; Wang, Cash, & Powers, 2000; Wang, Yi, Tao, & Carovano, 1998; Wilson, Minkler, Dasho, Wallerstein, & Martin, 2008; Zenkov & Harmon, 2009) and defined by many as *photovoice*. According to Wang, Burris, and Xiang (1996), photovoice is an intriguing tool that empowers youth with little money, power, or status by providing them with opportunities for critique and social change. Such a tool provides a springboard for students to highlight deficiencies they encounter in their society while writing for genuine, meaningful purposes and then using the oral language to present their ideas to an audience.

Such a process can be scaffolded by the teacher's guidance and modeling. The teacher can start by bringing a photograph or picture representing something that he or she sees as a problematic issue, displaying it on the board, and eliciting from students a caption and several sentences that can accurately describe the picture. The teacher writes the caption and sentences on the board and draws students' attention to grammatical points that can assist them while they compose their own sentences (e.g., capitalization and punctuation rules, subject-verb agreement, syntax rules). The teacher can also focus on the use of rich, descriptive language through asking students to add adjectives that further describe the nouns in the elicited sentences. Because students' written accounts of their own photos can be either expository (describing the photo and the event/issue it represents) or narrative (telling a personal story that the student has experienced concerning the portrayed issue), mini-lessons on both expository and narrative genres might be necessary. The teacher can bring examples of both and help students practice each genre.

Due to the potentially sensitive nature of this activity, it may be wise to get the consent of parents and the school principal before sending students to take photos. Additionally, students need to be aware that if they choose to photograph people, then they are required to ask them to sign release forms. After this preparation stage, students are encouraged to take photos and write a suitable title and a short paragraph in English describing the deficiencies each photo addresses. Students' photos and written accounts ("voices") are later displayed in a walk-in exhibit attended by leading figures in students' society, such as the mayor, political representatives, principals, and educators, in addition to parents and other students. Students share their criticism of the shortcomings they observe in their surrounding environment with the visitors and seek avenues for social change.

Examples of students' photos from my classes include an unpaved road next to the school, unattractive school walls with peeling and faded paint, lack of shaded areas at school, a woman holding a child on one arm and several (seemingly heavy) shopping bags in the other hand while her husband is walking next to her and not helping, and young children hazardously playing in the middle of a busy street due to the lack of a playground in their village (see Figure 1 for an example of an eighth-grade EFL student's photovoice).

Through sharing this tool with students, I could observe how they started using the language of critique (Shannon, 1995) to disrupt the status quo and demand social change (Lewison et al., 2008) and how they began developing powerful social identities. While using English to write short expository or narrative texts and to explain their photos orally to the audience, the students became more aware of social justice issues, and they became social activists who could highlight problematic issues to the wider community and act to improve their realities.

The benefits of this tool can be further intensified if teachers turn it into a class routine in which students can display their photos and written descriptions on the school bulletin board on a regular basis. After all, "schools need to provide the opportunity for literate occasions for students to . . . work in social relations that emphasize care and concern for others, to take risks, and to fight for a quality of life in which all human beings benefit" (Giroux, 1987, p. 181).

CONCLUSION

Social activism tools like writing letters of critique, composing a more empowering ending to a story, or reporting deficits in society through participatory

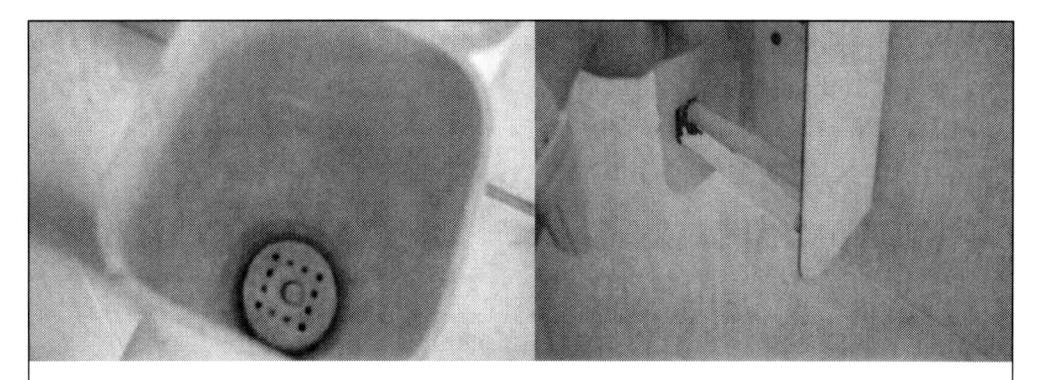

> The problem here is that there is absolutely no toilet paper or soap in the bathrooms of our school, which means the kids will not wash their hands. Therefore the kids (with dirty hands) will touch their lunch or even put their hands in their mouths which makes them sick. The school needs to provide soap and toilet paper so the kids stop being sick and absent from school.

Figure 1. Photovoice Example

documentary photography provide a platform for students to express their views and make their silenced voices heard while using English for real purposes. With the global socioeconomic, cultural, and political position of English in the world, real-life use of the language for social, cultural, and political purposes can better prepare students for life in a global world (Pennycook, 1994). English has truly become "the language of educational and socioeconomic advancement" in many countries, as Lin (1999, p. 396) describes, referring to the case of Hong Kong, where English had gained a dominant position although it was the first language of only a minority there. Indeed, it is believed by many that competence in English empowers speakers of other languages and positively influences their life chances and global mobility.

Language teachers can act as agents for social change through incorporating materials on students' life challenges in the language curriculum and encouraging students to take action. After all, students learn to read the word through reading the world and vice versa (Freire, 1983). As students express their ideas and critique in English and practice their oral and written language skills in a meaningful and powerful way, they also get empowered to effect some social change.

While equipping students with critical ways of practicing and using the English language, a language teacher can try to develop a counter-ideology and -culture "that provide an ethical alternative to the dominant hegemony, a lived experience of how the world can be different" (Lather, 1984, p. 55), a counter-reality to what he or she considers unethical, oppressing, and restricting. What might develop in the classroom can be, as Weiler (1988) describes, "democratic relationships, an alternative value system and a critique of existing society" (p. 54).

The application of the ideas presented in this chapter is especially relevant and essential in the current global reality, in which social injustices are abundant. However, it can potentially hide some risks in its folds. Unexpected issues may emerge that teachers might not be equipped to deal with; for example, students' discussions may be interrupted by insulting remarks or offensive objections. In such cases, it is essential for the teacher to remind the students that it is natural for different people to have different, and sometimes opposing, views. Respecting opposing views is an essential value in democratic societies, and establishing a classroom that promotes such respect is essential to the success of many of the activities described in this chapter.

Additionally, the activities presented here may sometimes fail to raise some students' awareness of such issues, and it would probably be overly idealistic to believe that social activism can affect everyone's views. Students may wish to remain encapsulated in their seemingly normal daily lives and choose to reject viewing any imperfections around them. What should teachers do in such a case? How can they awaken students' social justice awareness? On the other side of the continuum, students may be so intrigued by the social justice issues discussed in class that their responses become "too political" and stir opposition from principals and policymakers. One might wonder: What can be done to minimize opposition against turning students into powerful social activists? Such concern, however, reveals the power of such tools, which should be encouraged in democratic societies even if critiquing sensitive issues. As Hall (2003) proposes, literacy is not neutral but "bound up with ethnicity, gender, social class, disability, and so on. Its purpose is social justice, equality and democracy" (p. 189). It is my hope that after reading this chapter, you will be willing to take the challenge and start teaching like a social activist. Ask yourself: What can *you* do to promote social justice, equality, and democracy in your little part of the world?

RESOURCES FOR FURTHER EXPLORATION

Lewison, M., Leland, C., & Harste, J. C. (2008). *Creating critical classrooms: K-8 reading and writing with an edge.* New York, NY: Taylor and Francis Group.

> After succinctly describing the theoretical underpinnings of critical literacy theory and presenting the authors' four-resource framework of critical literacy, this rich book suggests several literacy activities and detailed K-8 language lessons that aim to raise students' awareness to social justice issues and encourage them to take action for social change.

Singer, J., & Shagoury, R. (2005). Stirring up justice: Adolescents reading, writing, and changing the world. *Journal of Adolescent & Adult Literacy, 49*(4), 318–339.

> This article details a unit on social activism for high school students that connects literacy to issues of equity. As a social justice educator, the literacy teacher described in the article encourages students to effect positive change in their lives while acquiring and practicing the literacy skills required for success in future work, study, and personal life choices.

Wang, C., Burris, M., & Xiang, Y. P. (1996). Chinese village women as visual anthropologists: A participatory approach to reaching policy makers. *Social Science and Medicine, 42*, 1391–1400.

> This article describes how the educational tool called photovoice or photo novella was used to empower rural underprivileged women through providing the means for them to capture photos that reflect their difficult life conditions and needs to the wider community. The authors especially focus on how such a tool can inform policymakers and effect some change.

REFERENCES

Browne, A. (1986). *Piggybook.* New York, NY: Dragonfly Books.

Cronin, D. (2000). *Click, clack, moo: Cows that type.* New York, NY: Simon & Schuster.

Edelsky, C. (1999). *Making justice our project.* Urbana, IL: National Council of Teachers of English.

Ewald, W. (2001). *I wanna take me a picture: Teaching photography and writing to children.* Boston, MA: Beacon.

Freire, P. (1970). *Pedagogy of the oppressed.* New York, NY: Continuum.

Freire, P. (1983). The importance of the act of reading. *Journal of Education, 165,* 5–11.

Gee, J. P. (2008). *Social linguistics and literacies.* London, England: Routledge.

Giroux, H. (1987). Critical literacy and student experience: Donald Graves' approach to literacy. *Language Arts, 64,* 175–181.

Hall, K. (2003). *Listening to Stephen read: Multiple perspectives on literacy.* Buckingham, England: Open University Press.

Hubbard, J. (1994). *Shooting back from the reservation: A photographic view of life by Native Americans.* New York, NY: New Press.

Hudelson, S. (1989). *Write on: Children writing in ESL.* Englewood Cliffs, NJ: Prentice Hall Regents.

Jackson, E. (1994). *Cinder Edna.* New York, NY: Mulberry Books.

Jensen, J. R., & Hammerback, J. C. (Eds.). (2002). *The words of Cesar Chavez.* College Station: Texas A&M University Press.

Kohl, H. (1998). Afterward: Some reflections on teaching for social justice. In W. Ayers, J. Hunt, & T. Quinn (Eds.), *Teaching for social justice* (pp. 285–287). New York, NY: Teachers College Press.

Kroeger, S., Burton, C., Comarata, A., Combs, C., Hamm, C., Hopkins, R., & Kouche, B. (2004). Student voice and critical reflection: Helping students at risk. *Teaching Exceptional Children, 36*(3), 50–57.

Lagonegro, M. (2005). *A dream for a princess.* New York, NY: Random House.

Lather, P. (1984). Critical theory, curricular transformation and feminist mainstreaming. *Journal of Education, 166*(1), 49–62.

Lewison, M., Leland, C., & Harste, J. C. (2008). *Creating critical classrooms: K–8 reading and writing with an edge.* New York, NY: Taylor and Francis.

Lin, A. M. Y. (1999). Doing-English-lessons in the reproduction or transformation of social worlds? *TESOL Quarterly, 33,* 393–412.

Luke, A., & Freebody, P. (1999). *Further notes on the four resources model.* Retrieved from http://www.readingonline.org/research/lukefreebody.html

Maynes, M., Pierce, J., & Laslett, B. (2008). *Telling stories: The use of personal narratives in the social sciences and history.* Ithaca, NY: Cornell University Press.

Pennycook, A. (1994). *The cultural politics of English as an international language.* London, England: Longman.

Shannon, P. (1995). *Text, lies, and videotape: Stories about life, literacy, and learning.* Portsmouth, NH: Heinemann.

Vygotsky, L. S. (1978). *Mind in society: The development of higher psychological processes* (Ed. and trans. M. Cole, V. John-Steiner, S. Scribner, & E. Souberman). Cambridge, MA: Harvard University Press.

Wang, C., Burris, M., & Xiang, Y. P. (1996). Chinese village women as visual anthropologists: A participatory approach to reaching policy makers. *Social Science and Medicine, 42,* 1391–1400.

Wang, C. C., Cash, J. L., & Powers, L. S. (2000). Who knows the streets as well as the homeless? Promoting personal and community action through photovoice. *Health Promotion Practice, 1,* 81–89.

Wang, C. C., Yi, W. K., Tao, Z. W., & Carovano, K. (1998). Photovoice as a participatory health promotion strategy. *Health Promotion International, 13*(1), 75–86.

Weiler, K. (1988). *Women teaching for change.* New York, NY: Bergin & Garvey.

Wilson, N., Minkler, M., Dasho, S., Wallerstein, N., & Martin, A. C. (2008). Getting to social action: The Youth Empowerment Strategies (YES!) project. *Health Promotion Practice, 9*(4), 395–403.

Zenkov, K., & Harmon, J. (2009). Picturing a writing process: Photovoice and teaching writing to urban youth. *Journal of Adolescent and Adult Literacy, 52,* 575–584.

AUTHOR BIOGRAPHY

Rawia Hayik is a recent PhD graduate from the Literacy, Culture, and Language Education Department at Indiana University, in the United States. Prior to pursuing her PhD, she worked as an elementary and middle school EFL teacher for 16 years. Her research focuses on working with Israeli-Arab EFL students and using children's literature on gender, religious diversity, and minority issues as a springboard for critical reader responses. Currently, Rawia teaches English methodology courses and works as a pedagogical advisor at Sakhnin College for Teacher Education, in Israel. She also serves as an adjunct faculty member at Indiana University, teaching a graduate course on using multicultural and international children's literature in the language classroom.

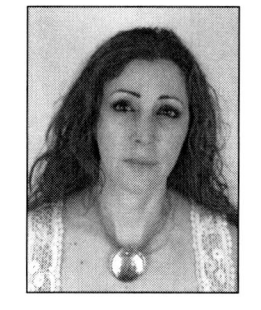

Developing as a Professional

CHAPTER 13

How Would a Public Speaker Hook 'Em Every Time?

John Schmidt

"Hook 'em!" That's the rallying cry at football games of my alma mater, the University of Texas at Austin. It's also a greeting on campus and a short variation of "Hook 'em, Horns!" referring to our school's mascot, the longhorn steer, in a battle of engagement.

Do you start class by saying, "Please open your books to page . . . . Today we're going to study . . . ."?

ZZZZZzzzzzzz.

Hook 'em when you start class or start a speech to immediately draw in your audience. Like an effective public speaker, an effective teacher starts strong, capturing students' attention and engaging them from the outset. The students stop and focus. They connect and respond (Proven, 2009).

I had been a Longhorn alumnus for over a decade, as well as a language teacher and public speaker, before discovering the significance of "hooking" my audience, as well as many other public speaking techniques useful for the classroom. When I was recruited to lecture on cruise ships in exchange for vacation trips, I realized that I would need to enhance my performance skills to give shipboard presentations, so I joined a Toastmasters club to study public speaking. Hooked on the well-developed methodologies and materials of Toastmasters International, I spent the next 5 years working through the entire Toastmasters communication and leadership programs, learning and practicing skills that could be applied in classrooms and lecture halls, even on the high seas.

A PUBLIC SPEAKER'S TIPS FOR LANGUAGE TEACHERS

As a student, teacher, and practitioner of foreign languages and public speaking, I've personally experienced and witnessed the same three fundamental aspects in both lessons and speeches. The first aspect is that of *the messenger*, a basic aspect that most teachers and speakers readily master but can enhance throughout their careers, which I explore in my first tip. The second aspect, t*he message*, is addressed in my second tip and involves ongoing development on a daily basis and throughout one's entire career. The third aspect, *the recipients*, involves the ultimate goal of focusing speeches and lessons on the audience.

Tip 1: Think about yourself as the messenger, and use your body effectively to deliver your message.

As messengers, language teachers and public speakers should focus on the facets that make up the physical message. These facets are body language, movement, gestures, expression and eye contact, and voice.

Body Language

A public speaker or a teacher usually stands up to project a presence and to command attention in front of a seated audience or group of students. Yet many teachers spend much of their time sitting down while they teach. At the end of semesters, I've read student evaluations of their language instructors in which they've written that their teachers are tired or lazy or uninterested because they seldom stand up while teaching. How can a teacher use movement and communicative gestures in class, readily access a chalkboard or a white board, circulate throughout the classroom, and project a command of the room while seated?

Movement

From the first words of a speech or a lesson, good posture and stance communicate confidence, comfort, and interest. Shifting, slouching, or leaning on a lectern, a desk, or a wall does not project a positive image to the viewer. Purposeful movement conveys involvement. It provides variety and thus keeps the listeners attentive and interested. It emphasizes enthusiasm and engagement, as well as a connection to everyone in the room.

Both teachers and public speakers can use movement and step into the audience to emphasize or dramatize a point, and both can benefit from rehearsal of movement. Stand up in an empty classroom or in your living room, and try out various movements from the front of the room and around the room. Teach a language point to an invisible audience as you move. Developing poise and a sense of purposeful movement enhances the effectiveness of any public speaker or teacher.

Gestures

A considerable amount of a message is conveyed through nonverbal language. Gestures significantly complement the oral message and facilitate understanding. The head, shoulders, arms, and hands can convey size, shape, weight, location, and direction. They can also express agreement and disagreement, comparison and contrast, emphasis and urgency (Gershon, 2008; Leanne, 2009).

Stand up and practice expressing all of these aspects of message through gestures. Use larger-than-life gestures for a big classroom or perhaps for students with a limited proficiency in the target language. Try this same exercise with students. How many different gestures can you demonstrate from head to toe? What do these gestures convey? Which are universal? Which gestures vary among your culture and the cultures of the students in your class? What gestures should be avoided when crossing cultures? It's useful for students to learn about these notions in the classroom instead of out in the world. A University of Texas graduate, I avoid the "Hook 'em, Horns" gesture, given its offensive interpretation in various cultures.

Expression and Eye Contact

The eyes have it—the ability to convey a range of emotions with your eyes. As an intern teacher of sixth-grade Spanish, my eyes were the most effective weapon in disciplining Jimmy, a mischievous student. He didn't want me to call his mother to report his misbehavior in class or else he wouldn't get a bicycle for his birthday. All it took was a stern look from me, and Jimmy immediately shaped up in class.

Eye contact is essential to maintaining an ongoing connection to an audience or a classroom of students (Arnold, 2010). Speakers or teachers who break eye contact to read too much of their message from a sheet of paper, a book, or PowerPoint slides, or who turn their backs on the audience to face a board or screen, may readily lose their listeners' interest and attention.

Voice

Another facet of the physical message is the voice. It should attract the listeners' attention and hold it, enhancing the words that are spoken. Good posture is important to the free flow of air through the lungs and vocal chords of both the public speaker and the teacher, significantly influencing voice quality. Vocal impact is greater when standing up than when sitting down. Abdominal breathing contributes to vocal quality, based on the depth and steadiness of the air flow (Jacobi, 2009).

Vocal characteristics include volume, pitch, rate, and quality. Volume control and variety are effective in maintaining listener attention. Avoiding a monotone voice through variety in pitch also fosters listener alertness (Leanne, 2009). As for rate, 125 to 160 words per minute is effective for standard communication (Toastmasters International, 2011). Full or resonant voice quality projects confidence, naturalness, and friendliness (Rodenburg, 1993).

Experiment with your voice, recording it if possible. Choose a topic. Talk about it for several minutes. Change your position from sitting to slouching to standing. How does your voice vary from position to position? Exaggerate for effect, and talk as you vary your rate of breathing. What differences do you notice as the rate changes? Vary your volume along a continuum. Vary the pitch and the rate. Vary your voice quality. What differences do you notice among the varieties? How would voice differences affect your listeners?

As a listener of your own recording, how do you react as your voice changes? Do you notice any verbal mannerisms that might be distracting? Are you speaking too fast for your students? Is there too much information for them to absorb? Are you pausing and adding emphases? Are you clear and articulate? A fellow ESL teacher reported to me that students asked her what the "festivals" were that she kept talking about in class. She realized that she should slow down and not overuse the phrase "First of all, ..."

While speaking with students, purposely pause or stop for a few moments. Did this have the desired effect—to focus the students' attention, to emphasize a point, or to punctuate a thought? Being expressive with the voice while giving a speech or teaching a lesson can increase your effectiveness. It can add meaning to words, enhance points, and increase the interest of the listener. Vocal features need to be balanced and used in moderation. An overly expressive voice becomes tiring, alienates the listeners, and does not achieve the intended purpose (Reinhart, 2002).

Think of voices that you personally know or those of newsmakers whom you've heard. Who has a pleasant voice? What aspects of the voice provide a positive sound and impression? Who has an unpleasant voice? What's unappealing about it? To further assess vocal characteristics, turn on your radio or television to identify a variety of vocal features and tones. Just like public speakers, teachers can enhance or modify their message significantly by purposefully employing vocal variety. Rehearse a segment of your lesson. If you don't already employ purposeful vocal variety as you teach, with practice you may begin to do so subconsciously.

Tip 2: Use practice, planning, and props to deliver the message effectively.

In addition to presenting oneself well, the messenger must craft a good message. It may be in the form of a speech script for the public speaker or a lesson plan for the teacher. Personal style and available time to prepare are major factors in planning a message for delivery. You may be a methodical person or a spontaneous one. You may be very creative. Whatever your style and attributes and whatever time you have available, organization is critical (Berkun, 2010).

Hooks and Props

Take just a few moments of creative thought to plan a hook for your next class. It may be a question: "Have you ever . . . ?" or "How many of you . . . ?" or "Why do . . . ?" It may be an imperative: "Tell me three . . . ." A hook can be an engaging quote or proverb, an entertaining anecdote or a short story (Perlman, 1998). Question and imperative hooks get attention and connect, as well as gain interest and solicit participation through oral responses (Koegel, 2007).

Effective hooks can appeal to the sense of sight. Props serve as a hook's visual stimuli. They might be as simple as a feather, a toy, or a piece of fruit. They can be an intriguing or hidden object or an article of clothing that a teacher dons. Putting on a hat, a pair of sunglasses, or something more unusual in class can attract students' interest and curiosity.

A hook might be a prop that is distributed to students to handle. Props should be vivid and visible; small ones can be used, if there are enough of them to go around. I've seen paperclips used in reading and writing classes to preface essays on invention and used in grammar classes to hook together two parts of a sentence. What topic are you teaching in your next class? How could you use paperclips as props with a hook?

Props can also take the form of a picture or two (three would be plenty) that are large enough for all to see. Projecting a visual on a screen is an alternative. No matter what prop a speaker or a teacher uses as a hook, it should relate to the message, not distract the audience and not take up a lot of time. With a transition, the hook can lead right to the introduction (Garmston, 2005). In addition to spoken words and props as oral and visual stimuli, sounds or music can serve as hooks. What sounds or short musical selections could you use as a hook in your next class to introduce a point that you will teach?

Interact

Opportunities can be built into any plan to invite and respond to input from listeners with segments that are interactive and open to improvisation. This is important to the captive audience members and extremely critical to language learners who should be using the language more than the teacher! Keep this in mind as you develop your lesson plan. Incorporating these unstructured segments into the overall plan and controlling them will allow you to fulfill your plan within the allotted amount of time and contribute to your overall message.

Timeframe

When planning a lesson or a speech, consider the total amount of time available, the amount of time each of your segments will take, and how to fit everything in. Many teachers and speakers plan their message without close attention to the time limit. I did this for years, usually planning too much content and cutting out important class segments or postponing them until another day, racing through the rest of a lesson or speech, and flipping through PowerPoint slides to cover the remaining content. At a minimum, quickly jot down your lesson plan or a speech outline, on a simple grid noting 5- or 10-minute intervals to strive for a realistic fit and to ensure ample coverage, along with a strong close, before your time is up.

Sample Activities

After developing your content and materials, extra time can be spent productively refining your message. What's your hook? How have you framed the message? How can you improve the "packaging" and sequencing of subsections so they can be better captured by the listeners? Can you add smooth transitions? Don't underestimate the value of the words you select and how you arrange them. Use vivid and colorful words in short sentences, as well as in paragraph construction that allows you to get to the point.

How can you enhance the physical, verbal, and visual aspects of your message? Public speakers are encouraged to practice their delivery a number of times. Some teachers might simply "wing it," especially if they are teaching many hours each and every day, but they could benefit from rehearsing short segments of their performance, particularly the introduction of a topic or the explanation of a grammar point.

Language teachers can readily incorporate public speaking skills into their performance in class by focusing on the physical aspects of a messenger—effective body language and voice quality. They can enhance their instruction by considering diverse characteristics related to the message. They can combine these factors to conduct the following effective activities in class that will facilitate students' production of the language:

Minute Message

When I first became a Toastmasters club member, I didn't know that I would eventually be teaching like a Toastmaster, discovering attributes and techniques that I could adapt to my ESL classes and, later, public speaking classes. Inspired at each Toastmasters meeting by the Table Topics segment, during which members think on their feet and give short, extemporaneous speeches in response to questions or stimuli, I developed the Minute Message activity for classes that I teach. Try out the following example of this activity in class.

1. Stand up and speak for a minute and answer this question:

   What's your favorite holiday and why?

2. For a minute:

   Tell us about a holiday memory from your childhood.

3. Answer this question:

   If you could invent a holiday, what holiday would you invent and why?

This is an example of a Minute Message theme with diverse questions, each of which would be asked of a different speaker.

Let's adapt this technique to language teachers by asking you the following:

Tell us one thing that you're going to teach tomorrow. Speak for 1 minute.

After talking for a minute, you've developed a rough lesson plan for tomorrow.

The Minute Message activity is based on a designated theme of the day from which prompts such as questions or other forms of stimuli (a single word, a phrase, or the start of a story line) are generated. When I'm conducting an in-service public speaking course for English language teachers from South Korea who will be interning in schools in the United States, our theme and questions relate to Korean or U.S. culture and personal topics, questions that curious students in the United States might ask the visiting teacher. In my classes at an intensive English program, students choose themes and create sets of questions. As a whole-class activity or in small groups, we dedicate the first segment of class to warming up with Minute Messages or save them for a lively grand finale at the end of class. Students preparing for job interviews or school admission interviews find this activity to be extremely practical.

Beyond the roles of asking and answering questions and keeping track of the time, I often add roles to involve all students at all times. Some of the roles are the same as those in Toastmasters meetings, such as the grammarian and the "*ah* counter," who, respectively, listen for good use of grammar and grammar errors and who count the number of times the speaker says *ah* and *um*.

Line Up, my paired variation of Minute Message, proceeds as follows:

- Students stand in two rows (A and B), face to face.

- Student A asks Student B a question related to the theme of the day.

- Student B responds by speaking for a minute while Student A listens.

- When the time is up, the students in row A move to the left. Students in Row B stay in place.

- Student B asks the new partner a different question, and Student A gives an uninterrupted Minute Message.

To provide extensive opportunities for fluency development, we make time in class for a Minute Message Marathon or a class contest. Varying the theme, the stimuli, and the format results in diverse, lively, and productive language classes.

Three in One

Three in One is a structured approach to public speaking for both teachers and students that I created for expedient development and delivery of speeches during a single class. As a teacher, experience how easy it is to develop and give a basic speech as the opening for your next lesson. Item 3 in italics has been adapted for you, the language teacher as public speaker in your classroom:

1. Start with five index cards or half sheets of paper.
2. Number the cards 1–5 at the top.
3. Title your first card with *a topic that you'll teach next Monday.*
4. On Cards 2–4 write three parallel points or aspects related to this topic.
5. Add a subpoint and an example to Cards 2–4.
6. On your first card, write a hook, an introductory statement, and a transition.
7. Start your fifth card with a transition, a summary, and a memorable line.
8. Stand up. Feel free to use your cards as notes to give a 3-minute speech.

With an introduction, body, and conclusion, you have three parts to a "speech" that you can use to begin teaching a new lesson. You started strong by getting the students' attention, you systematically and sequentially led them through a body of content with subpoints and examples, and as Powell (2002) adds, you finished strongly, which included a summary and an impactful conclusion. Your three points in this one speech, delivered in 3 minutes, demonstrate the *power of three*, the amount of oral information that students should be able to retain and recall (Hale, 2010). You now have the start to a lesson for next Monday.

Adapt Three in One as a technique in your language classes. This activity works well at any time and with any topic, particularly at the start of a new semester as the equivalent to a Toastmasters Ice Breaker speech, in which new members introduce themselves to the others.

Proving a Proverb is one of my variations of Three in One. I present several English proverbs, some of which have equivalencies in students' languages and cultures:

1. A bird in the hand is worth two in the bush.
2. Haste makes waste.
3. Don't count your chickens before they hatch.

Students choose any proverb and connect it to a personal experience. They develop their speech, starting with a hook and ending with a memorable line, perhaps the proverb itself. In the process, the speech exemplifies the motto of Bill Gove, the first president of the National Speakers Association: "Tell a story, make a point" (Brown, Lacroix, Fripp, Tate, & Valentine, 2010, p. 35).

Tip 3: Tailor your message to your audience.

During my development as a Toastmaster, I realized that accomplished public speakers and accomplished teachers had to be more than talented messengers with well-crafted messages. Although they continue to enhance both aspects of their performance with each speech or lesson that they produce and deliver, their major focus should be a third dimension—their audience or students.

While creating their message, public speakers should well understand the four major purposes or types of speeches: to inform, to entertain, to persuade, and to inspire (Garmston, 2005). Focusing on the third dimension of speeches, public speakers clearly direct their speeches accordingly to their audiences. Additionally, they often combine two or more of these purposes into a speech, particularly incorporating entertainment, putting into practice the common idea that when audiences laugh, they relax, and when they relax, they are more likely to learn. As a shipboard lecturer, I was often told by the cruise director to "edutain." As a language instructor, how often do you combine two or more of these four purposes in your teaching?

Teachers may start their lesson with a hook to connect with the students. They begin with an outline of their talk to facilitate students' ability to construct the components of the message, given the ephemeral nature of oral information. They use oral organizers such as restatement, definitions, and short, numbered lists of points. Visual organizers on a chalkboard, on a handout, or in a computer-based format such as PowerPoint can also benefit the listener. After such an effective start, don't simply proceed to inform and inform and inform. Regularly take time to reconnect, to check student understanding. Ask questions, ask students to restate a point, or better yet ask them to complete a task or activity that quickly tells you whether they have understood what you have taught.

Alternately, in small groups, one student can take on the role of "5-minute teacher," going over an exercise. Often peers understand best from each other and get the best out of each other, because students tend to excel in a peer context. Teachers should also reactivate interest and previous knowledge, and branch into other purposes of speech, inspiring student to action, which often involves a homework assignment to master specific content (Coombe, England, & Schmidt, 2008).

Handouts

A useful strategy to keep listeners focused is to have various tasks or roles for them to fulfill, as mentioned with the previous activities. An activity-based handout can focus, engage, and guide listeners while providing key information in a structured framework (Mandel, 2009). The timing of the distribution of a handout is critical; once it's in the listeners' hands, they shift from an auditory focus on the speaker to a visual focus on the document. Also, having too much information on the handout is distracting and defeats the purpose of the oral message (Lucas, 2011).

An effective handout has gaps, such as a limited number of blanks or sections to fill in or complete based on what the speaker is saying. It also has room for the listeners' own ideas and examples, as the speaker solicits their information, input, and involvement. Without being voluminous, the handout's sections may vary in format.

Technology

In addition to considerations about handouts for public speakers and teachers, a note of caution needs to be added about computer-based visuals, which have become common among public speakers and teachers. Traditionally, a speaker sets the scene or paints a picture in the listeners' minds through words. I strongly encourage this approach, which challenges listeners to pay attention and create their own visions of the picture in their minds. PowerPoint visuals circumvent this process. These visuals limit the picture to the one in the room, precluding the many different ones that would have been painted in each listener's mind. Of course, pictorial visuals, particularly entertaining pictures, can be useful to capture the listeners' attention and engage the listener. Too many pictures, however, diminish the pictorial attraction and emphasis, and too many pictures projected for too short a time frustrate listeners who can't keep up with the speaker (Hall, 2008).

Computer-based visuals with text present both benefits and distractions in the lecture hall and the classroom. They can spell out key terms or definitions. They can emphasize topics and facilitate framing, providing visual markers as headings to sequence the content of the message. A limited number of slides with a limited amount of text, combined with a few carefully selected pictures, can embellish the oral message (Mandel, 2009). However, PowerPoint presentations should never be a substitute for the speaker or teacher, but only a complement to them, providing visual focal points and guideposts for the listeners (Sweeney, 2004). They should be developed after the message has been constructed or outlined, perhaps after using the expedient method described earlier in the section on Three in One.

Used purposefully and selectively, PowerPoint presentations, video and audio clips, and other computer-based visual and auditory formats can increase listener interest and understanding, assuming there are no technological glitches. However, Koegel (2010, p. 10) emphasizes that "the technology can't do it for you" and encourages speakers to keep presentations relevant, engaging, and moving.

CONCLUSION

Having spent large amounts of time in front of television and computer screens, students in classrooms and members of audiences have become passive recipients of information. They have become overly dependent on visual media to convey much of the message. In the last few years, the presence of a cell phone in most every pocket, purse, and backpack has significantly exacerbated the problem of passive, unfocused listeners, providing them with a major distraction at hand. Additionally, many in the lecture hall or classroom audience think that recording the speech or lesson can substitute for listening to it in real time and taking notes. Some simply want to film the entire speech or lesson, take pictures of key slides or other written information, or get the entire computer-based presentation from the speaker or teacher. I wonder how many recorded speeches or lessons are ever actually played at a later date.

If there is not an attendance requirement nor interaction or tasks to complete in real time, many contemporary listeners wonder whether they even need to be present to get the message live and in person from the messenger. As a role model for our listeners, public speakers and teachers should try turning off their technology and that of their audience for an hour and turning on all of their talents by communicating interactively, engaging all members of the audience.

I've often suggested the following alternate use of technology to language teachers whom I observe: Record your class. Clock the oral participation of each of the students to determine the balance or lack thereof. Of equal importance is to clock the time dedicated to teacher talk versus student talk. Is your class too teacher centered? The recording can also provide you with a self-assessment as a messenger with important information to communicate. You don't have to share the recording with anyone; just listen to it by yourself for some valuable feedback. What can you do to enhance your delivery and message? How can you skillfully engage and connect with students? Get ready, so tomorrow you can "hook 'em" in class and teach like a public speaker!

ACKNOWLEDGMENTS

Liz England and fellow Toastmasters Christine Coombe and Neil Anderson have collaborated on related presentations at TESOL conventions and elsewhere. Hundreds of ESL students from around the world, including English language teacher trainees, have sparked my enthusiasm to enhance their abilities as public speakers and "hook 'em" every time. My thanks and appreciation to all!

RESOURCES FOR FURTHER EXPLORATION

At www.toastmasters.org, find a Toastmasters club near you that you can visit, or explore starting a new club. This global nonprofit organization today comprises 280,000 members giving speeches and serving in different meeting roles each week in 13,500 clubs in 116 countries (Toastmasters International, 2013). The five-level communication achievement program and four-level leadership achievement program of Toastmasters International are based on well-developed methodology, curriculum, and corresponding training materials. The approach is flexible and collegial; you can proceed at your own pace in a supportive environment of peers. In addition to the resources on the Toastmasters website, there are many more at district and club websites, such as www.tmd55.org and www.austintoastmasters.org, which correspond to my district and club.

The National Speakers Association (www.nsaspeaker.org) focuses on aspiring and accomplished professional speakers. It is a source of publications, conferences, and even a Laugh Lab, a training course where you can learn to be a more entertaining speaker.

There are numerous accomplished public speakers, including the following, who host their own websites to introduce their varied services and products.

Patricia Fripp: www.fripp.com

World Champion's Edge: www.fripp.com/world-champions-edge (featuring four Toastmasters International World Champions of Public Speaking)

Darren LaCroix: darrenlacroix.com

The Art of Public Speaking (11th ed.) is one of the most widely used academic textbooks designed for university instruction in public speaking. Written by Stephen Lucas of the University of Wisconsin, it is supplemented by materials at highered.mcgraw-hill.com/sites/0073406732.

REFERENCES

Arnold, K. (2010). *Boring to bravo: Proven presentation skills to engage, involve, and inspire your audience to action.* Austin, TX: Greenleaf.

Berkun, S. (2010). *Confessions of a public speaker.* Sebastopol, CA: O'Reilly.

Brown, M., Lacroix, D., Fripp, P., Tate, E., & Valentine, C. (2010). *Speaker's edge: Secrets and strategies for connection with any audience.* Rogers, AR: Soar with Eagles.

Coombe, C., England, L., & Schmidt, J. (2008). Public speaking skills for ELT educators. In C. Coombe, N. J. Anderson, M. L. McCloskey, & L. Stephenson (Eds.), *Leadership in English language teaching* (pp. 50–62). Ann Arbor: University of Michigan Press.

Garmston, R. (2005). *The presenter's fieldbook: A practical guide* (2nd ed.). Norwood, MA: Christopher-Gordon.

Gershon, S. (2008). *Present yourself* (1–2). New York, NY: Cambridge University Press.

Hale, J. (2010). *The art of public speaking: Lessons from the greatest speeches in history.* Chantilly, VA: The Great Courses.

Hall, R. (2008). *Brilliant presentation: What the best presenters know, do and say* (2nd ed.). Harlow, England: Pearson.

Jacobi, J. (2009). *How to say it with your voice.* Paramus, NJ: Prentice Hall.

Koegel, T. (2007). *The exceptional presenter: A proven formula to open up! and own the room*. Austin, TX: Greenleaf.

Koegel, T. (2010). *The exceptional presenter goes virtual*. Austin, TX: Greenleaf.

Leanne, S. (2009). *Say it like Obama: The power of speaking with purpose and vision*. New York, NY: McGraw-Hill.

Lucas, S. (2011). *The art of public speaking* (11th ed.). New York, NY: McGraw-Hill.

Mandel, S. (2009). *Presentation skills: Captivate and educate your audience* (4th ed.). Rochester, NY: Axzo Press.

Perlman, A. (1998). *Writing great speeches: Professional techniques you can use*. Needham Heights, MA: Allyn & Bacon.

Powell, M. (2002). *Presenting in English: How to give successful presentations*. Boston, MA: Heinle.

Proven, D. (2009). *Giving great presentations*. Southam, England: Easy Steps.

Reinhart, S. (2002). *Giving academic presentations*. Ann Arbor: University of Michigan Press.

Rodenburg, P. (1993). *The right to speak: Working with the voice*. New York, NY: Routledge.

Sweeney, S. (2004). *Communicating in business* (2nd ed.). Cambridge, England: Cambridge University Press.

Toastmasters International. (2011). *Competent communication*. Rancho Santa Margarita, CA: Author.

Toastmasters International. (2013). *About us*. Retrieved from http://www.toastmasters.org/Members/MembersFunctionalCategories/AboutTI.aspx

AUTHOR BIOGRAPHY

Texas International Education Consortium administrator and Texas Intensive English Program instructor John Schmidt has taught Spanish and English as a foreign/second language. He has also trained English language teachers and students on five continents. After having studied at the Universities of Wisconsin, Madrid, Illinois, and Barcelona, he completed his doctorate in foreign language education at the University of Texas at Austin. A Distinguished Toastmaster, he has served as a district leader of Toastmasters International. In addition to having served on the TESOL Board of Directors, he is the TESOL International Association 2012 and 2013 associate convention chair and the 2014 convention program chair.

CHAPTER 14

How Would a Document Designer Create Classroom Materials?

Tammy R. Jones and Gabriela Kleckova

Mr. Selenko had done a good job planning a content-based thematic unit on the importance of rice as a world commodity. He had designed hands-on projects that gave students the opportunity to test what kind of soil produced higher yielding plants, and he had scaffolded the middle school social studies textbook his district used with full-color photographs, flow charts of rice production phases, and maps of export trade routes. Students had created their own word walls with important vocabulary, written poems on rice paper about rice, and investigated resources that detailed the cultural importance of rice in various countries. In short, the unit had been a great success, and Mr. Selenko had been looking forward to the high marks the students would undoubtedly enjoy on their summative evaluation. Indeed, the students similarly felt confident going into their unit exam; they knew they had learned a great deal, and they were eager to show it.

However, as Mr. Selenko handed out the test, he noticed an uncharacteristic silence had fallen on his normally lively classroom. The students were utterly still. No one was even writing his or her name. When he looked around, they appeared stricken. After a few moments, he finally asked, "What is going on? You all know this stuff." The students' replies shocked him. Variations of the same answer came from every part of the classroom: "This test is too hard. Why did you give us this test?" Mr. Selenko could not understand that complaint, and irritation flared briefly as he considered whether this might be some sort of staged coup against the test. But as he looked around at the faces of students he knew very well, his suspicions evaporated, and he started with Item 1 in the vocabulary section. As he coached his class through Items 1–3, he could tell that they had relaxed into their knowledge again. They were ready to take the test. Still, he pondered the mystery until a student remarked as he turned in his test, "That looked like a college test!" That's when Mr. Selenko suddenly understood. In his efforts to conserve the limited resources of both his school and the environment, he had prepared a test that featured 36 questions on the first page. He had shrunk the margins to nearly nothing on every side, and he had used a 10-point font in Times New Roman. In other words, his test was dense with text. To his students, it looked hard—like text more suitable for college! In spite of the fact that they knew the content and ultimately performed well on that exam, their first impression—created by the visual appearance of the test—produced a tremendous amount of anxiety and even confusion. The overall look of the document initially trumped everything else they knew.

Like Mr. Selenko, most language professionals must apply many skills to successful teaching, including designing their own classroom tests. Although many publishing companies and language teaching materials writers provide a broad range of useful textbooks and supplements, sometimes these resources are not sufficient to meet all of a classroom teacher's needs. Consequently, teachers develop and prepare their own materials such as worksheets, checklists, surveys, tests and quizzes, assignment sheets, and even notices to parents. Language teacher training programs focus on helping teachers develop pedagogies for creating their own instructional content, but not much—if any—training is provided in how to present materials visually in print or digitally.

Our PhD program in applied linguistics at the University of Memphis required us to take a number of courses outside our concentration, specifically courses in professional writing. Professional writing programs can vary widely among universities, but students who specialize in that discipline are generally learning how to communicate technical information effectively, and a course in document design is almost always foundational. It was that course in document design that we took to fulfill our interdisciplinary degree requirement, and because of our backgrounds in TESL/TEFL, it was natural for us to focus on classroom contexts and materials. Examining our own accumulated repertoires of classroom worksheets, quizzes, and assignments through the lens of document design principles was a minor professional epiphany. We had so much room for improvement! Consequently, through our own experiences, and in conversations with other language teaching professionals and learners, we have realized that insights from the field of document design can enhance efforts to provide quality instruction. In other words, the success of materials developed by language teaching professionals depends on many factors, including the way they appear visually. In this chapter we share tips and principles from the field of document design that can increase the effectiveness of teacher-made classroom materials.

DOCUMENT DESIGN TIPS FOR LANGUAGE TEACHERS

The field of document design examines ways of improving documents through good writing and good visual design (Schriver, 1997). It draws on research from a number of disciplines to discover the best ways of presenting information in printed texts. For example, designers learn from cognitive psychologists how the human brain processes visual input, and they use information from a number of medical fields about how our eyes move and respond to various stimuli. Good document designers, then, use those findings to build sound theoretical principles for creating effective documents that are not only aesthetically attractive, but also more readable and easier to navigate in general. Therefore, the purpose of good document design is to structure information in a way that allows readers to use it effectively and to make the information visually appealing (Kramer & Bernhardt, 1996). Moreover, Kostelnick and Roberts (1998) explain that "a well-designed [page] enables readers to glide effortlessly through the text; a poorly designed one makes their work hard" (p. 188). And Ware (2008) notes that when documents are designed well, "visual [elements] are processed both rapidly and correctly for every important cognitive task the [design] is intended to support" (p. 14). In other words, well-designed documents communicate information not only through textual content but also through carefully crafted visual design elements that scaffold the overall meaning.

Tomlinson (1998) arrives at 12 characteristics of effective language teaching materials based on research in second language acquisition, and 3 of the suggested qualities apply directly to the visual appearance/graphic design of the materials and form the basis of our first three tips.

Tip 1: Raise language learners' interest and curiosity.

For materials to engage learners successfully, they should raise language learners' interest and curiosity. Consequently, as Tomlinson (1998) argues, "there is a better chance that some of the language in the materials will be taken in for processing" (p. 7). One obvious way to capture learners' attention is by presenting attractive materials that make effective use of colors, white space, and photographs. However, one common mistake is to use too many visual elements in a single document, which distracts learners' attention rather than directing it. Another pitfall is using visuals simply for the sake of using them. As we point out later in the chapter, good document design decisions should support the content and purpose of the materials, and adding visuals that are not directly related to the language tasks can significantly affect learners' abilities to use materials effectively.

Tip 2: Make materials easy to use.

Language learners need to feel the materials they work with are easy to use; establishing an acceptable level of confidence in using materials can also be achieved through document design. As Tomlinson (1998) points out, learners "feel more comfortable with materials with lots of white space than they do with materials in which lots of different activities are crammed together on the same page" (p. 8). Our friend Mr. Selenko could attest to that. Remembering how students responded to the crowded first page of a poorly designed unit exam, he learned to reduce test anxieties by sticking with default margins, using standard font sizes, and keeping the pages of the test free of visual clutter.

Tip 3: Use materials to build learners' confidence in themselves.

Materials should allow learners to develop confidence about their language skills and themselves as language learners. Their performance with the materials should be successful. In other words, the visual design of language teaching supplements must serve multiple purposes: providing visual guidance for the text itself, motivating students toward effective use of the materials, and supporting the language content in a consistent and accessible way for the learners. Therefore, the visual presentation of information needs to be considered, for it is a significant aspect of how learners perceive and interact with the content (Kostelnick & Roberts, 1998; Schriver, 1997).

Sample Activity: First Impressions

Look at Figure 1, in which an image is used to supplement and support a language task. Consider the following questions as you think about how a language student might interpret the document and the activity:

- What do you notice first? What stands out?

- What background knowledge does the picture activate? What associations might be connected with the image?

- What expectations does the picture raise about the activity? Based on the image, what topic might a language student think the task is about?

Perhaps as proficient readers of English, we can easily navigate the requirements of the task and the mismatched image that accompanies it. However, if we put ourselves in the position of a language learner who depends on visual cues to scaffold everything from the instructions to the topic of the activity, then we can see how problems arise. For example, the first thing most people notice about the document is the picture. Because we notice the image before we even begin to decode the instructions, a natural first assumption is that the topic of the activity will be about a girl on a scooter, and the instructions do not contradict that visual cue. In fact, after reading the instructions, it is still very plausible to

How Would a Document Designer Create Classroom Materials?

> 3) What about your friend? Fill in the missing words.
> A: _____ is this?
> B: *This is my friend. Her* _____ *is Cathy, and she's* _____ *Leeds.*
> A: _____ is Cathy?
> B: *She is five today.*
> A: Oh, is it her _____ today?
> B: *Yes, it is.*

Figure 1. Test Sample

think that the language task will involve filling in the blanks with details about a girl on a scooter who is our friend. However, as students continue the activity, they may experience some confusion because the predictions they made about the likely topic do not correspond to the actual subject—a girl celebrating her fifth birthday. When students experience that kind of cognitive disorientation, it costs valuable time and energy to reorganize subsequent attempts to complete the cloze activity. Moreover, even if students recover from the confusion, their motivation and confidence to finish the task successfully have undoubtedly suffered. In this example, then, the language learner's natural reliance on visual cues negatively influences language performance because the visual element hasn't been implemented effectively.

Teachers as materials developers often think about the textual content first—what to teach and what instructional strategies to use when presenting the lessons. The visual arrangement of the materials usually comes last as teachers finalize their ideas. Although selecting appropriate content and figuring out effective activities to help students learn is imperative, the visual appearance of the materials we ultimately come up with must not be neglected, for it can enhance or hinder even the most pedagogically innovative ideas. In fact, when language teachers develop materials, they become document designers who bring "together prose, graphics . . . and typography for purposes of instruction, information, or persuasion" (Schriver, 1997, p. 10).

The question that emerges, then, is how we can improve the materials we prepare for English language learners. Many resources on document design and graphic design offer everything from practical to theoretical advice about how to make use of visual elements, but we particularly like *The Non-Designer's Design Book,* by Robin Williams (2008) because of its accessibility for novices, since many other texts aimed at design veterans can present an overwhelming array of design choices. Indeed, professional document designers successfully and simultaneously manipulate a very broad range of visual elements such as color, headings, type, numbers, letters, symbols, icons, boxes/borders, lines, headers and footers, layout, space, and pictures. The next four tips identify basic principles that are easy to implement without having much background knowledge in visual design: contrast, proximity, alignment, and repetition.

Tip 4: Use contrast to emphasize important information.

Document designers use contrast to emphasize important information. The design principles that govern the use of contrast are the same ones that we use in verbal rhetoric. Simply put, contrast is achieved by highlighting differences. In terms of visual design, effective use of contrast involves giving similar items a similar appearance and making different parts visually distinct. Strong elements of contrast provide readers with the ability to determine the organization of a document quickly so that they understand what to pay attention to first and the order in which information should be processed.

Look at Figure 2. The text on the left offers very little contrast as a visual cue for understanding the content. However, we immediately understand the hierarchy of the content presented in the text on the right because of the larger contrast provided in both font size and boldface. In fact, there are many ways to create contrast in a document such as through type, color, size, shapes, and layout. For example, notice the additional line added underneath the heading of each section. It is important to keep in mind, however, that contrast is achieved through a big difference between two items—not a subtle or minor one.

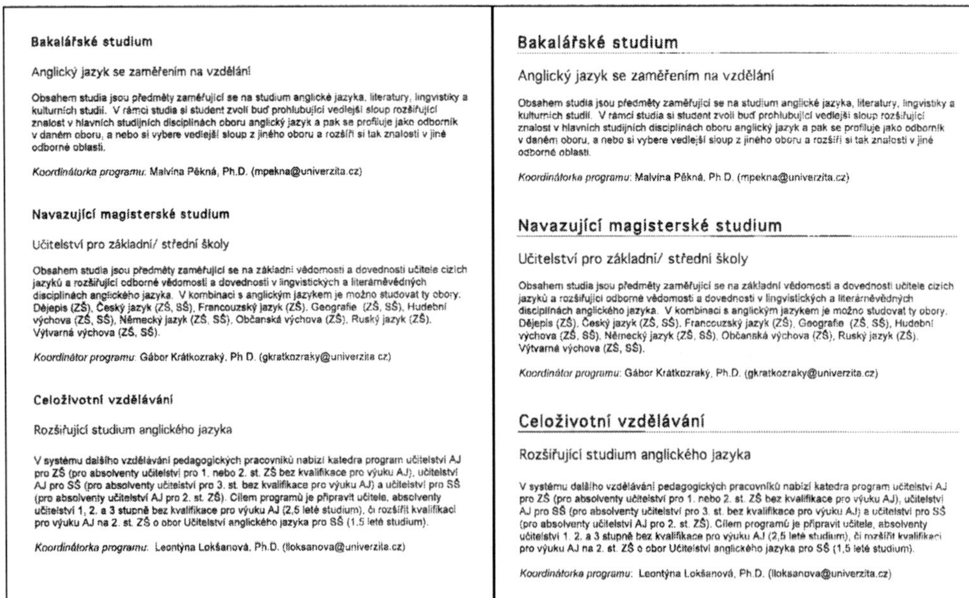

Bakalářské studium

Anglický jazyk se zaměřením na vzdělání

Obsahem studia jsou předměty zaměřující se na studium anglické jazyka, literatury, lingvistiky a kulturních studií. V rámci studia si student zvolí buď prohlubující vedlejší sloup rozšiřující znalost v hlavních studijních disciplinách oboru anglický jazyk a pak se profiluje jako odborník v daném oboru, a nebo si vybere vedlejší sloup z jiného oboru a rozšíří si tak znalosti v jiné odborné oblasti.

Koordinátorka programu: Malvína Pěkná, Ph.D. (mpekna@univerzita.cz)

Navazující magisterské studium

Učitelství pro základní/ střední školy

Obsahem studia jsou předměty zaměřující se na základní vědomosti a dovednosti učitele cizích jazyků a rozšiřující odborné vědomosti a dovednosti v lingvistických a literárněvědných disciplinách anglického jazyka. V kombinaci s anglickým jazykem je možno studovat ty obory. Dějepis (ZŠ), Český jazyk (ZŠ, SŠ), Francouzský jazyk (ZŠ), Geografie (ZŠ, SŠ), Hudební výchova (ZŠ, SŠ), Německý jazyk (ZŠ, SŠ), Občanská výchova (ZŠ), Ruský jazyk (ZŠ), Výtvarná výchova (ZŠ, SŠ).

Koordinátor programu: Gábor Krátkozraký, Ph.D. (gkratkozraky@univerzita.cz)

Celoživotní vzdělávání

Rozšiřující studium anglického jazyka

V systému dalšího vzdělávání pedagogických pracovníků nabízí katedra program učitelství AJ pro ZŠ (pro absolventy učitelství pro 1. nebo 2. st. ZŠ bez kvalifikace pro výuku AJ), učitelství AJ pro SŠ (pro absolventy učitelství pro 3. st. bez kvalifikace pro výuku AJ) a učitelství pro SŠ (pro absolventy učitelství AJ pro 2. st. ZŠ). Cílem programů je připravit učitele, absolventy učitelství 1, 2. a 3 stupně bez kvalifikace pro výuku AJ (2,5 leté studium), či rozšířit kvalifikaci pro výuku AJ na 2. st. ZŠ o obor Učitelství anglického jazyka pro SŠ (1,5 leté studium).

Koordinátorka programu: Leontýna Lokšanová, Ph.D. (lloksanova@univerzita.cz)

Bakalářské studium

Anglický jazyk se zaměřením na vzdělání

Obsahem studia jsou předměty zaměřující se na studium anglické jazyka, literatury, lingvistiky a kulturních studií. V rámci studia si student zvolí buď prohlubující vedlejší sloup rozšiřující znalost v hlavních studijních disciplinách oboru anglický jazyk a pak se profiluje jako odborník v daném oboru, a nebo si vybere vedlejší sloup z jiného oboru a rozšíří si tak znalosti v jiné odborné oblasti.

Koordinátorka programu: Malvína Pěkná, Ph.D. (mpekna@univerzita.cz)

Navazující magisterské studium

Učitelství pro základní/ střední školy

Obsahem studia jsou předměty zaměřující se na základní vědomosti a dovednosti učitele cizích jazyků a rozšiřující odborné vědomosti a dovednosti v lingvistických a literárněvědných disciplinách anglického jazyka. V kombinaci s anglickým jazykem je možno studovat ty obory. Dějepis (ZŠ), Český jazyk (ZŠ, SŠ), Francouzský jazyk (ZŠ), Geografie (ZŠ, SŠ), Hudební výchova (ZŠ, SŠ), Německý jazyk (ZŠ, SŠ), Občanská výchova (ZŠ), Ruský jazyk (ZŠ), Výtvarná výchova (ZŠ, SŠ).

Koordinátor programu: Gábor Krátkozraký, Ph.D. (gkratkozraky@univerzita.cz)

Celoživotní vzdělávání

Rozšiřující studium anglického jazyka

V systému dalšího vzdělávání pedagogických pracovníků nabízí katedra program učitelství AJ pro ZŠ (pro absolventy učitelství pro 1. nebo 2. st. ZŠ bez kvalifikace pro výuku AJ), učitelství AJ pro SŠ (pro absolventy učitelství pro 3. st. bez kvalifikace pro výuku AJ) a učitelství pro SŠ (pro absolventy učitelství AJ pro 2. st. ZŠ). Cílem programů je připravit učitele, absolventy učitelství 1. 2. a 3 stupně bez kvalifikace pro výuku AJ (2,5 leté studium), či rozšířit kvalifikaci pro výuku AJ na 2. st. ZŠ o obor Učitelství anglického jazyka pro SŠ (1,5 leté studium).

Koordinátorka programu: Leontýna Lokšanová, Ph.D. (lloksanova@univerzita.cz)

Figure 2. Contrast

Bakalářské studium
Anglický jazyk se zaměřením na vzdělání

Obsahem studia jsou předměty zaměřující se na studium anglické jazyka, literatury, lingvistiky a kulturních studií. V rámci studia si student zvolí buď prohlubující vedlejší sloup rozšiřující znalost v hlavních studijních disciplínách oboru anglický jazyk a pak se profiluje jako odborník v daném oboru, a nebo si vybere vedlejší sloup z jiného oboru a rozšíří si tak znalosti v jiné odborné oblasti.

Koordinátorka programu: Malvína Pěkná, Ph.D. (mpekna@univerzita.cz)

Navazující magisterské studium
Učitelství pro základní/ střední školy

Obsahem studia jsou předměty zaměřující se na základní vědomosti a dovednosti učitele cizích jazyků a rozšiřující odborné vědomosti a dovednosti v lingvistických a literárněvědných disciplínách anglického jazyka. V kombinaci s anglickým jazykem je možno studovat ty obory: Dějepis (ZŠ), Český jazyk (ZŠ, SŠ), Francouzský jazyk (ZŠ), Geografie (ZŠ, SŠ), Hudební výchova (ZŠ, SŠ), Německý jazyk (ZŠ, SŠ), Občanská výchova (ZŠ), Ruský jazyk (ZŠ), Výtvarná výchova (ZŠ, SŠ).

Koordinátor programu: Gábor Krátkozraký, Ph.D. (gkratkozraky@univerzita.cz)

Celoživotní vzdělávání
Rozšiřující studium anglického jazyka

V systému dalšího vzdělávání pedagogických pracovníků nabízí katedra program učitelství AJ pro ZŠ (pro absolventy učitelství pro 1. nebo 2. st. ZŠ bez kvalifikace pro výuku AJ), učitelství AJ pro SŠ (pro absolventy učitelství pro 3. st. bez kvalifikace pro výuku AJ) a učitelství pro SŠ (pro absolventy učitelství AJ pro 2. st. ZŠ). Cílem programů je připravit učitele, absolventy učitelství 1, 2. a 3 stupně bez kvalifikace pro výuku AJ (2,5 leté studium), či rozšířit kvalifikaci pro výuku AJ na 2. st. ZŠ o obor Učitelství anglického jazyka pro SŠ (1,5 leté studium).

Koordinátorka programu: Leontýna Lokšanová, Ph.D. (lloksanova@univerzita.cz)

Bakalářské studium
Anglický jazyk se zaměřením na vzdělání

Obsahem studia jsou předměty zaměřující se na studium anglické jazyka, literatury, lingvistiky a kulturních studií. V rámci studia si student zvolí buď prohlubující vedlejší sloup rozšiřující znalost v hlavních studijních disciplínách oboru anglický jazyk a pak se profiluje jako odborník v daném oboru, a nebo si vybere vedlejší sloup z jiného oboru a rozšíří si tak znalosti v jiné odborné oblasti.

Koordinátorka programu: Malvína Pěkná, Ph.D. (mpekna@univerzita.cz)

Navazující magisterské studium
Učitelství pro základní/ střední školy

Obsahem studia jsou předměty zaměřující se na základní vědomosti a dovednosti učitele cizích jazyků a rozšiřující odborné vědomosti a dovednosti v lingvistických a literárněvědných disciplínách anglického jazyka. V kombinaci s anglickým jazykem je možno studovat ty obory: Dějepis (ZŠ), Český jazyk (ZŠ, SŠ), Francouzský jazyk (ZŠ), Geografie (ZŠ, SŠ), Hudební výchova (ZŠ, SŠ), Německý jazyk (ZŠ, SŠ), Občanská výchova (ZŠ), Ruský jazyk (ZŠ), Výtvarná výchova (ZŠ, SŠ).

Koordinátor programu: Gábor Krátkozraký, Ph.D. (gkratkozraky@univerzita.cz)

Celoživotní vzdělávání
Rozšiřující studium anglického jazyka

V systému dalšího vzdělávání pedagogických pracovníků nabízí katedra program učitelství AJ pro ZŠ (pro absolventy učitelství pro 1. nebo 2. st. ZŠ bez kvalifikace pro výuku AJ), učitelství AJ pro SŠ (pro absolventy učitelství pro 3. st. bez kvalifikace pro výuku AJ) a učitelství pro SŠ (pro absolventy učitelství AJ pro 2. st. ZŠ). Cílem programů je připravit učitele, absolventy učitelství 1, 2. a 3 stupně bez kvalifikace pro výuku AJ (2,5 leté studium), či rozšířit kvalifikaci pro výuku AJ na 2. st. ZŠ o obor Učitelství anglického jazyka pro SŠ (1,5 leté studium).

Koordinátorka programu: Leontýna Lokšanová, Ph.D. (lloksanova@univerzita.cz)

Figure 3. Proximity

Tip 5: Use proximity to group related pieces of information.

Though contrast can be achieved through layout, it is more common to refer specifically to this principle as proximity. Good document designers know that it is important to group related pieces of information close together on the page. We have seen some bad examples of classroom activities in which students were asked to use a word bank at the top of the front of a page to complete an exercise that didn't appear until the bottom of the back of the page! That arrangement definitely did not make good use of proximity to help students understand which parts of the worksheet were related to each other. Indeed, not only was it confusing, but it was also very difficult to complete the activity because of all the flip-flopping necessary to identify the correct words. In Figure 3, the text on the right illustrates how good use of proximity improves the ability to navigate the information more easily than the information on the left.

Tip 6: Use alignment to guide the reader's eyes.

Another useful way to create visual connections and unity between related items is to use alignment effectively. Riley and Mackiewicz (2011) refer to alignment as a "design attribute that no item should be placed on the page arbitrarily; every item should have a visual connection with something else on the page" (p. 236). Whether we are aware of it or not, alignment is the visual element that guides our eyes over the entire appearance of the document. Many different alignments on a page create visual confusion and result in a cluttered or incoherent visual appearance, which can make it difficult to read. Simple, effective alignments not only make documents easier to navigate, but they also result in a more pleasing aesthetic appearance, which can affect our willingness to use a document. Most professional designers suggest choosing one alignment scheme and sticking with it for the whole document: flush left, flush right, centered, or justified. However, when using more than one alignment, items that are related should be aligned with each other as much as possible in a way that makes sense visually. Consider the difference that alignment makes in Figure 4.

Tip 7: Create unity through repetition.

The last principle of design that we discuss here is repeating visual elements to provide structure. Designers use repetition to create consistency within and across documents. Moreover, effective use of repetition creates a unity and a visual rhythm for readers that reduce the effort necessary to access information within the document. Many different elements can be used to create visual repetition. Icons, shaded boxes, font size and style, and even page layout can be repeated to create the visual rhythm of a document. For example, page numbers are usually situated in the top or bottom corners of a page, and very few designers place page numbers anywhere outside a header or footer because that element has been repeated in that position so frequently that it has become conventional to place it there. For a different example of a repeated visual element, look at Figure 5, in which boldface, italics, and symbols are used to create visual consistency across the text on the right.

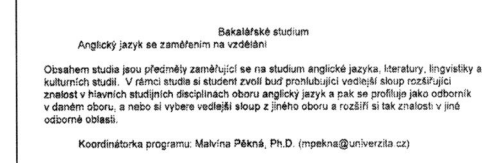

Figure 4. Alignment

Bakalářské studium
Anglický jazyk se zaměřením na vzdělání

Obsahem studia jsou předměty zaměřující se na studium anglické jazyka, literatury, lingvistiky a kulturních studií. V rámci studia si student zvolí buď prohlubující vedlejší sloup rozšiřující znalost v hlavních studijních disciplínách oboru anglický jazyk a pak se profiluje jako odborník v daném oboru, a nebo si vybere vedlejší sloup z jiného oboru a rozšíří si tak znalosti v jiné odborné oblasti.

Koordinátorka programu: Malvína Pěkná, Ph.D. (mpekna@univerzita.cz)

Navazující magisterské studium
Učitelství pro základní/ střední školy

Obsahem studia jsou předměty zaměřující se na základní vědomosti a dovednosti učitele cizích jazyků a rozšiřující odborné vědomosti a dovednosti v lingvistických a literárněvědných disciplínách anglického jazyka. V kombinaci s anglickým jazykem je možno studovat ty obory: Dějepis (ZŠ), Český jazyk (ZŠ, SŠ), Francouzský jazyk (ZŠ), Geografie (ZŠ, SŠ), Hudební výchova (ZŠ, SŠ), Německý jazyk (ZŠ, SŠ), Občanská výchova (ZŠ), Ruský jazyk (ZŠ), Výtvarná výchova (ZŠ, SŠ).

Koordinátor programu: Gábor Krátkozraký, Ph.D. (gkratkozraky@univerzita.cz)

Celoživotní vzdělávání
Rozšiřující studium anglického jazyka

V systému dalšího vzdělávání pedagogických pracovníků nabízí katedra program učitelství AJ pro ZŠ (pro absolventy učitelství pro 1. nebo 2. st. ZŠ bez kvalifikace pro výuku AJ), učitelství AJ pro SŠ (pro absolventy učitelství pro 3. st. bez kvalifikace pro výuku AJ) a učitelství pro SŠ (pro absolventy učitelství AJ pro 2. st. ZŠ). Cílem programů je připravit učitele, absolventy učitelství 1, 2. a 3 stupně bez kvalifikace pro výuku AJ (2,5 leté studium), či rozšířit kvalifikaci pro výuku AJ na 2. st. ZŠ o obor Učitelství anglického jazyka pro SŠ (1,5 leté studium).

Koordinátorka programu: Leontýna Lokšanová, Ph.D. (lloksanova@univerzita.cz)

Bakalářské studium
Anglický jazyk se zaměřením na vzdělání

① Obsahem studia jsou předměty zaměřující se na studium anglické jazyka, literatury, lingvistiky a kulturních studií. V rámci studia si student zvolí buď prohlubující vedlejší sloup rozšiřující znalost v hlavních studijních disciplínách oboru anglický jazyk a pak se profiluje jako odborník v daném oboru, a nebo si vybere vedlejší sloup z jiného oboru a rozšíří si tak znalosti v jiné odborné oblasti.

Koordinátorka programu: Malvína Pěkná, Ph.D. (mpekna@univerzita.cz)

Navazující magisterské studium
Učitelství pro základní/ střední školy

① Obsahem studia jsou předměty zaměřující se na základní vědomosti a dovednosti učitele cizích jazyků a rozšiřující odborné vědomosti a dovednosti v lingvistických a literárněvědných disciplínách anglického jazyka. V kombinaci s anglickým jazykem je možno studovat ty obory: Dějepis (ZŠ), Český jazyk (ZŠ, SŠ), Francouzský jazyk (ZŠ), Geografie (ZŠ, SŠ), Hudební výchova (ZŠ, SŠ), Německý jazyk (ZŠ, SŠ), Občanská výchova (ZŠ), Ruský jazyk (ZŠ), Výtvarná výchova (ZŠ, SŠ).

Koordinátor programu: Gábor Krátkozraký, Ph.D. (gkratkozraky@univerzita.cz)

Celoživotní vzdělávání
Rozšiřující studium anglického jazyka

① V systému dalšího vzdělávání pedagogických pracovníků nabízí katedra program učitelství AJ pro ZŠ (pro absolventy učitelství pro 1. nebo 2. st. ZŠ bez kvalifikace pro výuku AJ), učitelství AJ pro SŠ (pro absolventy učitelství pro 3. st. bez kvalifikace pro výuku AJ) a učitelství pro SŠ (pro absolventy učitelství AJ pro 2. st. ZŠ). Cílem programů je připravit učitele, absolventy učitelství 1, 2. a 3 stupně bez kvalifikace pro výuku AJ (2,5 leté studium), či rozšířit kvalifikaci pro výuku AJ na 2. st. ZŠ o obor Učitelství anglického jazyka pro SŠ (1,5 leté studium).

Koordinátorka programu: Leontýna Lokšanová, Ph.D. (lloksanova@univerzita.cz)

Figure 5. Repetition

Sample Activity: Contrast, Proximity, Repetition, and Alignment

To illustrate how using these four principles, even in simple ways, can dramatically improve classroom materials, we've developed a sample that highlights some of the typical features of many classroom handouts. (Keep in mind that our purpose here is to demonstrate the effects of design; we are not concerned in this instance about the pedagogy of the activity itself. In fact, our sample handout is an amalgamation of several different activities designed by classroom teachers.)

To begin, look at the original sample in Figure 6. As you examine the document, think about the principles of contrast, proximity, repetition, and alignment. Then consider the following questions: What do you see first? How is the activity organized? What parts go together? Is there a hierarchy within each part that is immediately visible? Is the document easy to read? Do any of the parts seem too far away from the rest of the items on the page? Do any of the parts seem too crowded visually?

Notice how the sample document doesn't capitalize on opportunities to use contrast, proximity, repetition, or alignment in ways that can scaffold the tasks. For example, although there are clearly three tasks for students to complete, the tasks have not been differentiated visually other than simple labels—Task 1, Task 2, Task 3. Additionally, the document does not make the best use of space to group the activities so that they are visually identifiable as three separate tasks. There are spaces between activities, but the use of a number of different tabs along with the absence of other contrasting elements largely cancel out that token observance of the proximity principle. Indeed, mismatched indentions create visual confusion for students, and the only repetition used in the document—the

---

Revision test

Task 1
Answer these questions in complete sentences. 4points
- Where is your school situated?
  _____
- What are the parts of your school?
  _____
- What material is the building built of?
  _____
- What study programs can students study at our school?
  _____

Task 2
Name 3 examples of common and special school subjects (according to your branch) and write what they are focused on: 6points (1point- 1sentence)
a) Common school subjects:
   1._____
   2._____
   3._____

b) Special school subjects:
   1._____
   2._____
   3._____

Task 3
Fill in these suitable words into the text./ 4,5points
A site – manager, materials, externship, finishing, focused on, provides, budget, construction, companies
The branch of study: Civil Engineering
This branch is _____ basic knowledge of civil engineering - principles of _____,
construction technologies and building _____.
It also _____ technical _____ in construction _____.
After _____ this branch, students are able to work as a assistant -designer, a foreman,
_____ on a smaller building site or make a simple _____ of construction as a quantity surveyor.

Figure 6. Problematic Design

task labels—are also lost in the jumbled alignments and therefore don't enhance usability either.

Before looking at the revised worksheet (Figure 7), take a few moments to jot down improvements that you would make to the document. How would you add contrast to attract attention to the items students should see first? How would you rearrange the parts of the worksheet so that the hierarchy of the document is instantly discernible visually? What visual elements of repetition would you create to improve the coherence of the document? How would you adjust the alignments in the document to eliminate the visual clutter?

Ultimately, there are many ways that our sample could be improved. In fact, we both prepared revised documents, and we came up with entirely different solutions to the problems we had noted! Both revisions were the products of our own understandings of the constraints of the teaching contexts, and both were effective renditions of the originals we had started with. What we present here, then, may be different from the improvements you might have noted, but we believe the improvements are solid examples of how to use contrast, proximity, repetition, and alignment effectively on a typical classroom worksheet.

How Would a Document Designer Create Classroom Materials?

First, notice how the revised worksheet (Figure 7) uses contrast to draw attention to the elements students should read first—the instructions. By using boldface, the directions are visually highlighted and effectively set apart from the activities that students are asked to complete. Using boldface for the instructions also creates a visual hierarchy both for the entire document and for each task. It is immediately clear, for example, that there are three tasks, and a quick glance also reveals that the directions and corresponding activities are distinct.

The revised document also groups elements effectively to reinforce the overall organization of the worksheet. Notice how the space between tasks has been increased, and look at how eliminating the short labels (Task 1, etc.) has

Figure 7. Redesigned Document

streamlined the visual appearance of the sections, which supports rather than undermines the proximity principle.

Perhaps the most effective revision, though, is establishing alignments in the document that create visual coherence rather than visual confusion. Although the original worksheet attempted to use alignment as an element to create contrast, the result was a cluttered visual field. By moving all of the elements to the left, getting rid of complicated indents to show the hierarchy of the tasks, and keeping activities simply aligned with the margin of the directions, the visual appearance is much cleaner and therefore easier to navigate visually.

And finally, the revised worksheet makes use of visual repetition through boldface, parentheses for scoring information, and uniform lengths for fill-in-the-blanks. Overall, though, the revised sample doesn't make use of any fancy design elements. We used only the four basic principles of contrast, proximity, repetition, and alignment, but it's easy to see how careful attention to those elements can result in a document that is substantially more usable for English learners.

Tip 8: Understand cultural differences in design principles.

Although it is possible to improve the design of classroom materials dramatically by using principles of visual organization, cultural considerations remain a tricky area for designers in every field. As Kostelnick and Hassett (2003) point out, "icons, symbols, and colors have different associations across cultures, creating a minefield of potential faux pas for information designs intended for international or multicultural audiences" (p. 92). And because language classrooms are often culturally heterogeneous, language teachers may face document design dilemmas that are difficult to resolve. Consider, for instance, the use of white space. Research confirms that skillful use of the conventions of white space increases readability. Nevertheless, readers' interpretations of white space may vary widely. Maitra and Goswami (1995), for example, report that Japanese readers may prefer minimal text, expanses of white space, and ambiguity; Western readers, on the other hand, prefer textual clarity and white spaces that do not dominate the page.

Another example of cultural difference relates to the practice of using cartoons in language materials. Many teachers use funny little illustrations to help put students at ease, and indeed, students with backgrounds in Japanese culture probably are encouraged by images used in such decontextualized ways apart from the language tasks. Fukoka, Yukiko, and Spyridakis (1999) found that Japanese readers, in fact, prefer cartoon images to other types of illustrations, even in complex texts, because of the familiar presence of manga comics in Japanese media and a cultural emphasis on harmony, which is perceived to be maintained through the use of whimsical images. Non-Japanese readers, on the other hand, preferred more literal and three-dimensional illustrations to accompany complex texts. And though half of the non-Japanese readers did not object to the cartoons, about one third of them found their presence distracting and frustrating because the illustrations didn't offer any clues for understanding the activity to be completed.

The use of images can cause other cultural dilemmas as well. Wang and Wang (2009) found that German and Chinese students connect text and visuals very differently. Whereas Chinese readers associate visuals with text above or below the images, German readers connect visuals with text that is arranged horizontally on a parallel with the images. In both cases, when the readers were presented with documents that asked them to perform actions based on images that were arranged contrary to their preferred cultural orientations, their abilities to complete the tasks were slowed down significantly, which confirms that cultural expectations of how a document should appear affect cognitive interaction with the information in the document.

One solution to these kinds of competing aesthetics is to create a strong sense of discourse community in the class itself. Help students understand the rhetorical, visual, and language conventions you observe as you prepare materials for the class. Identify the rationales for your design decisions, and make them transparent to students. Explicitly teach students how to use the visual elements of documents and how to benefit from them. As Kostelnick and Hassett (2003) point out, "although the degree of consensus may vary, discourse communities . . . supply the social cohesion for visual language to coalesce and to develop currency among group members" (p. 96). In other words, guiding students to an understanding that they are stakeholders in a discourse community can help them accept a new way of regarding visual design elements without invalidating cultural aesthetics.

CONCLUSION

As materials designers, we need to keep in mind that the purpose of visual design is to guide learners through the textual content of what we've prepared. To use visual elements effectively, here is a checklist of the initial steps to take when designing documents:

- Decide what students should see first.
- Arrange information into logical groups.
- Create alignments and keep consistent.
- Identify items that have a connection, and create visual repetition.
- Remember to have strong contrasts to attract the student's eye.

Growing scholarship on document design provides many guidelines for the effective presentation of information. Of course, there is much more to visual composing than the principles we have discussed (see Resources for Further Exploration to learn more about visual design). However, following these basic rules will improve the design of our materials to better serve language learners and enhance their chances of success in the language classroom.

RESOURCES FOR FURTHER EXPLORATION

Jones, T. R., & Kleckova, G. (2009). Unlocking the visual puzzle: Understanding textbook design. In L. Savova (Ed.), *Using textbooks effectively* (pp. 119–129). Alexandria, VA : TESOL.

> This chapter introduces the role of visual elements in professionally published teaching materials and provides tips to help teachers empower language learners to use visual cues of their textbooks more effectively. Specifically, Jones and Kleckova present an activity that gives teachers and students a key to navigating the visual conventions typical of language workbooks more effectively.

Kostelnick, C., & Roberts, D. D. (1998). *Designing visual language: Strategies for professional communicators.* Boston, MA: Allyn & Bacon.

> Although written for professionals in technical writing, this book is very comprehensible to nonexpert audiences. Kostelnick and Roberts first provide readers with rhetorical principles of visual language and then focus on visual language elements and their use in text design. The comprehensive discussion makes use of a wide variety of examples, from the word level to lengthier documents. The book as a whole teaches a framework of visual language strategies that can be implemented to create usable documents.

Riley, K., & Mackiewicz, J. (2011). *Visual composing.* Upper Saddle River, NJ: Prentice Hall.

> This book is a publication intended for the world of professional communicators. As such, it nevertheless provides extensive fundamental guidance on designing effective documents. Specifically, it explains principles of typography and how to create a visual hierarchy of information. Additionally, the text covers how to use layout, color, graphs, and charts, and Riley and Mackiewicz give useful tips for designing common print documents, presentations, and websites. The glossary at the end of the book can help readers understand the discipline-specific terminology.

White, A. W. (2002). *The elements of graphic design.* New York, NY: Allworth Press.

> This book is oriented more toward graphic rather than document design and familiarizes readers with basic graphic design principles in four sections: space, unity, page architecture, and type. White takes a very practical approach and includes a designer's checklist, which summarizes the main tips for successful visual design as well as what pitfalls to avoid. The book is an easy and enjoyable read with no requirements for the readers to have a background in graphic design.

Williams, R. (2008). *The non-designer's design book: Design and typographic principles for the visual novice* (3rd ed.). Berkley, CA: Peachpit Press.

> The subtitle of this publication completely captures the essence of the book. In a user-friendly style, Williams writes about the four design principles introduced in our chapter. Additionally, she discusses the effective use of color and type, and includes tips for design projects from business cards to websites. She also has selected relevant examples that support the text and give readers a clear understanding of the basic design principles.

REFERENCES

Fukoka, W., Yukiko, K., & Spyridakis, J. (1999). Illustrations in user manuals: Preference and effectiveness with Japanese and American readers. *Technical Communication, 46*(2), 167–176.

Kostelnick, C., & Hassett, M. (2003). *Shaping information: The rhetoric of visual conventions.* Carbondale: Southern Illinois University Press.

Kostelnick, C., & Roberts, D. D. (1998). *Designing visual language: Strategies for professional communicators.* Boston, MA: Allyn & Bacon.

Kramer, R., & Bernhardt, S. A. (1996). Teaching text design. *Technical Communication Quarterly, 5,* 35–60.

Maitra, K., & Goswami, D. (1995). Responses of American readers to visual aspects of a mid-sized Japanese company's annual report: A case study." *IEEE Transactions on Professional Communication, 38,* 197–203.

Riley, K., & Mackiewicz, J. (2011). *Visual composing.* Upper Saddle River, NJ: Prentice Hall.

Schriver, K. A. (1997). *Dynamics in document design.* New York, NY: John Wiley & Sons.

Tomlinson, B. (1998). *Materials development in language teaching.* New York, NY: Cambridge University Press.

Wang, Y., & Wang, D. (2009). Cultural contexts in technical communication: A study of Chinese and German automobile literature. *Technical Communication, 56*(1), 39–50.

Ware, C. (2008). *Visual thinking for design.* Burlington, MA: Morgan Kaufmann.

Williams, R. (2008). *The non-designer's design book* (3rd ed.). Berkeley, CA: Peachpit Press.

AUTHOR BIOGRAPHIES

Tammy R. Jones is an instructor in the English Department at the University of Memphis, in the United States, where she teaches ESL methodology to preservice teachers. She is interested in investigating how rhetorical elements—including elements of visual rhetoric—influence learners in multicultural classroom contexts. (trjones1@memphis.edu)

Gabriela Kleckova is an assistant professor in the English Department, College of Education, at the University of Western Bohemia, in Plzen, the Czech Republic, where she teaches TESOL methodology courses to preservice and in-service teachers. Her research, among other interests, focuses on effectiveness and utility of visual design of language teaching materials. (gabriela_kleckova@yahoo.com)

CHAPTER 15

How Would a Researcher Conduct a Language Course Evaluation?

Cynthia Quinn and Gregory Sholdt

In simple terms, research means searching for answers to questions we have about problems or curious phenomena. Whether shopping for a new car, searching for the cheapest route to Bali, investigating ways to fend off the common cold, or considering which school is right for your child, all involve doing research: gathering information, reviewing the details, and making conclusions based on what was read or observed. At this commonplace level, we are all researchers in that we try to make informed, practical, effective decisions about our daily lives.

At the professional level, researcher is typically a project-oriented occupation in which someone systematically collects, analyzes, and reports data in response to a defined inquiry. Although the profession may require a good deal of independent work managing and organizing data, being a researcher also involves liaising with others to accomplish research goals and share findings.

Different from the conception of everyday research illustrated above, we expect professional researchers to use a more scientific approach, which can be regarded as a "systematic controlled extension of common sense" that is logical, objective, and based on observable phenomena (Drew & Hardman, 1985, p. 11). A critical goal of the scientific approach is to reduce the influence of personal beliefs or feelings, make unbiased observations, and draw logical evidence-based conclusions (McMillan, 1996). This is a basic aim of any researchers, regardless of whether they are collecting unemployment data, investigating migration patterns, or studying social interaction. For this chapter, we share how we have applied our training in research methodology and our educational research experience to the language learning classroom, specifically as to how these research skills can support teachers in assessing the success of their courses while also maintaining the goals of a scientific approach.

Researchers using this standard approach face some challenges, however, such as coping with barriers to direct assessment. Especially in cases where the aim is to uncover mental or emotional factors for some occurrence, researchers are limited to measuring only what can be observed and therefore cannot make direct, completely accurate conclusions. This inherent barrier requires the researcher to speculate based on what is actually observed and to then make well-reasoned, informed generalizations. This is likewise a challenge when surveying students to assess satisfaction, as teachers attempt to uncover learner response to a course and the factors that influence those views. To accomplish such goals, researchers rely on indirect routes of observation.

Consider the fragrance industry, in which products are associated with emotions and sensations, rather than practical benefits, and image is the sole means to convey the product's nuances to the consumer (Gobé, 2009). In order to elicit observable patterns in product perception, market researchers may survey consumers on their fragrance usage, observe individual reactions to new scent combinations, or conduct focus groups to uncover emotional associations in response to various aromas. In addition, they may set up experimental studies to assess physiological reactions to different smells in order to make advertising claims about the product's effects. Ultimately, all of these methods set out to discover patterns in consumer behavior and can help a researcher make an educated guess about what characteristics appeal to buyers.

Another major challenge to the researcher is subject variety and complexity; in a given situation, human behavior can be influenced by a range of individual factors, making it difficult to predict outcomes. If a market researcher asks a consumer, "Why do you wear fragrance?" the answer to this question will inevitably vary from person to person. Similarly, learners join a course for a number of reasons and will each bring his or her own set of needs and goals to the classroom. At the same time, contextual factors affect a researcher's ability to collect accurate data. A social researcher interviewing immigrant families about cultural assimilation might face challenges in accessing participants, managing interpersonal dynamics, dealing with technological mishaps (e.g., with data collection), coping with the *observer's paradox* (Labov, 1972), or minimizing the researcher's effect on participant behavior. Likewise, research into student satisfaction can be influenced by the learning materials, the teacher's implementation of those materials, testing procedures, teacher feedback, and the pace of the course, among other factors.

In cases where researchers and participants work together for a period of time, they will inevitably develop some degree of relationship. This situation brings a number of personal and ethical issues into the interpretive research process (Creswell, 2009), making it difficult for researchers to maintain an objective stance when drawing conclusions and reporting results. Much like a cultural anthropologist living in some community as a long-term participant-observer, a teacher investigating student satisfaction must take on a similarly dual role of teacher-researcher. Being closely involved with student progress can make it difficult for teachers to assess the situation independent of their own involvement and accurately view circumstances from the participant's perspective, a case that illustrates one type of threat to interpretive validity (Rovai, Baker, & Ponton, 2012).

In response to these challenges, this chapter introduces methodological issues that are especially relevant to teachers and offers some practical advice for designing and administering surveys for the purpose of assessing overall course success. A major aim of this advice is to guide teachers in preparing valid survey instruments and to maximize their use of other classroom data to make informed conclusions.

A RESEARCHER'S TIPS FOR LANGUAGE TEACHERS

Tip 1: Carefully plan out your questionnaire before you write it.

One simple mistake is to give a survey based on questions that have simply popped into your head. Carpenters operate by a rule of thumb: Measure twice, cut once. You only have one chance to cut the wood, so make sure your measurements are precise. For researchers, it is extremely important to consider every aspect of their questionnaires in order to collect the right data to answer a research question. Likewise, as teachers, you really have only one chance to have students evaluate your course, and a poorly planned questionnaire means that you could miss out on critical data. In the planning stage, there are two central interrelated issues to consider: what you are hoping to learn and, then, how you can best get that information.

The first step is to think carefully about what you hope to accomplish by administering this questionnaire. It can simply be to get a sense of how satisfied the students are with the course you provided, but it can also serve additional purposes. These could include providing feedback for course improvement, self-reports on time and effort devoted to the course, or a teaching evaluation for your school's administration.

Next, for each goal, brainstorm what viewpoints you would like to get from students. In other words, what attitudes, opinions, and experiences relate to the different goals of your questionnaire? For student satisfaction, try to think about what different components of their involvement in your course could affect overall satisfaction. These could include how happy they were with your teaching, how fair they thought your grading system was, and how appropriate they found the workload. A brainstorming session should provide you with a list from which you can consolidate and condense into a manageable set of viewpoints to assess for each goal. Table 1 includes some example goals and viewpoints.

Once you have identified the student viewpoints you want to assess for each

Table 1. Questionnaire Goals and Student Viewpoints

Student satisfaction	Teacher evaluation	Course feedback
• amount of learning • enjoyment of course • fairness of grading • appropriate workload • interaction with students • quality of teaching	• well prepared for class • knowledgeable of subject • ability to teach • quality of feedback • quality of tests • accessibility	• activities that worked • what should be changed • relevance of content • test fairness • difficulty of material • speed of the course

goal, it can help to further specify them. For example, enjoyment of the course could include how much students enjoyed the lectures, group discussions, readings, projects, or other components of the course. It is possible that they enjoyed your lectures but found the readings to be too difficult. Table 2 includes some more specific components of the viewpoints you plan to assess.

One important consideration during the planning stage is how you will collect and analyze your data. Using a word processor and printing out copies allows you to have full control of the administration process. However, entering all of the data by hand into a spreadsheet application such as Microsoft Excel can be time-consuming. If you go this route, try to line up blanks for answers in one column on the side of your questionnaire. This will speed up data entry because you do not have to move your eyes over different areas of the questionnaire to find answers. Additionally, you may need to spend time learning various functions of the word-processing program to create an easy-to-read and neat-looking questionnaire. Knowledge of certain functions of the database program will be necessary to properly analyze the data once it is entered.

If students have access to the Internet, several online applications (e.g., SurveyMonkey, Google Docs) make creating questionnaires and analyzing data quite fast and easy. You may end up saving quite a bit of time, especially with the management of the quantitative data. One possible risk is that students may not complete the questionnaire on their own. It would be a good idea to assign the questionnaire with enough time before the end of the course so that you can follow up with any students who do not complete it.

Table 2. Example Viewpoints and Specific Components

Amount of learning	Enjoyment of course	Fairness of grading
• from instruction • from texts • from projects • from homework	• lectures • text • projects • homework	• tests covered material we studied • breakdown of course grade was reasonable • my efforts affected my grade

Tip 2: Use Likert scale items to cover a broad range of topics.

Once you have identified the relevant viewpoints and specific components you want to assess, you will need to convert them into items for your questionnaire. Researchers know that one of the advantages of collecting quantitative data is that the items can be simple and require only a short time to answer. In this way, you can add many items to your questionnaire that cover a broad range of topics. Although there are a few different techniques for item construction, Likert scale-based items are generally easy to write. In addition, they are familiar to students, which reduces confusion and misinterpretation.

There are a couple of points to keep in mind when working with Likert scale items. First, create one scale and use it throughout your questionnaire; the simplest one is a 5-point scale that ranges from *strongly disagree* to *strongly agree*. You can explain the scale at the top of the questionnaire and then just list all of the items underneath. This will save space and allow students to work through the items quickly. However, if the item statements are too repetitive, the students may not take time to think carefully about each response. Mix up the grammar structures and wording so they must be processed carefully for meaning. Finally, keep each item focused on one specific issue. For example, "The textbook was interesting and the reading assignments were the perfect length" is better split into two items because a student could find the book interesting but the assignments too long.

Figure 1 shows an example layout and some items focused on student perceptions of the amount of learning they gained in your course.

Tip 3: Explore different aspects of your data.

After administering your questionnaires and entering the scores into a database (or using an online survey system), it is time do the analysis. Simply looking over the raw data—the individual scores from each question for each student—does little to help you make sense of what you collected. This is where statistical tools come in handy because they allow us to summarize a large set of numbers with a single value. Whereas quantitative researchers delight in spending hours running a variety of abstract statistical manipulations and analyses with their data, our purpose really only requires two main statistics to help us reach our goals: *means* and *frequencies*.

The mathematical average, or the mean, indicates the central tendency of a group of scores and is a kind of representative value for the whole group. Means give us one simple number to summarize all students' responses. Both spreadsheet and online applications will provide ways to calculate a mean for each item in your questionnaire. Looking at each mean can help you pinpoint specific trouble spots or points of success. Also, if you have several different items that relate to one single topic (e.g., fairness of grading), you can add those item scores together for each student and then get an overall mean for that topic. This can

Course Evaluation Questionnaire
Instructions The purpose of this questionnaire is to learn about your viewpoints and experiences in this course. Your responses are anonymous and will not affect your grade in any way. Please read each item carefully and choose the response that best fits your experience or feelings. It is very important that you respond to every item. Check with the instructor if you have any questions.
Use the following scale to respond to the statement in each item: Strongly Disagree   Disagree   Neutral   Agree   Strongly Agree 1   2   3   4   5
Item Responses 1. I learned a lot from the lectures we received in class. _____ 2. The readings were a useful supplement to the lectures. _____ 3. Doing the projects helped me deepen my understanding of the topics. _____

Figure 1. Example Questionnaire Layout

simplify your results into a handful of means for major viewpoint topics. However, means do not always give a complete picture and can be misleading. There are other ways to look at data that may reveal information the mean does not.

Along with the mean, it is important to get a sense of how the scores are spread out for each item. A good way to do this for our questionnaires is to look at frequency counts in a table. A frequency table simply tells you how many students chose a particular value on the scale for one item. Again, spreadsheet and online applications both offer quick ways to produce these tables. An example is provided in Table 3.

Looking over frequency tables can reveal a lot of information. First, we can see which values were selected the most, another measure of central tendency called the *mode*. In Table 3, the large number of students selecting value 5 for *strongly agree* shows that the majority of students found the readings very useful. However, the table reveals that there is a sizeable group who did not find the textbook useful at all. Just looking at the mean for this item, 3.65, might lead you to believe that students found the textbook moderately useful, but the frequency table for this item tells a different story. In most cases, the mean will be a good representative of student viewpoints, but close inspection of frequency tables is an important step in determining how representative a mean truly is.

As stated previously, the advantage of working with quantitative data is that we can quickly assess student viewpoints on a wide variety of topics. However, as shown in the previous example, the numbers do not always give the complete

Table 3. Example Frequency Table

Item 3. The readings were a useful supplement to the lectures.

Value	Number	Percentage
1 Strongly disagree	6	30
2 Disagree	0	0
3 Neutral	1	5
4 Agree	1	5
5 Strongly agree	12	60

picture. Even though we have tried to get a clear picture of student viewpoints on our course, we can never be sure that we have perfectly reached our goal. Good quantitative researchers recognize the limitations of numbers and cautiously draw conclusions based on them. The numbers you produce with your questionnaire look very precise, but they are based on imprecise measurements. They can give you a general idea of the reaction to your course but should never be used as clear-cut, irrefutable evidence for any kind of serious conclusion or decision.

Tip 4: Write effective open-ended questions and prepare students to respond.

Qualitative questioning can play an important role in expanding on the closed-ended questions by giving us more insight into why students make certain choices. For this reason, preparing open-ended questions that build on the closed ones can help create cohesion between the quantitative and qualitative parts of the questionnaire and build a unified survey.

Table 4 shows open questions that are designed to expand on corresponding closed questions through various strategies, such as exemplification, clarification, and short answer. Through the sentence completion task in #1, we can get a specific example to reinforce and build on the response we get from the closed question. In #2, the open question clarifies the closed response, because we can learn more specifically how students used the readings in relation to the lectures. In #3, the closed question asks whether the learning purpose was transparent and is then complemented by a short-answer question that asks how students regarded the journal-writing component of the course. By writing the qualitative section of the survey in direct relation to the quantitative section, we are able to keep the focus of the survey on our chosen constructs and expand on those selected points.

When phrasing open-ended questions, aim to use concise, simple, natural language and prepare questions that students are capable of answering on their own. Asking learners a relatively specialized question such as "Did the journal

Table 4. Corresponding Closed and Open Questions

	Closed question	Open question
1	I learned a lot from the lectures we received in class.	From the class lectures, I remember learning about _____.
2	The readings were a useful supplement to the lectures.	How did the readings help you understand the lectures?
3	I was able to see how the topics related to my life by writing in my journal each week.	Did you enjoy writing about class topics in your journal? Why or why not?

writing in this course help raise your background knowledge on each topic?" will probably not elicit as useful of a response as "Did the journal writing in this course help you prepare ideas for class discussion?" The latter example is more accessible to students and uses common classroom vocabulary. In addition, as discussed in Tip 2, take care to ask only one question. In relation to class readings, asking "Would you like to spend more time on the readings in class or could you understand them well on your own?" addresses both how the readings are processed in class and how comprehensible the texts were for students. These two issues should be dealt with in two separate questions.

Once you have written the open-ended portion of the questionnaire, a very important step is to prepare students for the task, just as you would any other classroom activity. Distributing the questionnaire hurriedly in the last 10 minutes of class doesn't give students enough time to write thoughtful answers, and it sends the message that the course survey is not especially important. To make the most of your preparation efforts, spend time in class remembering and reflecting on the entire course. At a minimum, draw up a list of assignments and activities to help students recall specific course details. Students enrolled in several courses may not remember assignments and tasks completed earlier in the term, so taking a few minutes to review class activities on the board helps them give responses that take the entire course into consideration. If you feel that the students are independent and mature enough to uphold views that diverge from the group, then you could go one step further with discussion-oriented preparation tasks, such as having them rank preferences, exchange opinions, or formulate future learning objectives.

Finally, teachers should review the open-ended questions carefully and be sure that students understand what they are being asked to do. This is especially necessary if the questionnaire is being administered in the foreign language (L2). Responding to questions in the L2 will undoubtedly result in more limited responses than surveys in the native language (L1): Students may not fully understand a question, they may not have the language skills to express what they want to say, and they may become fatigued and start to give up toward the end of the questionnaire. If it is not feasible to administer the survey in the students' native language, then in-class preparation efforts like the ones discussed earlier can help students attempt to overcome these hurdles.

Tip 5: Complement questionnaire results with data from classwork.

Reviewing classwork can provide quantitative and qualitative data that inform questionnaire results and help give a more accurate perspective on student satisfaction. Journal entries, discussions, learner logs, blog entries, peer or self-evaluations, reflection tasks, and assignment grades and attendance can all function as useful data. Table 5 presents two examples to illustrate this process.

In Example 1, suppose that responses to the closed question are varied with a mean of 3.2 on a Likert scale of 1 to 5. The open question responses reveal that students had a hard time finding articles to support their research topics, which helps to explain the relatively low mean. Based on this information, a teacher might conclude that more class time spent learning how to find articles is necessary. But what is it about finding articles that is difficult? The data generated from this survey might direct the teacher to review students' research logs and course portfolios. Here it is discovered that the majority of students are using the same L1 search engine and not searching in the L2 and that most students have pulled information solely from Wikipedia. Knowing this, a teacher can target these problems in the next course plan and better anticipate challenges students will face in their research process.

The second example (Table 5) shows the same kind of process for an oral communication course. In this case, the closed question yields a fairly high mean of 4.6, but in the open question responses, the teacher finds that the least popular discussion topic by far was adoption. To better understand why this topic was so unappealing, the teacher looks through discussion self-evaluations for that topic and finds comments like "This was difficult to discuss," "I have no ideas about this," "I don't know anyone who's adopted," and so on. Also, the teacher recalls that, compared to other topics, student discussions on adoption ended relatively quickly, and the discussion question preparation in their class notebooks was weak. Based on these details, it is concluded that students did not have enough

Table 5. Classwork Employed as Qualitative Data

	Example 1: Writing course	Example 2: Communication course
Closed question	*The research paper assignment was useful for me.*	*I enjoyed the reading-based group discussions.*
Open question	*What difficulties did you have with the research paper?*	*Which discussion topic did you like the least and the most?*
Classwork	*Research logs and course portfolios*	*Discussion self-evaluations, teacher's observations, class notebooks*

experience and background knowledge on the topic. So for next time, the teacher decides to spend more time in class introducing the subject and exploring relevant issues and may change the reading to one that treats the topic differently.

CONCLUSION

Conducting course surveys is an efficient means to elicit learner perceptions: Researchers can explore student satisfaction broadly and can validate informal observations with systematic data. Many teachers survey students to get feedback on course success, but these efforts can be maximized by designing a well-thought-out questionnaire and by conducting organized data analysis that incorporates both qualitative and quantitative data sources.

Overall, what is gained through this process of course assessment? An obvious advantage is improvements in course planning that help teachers better meet students' needs. Without a systematic approach, it is extremely difficult to make accurate judgments regarding students' reactions to and experiences with lesson content; with reliable data, teachers can better focus their efforts on productive change.

At the same time, teachers improve their own practice by building the core components of teacher knowledge (Roberts, 1998), such as their practical knowledge of classroom techniques, their understanding of the learners and of the cultural context, their personal teaching beliefs and principles, and their professional self-awareness. Students also benefit from course evaluation because it leads them to reflect on their accomplishments in the course and encourages self-assessment of personal learning goals and outcomes. These activities represent forms of learner involvement in the curriculum (Tudor, 1996) through the opportunity for students to voice their reactions to and perceptions of lesson content. Ultimately, teachers will find that the overall evaluation process can help them uncover learning opportunities for students and improve their own teaching practice.

RESOURCES FOR FURTHER EXPLORATION

Brown, J. D. (2005). *Using surveys in language programs.* Cambridge, England: Cambridge University Press.

> This is a dedicated text on survey or questionnaire design for research in language classrooms. Although it does get technical and addresses some advanced statistical procedures, it is written for the language teacher with limited to no research training. Lots of great, specific advice here, but slow and careful reading is recommended.

Cohen, L., Manion, L., & Morrison, K. (2007). *Research methods in education.* Abingdon, England: Routledge.

> This is a great introduction to educational research that is logically organized and presented in easy-to-follow language. The topics cover big-picture concepts and specific strategies that focus on research in general but apply extremely well to course evaluations.

Fowler, F. J., Jr., & Cosenza, C. (2009). Design and evaluation of survey questions. In L. Bickman & D. Rog (Eds.), *The Sage handbook of applied social research methods* (pp. 375–412). Thousand Oaks, CA: Sage.

> This text addresses the major source of error in surveys: the design of survey questions. It is full of clear explanations and practical tips that can help teachers design and trial survey questions that avoid "noise" and measure precisely what they set out to measure.

Richards, J. C., & Lockhart, C. (1996). *Reflective teaching in second language classrooms.* Cambridge, England: Cambridge University Press.

> This text presents goals and strategies for conducting reflective teaching activities. Richards and Lockhart take the idea of a course evaluation that is usually conducted at the end of a course and apply it to evaluating or reflecting on your classroom experiences and teaching practices while you are teaching your class or as a way to look at your teaching approach in general.

REFERENCES

Creswell, J. (2009). *Research design: Qualitative, quantitative, and mixed methods approaches.* Thousand Oaks, CA: Sage.

Drew, C. J., & Hardman, M. (1985). *Designing and conducting behavioral research.* New York, NY: Pergamon Press.

Gobé, M. (2009). *Emotional branding: The new paradigm for connecting brands to people.* New York, NY: Allworth Press.

Labov, W. (1972). *Sociolinguistic patterns.* Philadelphia: University of Pennsylvania Press.

McMillan, J. (1996). *Educational research: Fundamentals for the consumer.* New York, NY: HarperCollins.

Roberts, J. (1998). *Language teacher education.* London, England: Arnold.

Rovai, A., Baker, J., & Ponton, M. (2012). *A practitioner's guide to research methods and SPSS analysis.* Chesapeake, VA: Watertree Press.

Tudor, I. (1996). *Learner-centeredness as language education.* Cambridge, England: Cambridge University Press.

AUTHOR BIOGRAPHIES

Cynthia Quinn teaches in the Graduate School of Intercultural Studies at Kobe University, in Japan. Through her work in second language writing, she has developed an interest in qualitative methodologies for exploring teacher feedback and student approaches to revision. Recently, she has been investigating learner self-correction through corpus use and other online writing tools with the aim of helping students become more independent, resourceful writers. Aside from second language

writing, she has presented and published on English program management, curriculum design, and business English.

Gregory Sholdt teaches in the School of Languages and Communication at Kobe University, in Japan. His graduate training is in educational psychology, for which he specialized in statistics and quantitative methods for educational research. His academic interests center on facilitating professional development for language teachers interested in classroom-based quantitative research. In pursuit of these interests, he has created a series of workshops, online courses, and special projects to foster the development of fundamental knowledge and critical skills in quantitative methods. He currently serves as a consulting editor for JALT Journal.

Index

Page numbers followed by an *f* or *t* indicate figures and tables.

A

Abstract conceptualization, 78–79, 78*f*
Accomplishments
 making progress visible, 30
 recognizing, 26–27
Accuracy, 96–97
Active experimentation, 78*f*, 79
Active learning, 79
Activism. *see* Social activist; Social injustice
Actors
 curiosity, 96–97
 find the story, 92–93
 identifying objectives, 90
 improvisation, 91–92
 observations from the audience, 93–95
 overview, 89–90, 97–98
 unsolved mysteries, 95–96, 95*t*
Alice in Wonderland (Carroll), 93–95
Alternative endings activity, 129–130
Anonymity, 39–40, 41*f*
Approachability, 11–12
Architects
 build a foundation with visuals, 103–104, 104*f*
 communicating the big picture, 105–106, 106*f*
 explore structure, 104–105, 105*f*
 overview, 101–103, 108–109
 poster presentations, 106–108, 107*f*
Art, 102
Assessment
 character sheets, experience points, and leveling-up, 43, 44*f*
 needs assessment, 53
 zen master insights into, 64–65
Audio clips, 151
Avatar use, 39–40, 41*f*
Awareness, 128, 133–135

B

Bartender
 addressing the needs of students, 15–18
 overview, 11–12, 19–20, 19*f*
 rapport building, 12–15, 13*f*, 15*f*
 staying positive, 18
Basketball coach
 glossary of basketball terminology, 122–123
 motivation, 117–118
 overview, 111–112, 118–120, 119*f*
 physical and verbal components of communication, 112–114, 113*f*
 playbook of language drills, 114–117, 114*f*, 115*f*, 116*f*
Belt system, 26–27
Body language, 142
Breathing exercises, 61–63

C

Celebration of students' growth, 26–27
Challenges, 30
Character sheets, 41–44, 42*f*, 43*f*, 44*f*
Chávez, César, 126
Choice theory, 61
Choiceless awareness
 challenges to achieving, 63–64
 meditation and, 61–63
 overview, 60, 61, 64–65
Cinder Edna (Jackson, 1994), 129–130
Cinderella, 128–129
Click, Clack, Moo: Cows That Type (Cronin, 2000), 125
Coach, basketball. *see* Basketball coach
Collocations, 115
Communication, 56, 112–114, 113*f*
Compassion, 60–63
Computer-based visuals, 150
Concern for students, 60–63
Concrete experience, 78–79, 78*f*

Confidence
    document design and, 158–160, 159*f*
    recognizing accomplishment and, 27
Constructive criticism, 117
Conversations
    overview, 4–6, 5*f*
    physical and verbal components of communication, 112–114, 113*f*
    playbook of language drills, 114–117, 114*f*, 115*f*, 116*f*
Critical questions activity, 128–129
Cronin, Doreen, 125
Cultural differences, 166–167
Curiosity, 96–97, 157

D

Damon, William, 90
Data analysis, 175–177, 177*f*, 179–180, 179*f*
Debate activity, 131
Design. *see also* Document designer
    build a foundation with visuals, 103–104, 104*f*
    communicating the big picture, 105–106, 106*f*
    cultural differences in design principles, 166–167
    explore structure, 104–105, 105*f*
    overview, 101–103, 108–109
    poster presentations, 106–108, 107*f*
Document designer. *see also* Design
    building confidence, 158–160, 159*f*
    creating unity through repetition, 162–166, 163–166, 163*f*
    cultural differences in design principles, 166–167
    making materials easy to use, 158
    overview, 155–156, 167
    raising interest and curiosity of learners, 157
    using alignment to guide the reader's eyes, 161–162, 162*f*, 163–166
    using contrast to emphasize important information, 160, 160*f*, 163–166
    using proximity to group information, 161, 161*f*, 163 166
Documentary photography, 132–133, 133*f*

E

Ego, 63–64
Empty mind, 24
Energy levels, 31
Engagement
    document design and, 157
    quest engagement, 37–38
    set-up and teamwork and, 38–39
Environment, learning. *see* Learning environment
Equanimity, 59–60
Equipment inventory, 44–45
Expectations
    making progress visible, 30–31
    routine framework and, 24
Experience points, 41–44, 42*f*, 43*f*, 44*f*
Experiential learning, 78, 78*f*
Expression, 143
Eye contact, 143

F

Family involvement, 30–31
Feedback
    individualized feedback, 82
    motivation and, 117–118
    practice and, 27, 28
    thick description and, 72–73
    videotaping technique and, 82–83, 85–86
    writing feedback, 70–74
Field trips, 56
First Impressions activity, 158–160, 159*f*
Flexibility
    needs of students and, 97–98
    planning, 53, 54
Fluency development
    curiosity, 96–97
    improvisation and, 91–92
Frequencies in data analysis, 175–177, 177*f*
Friendliness, 11–12
Fripp, Patricia, 152

Index

G

Games, 56
Gamification, 36. *see also* Role-playing game master
Gaming, 36. *see also* Role-playing game master
Gehry, Frank, 101, 109
Gestures, 143
Glasser, William, 61
Goals
    character sheets, experience points, and leveling-up, 41–44, 42*f*, 43*f*, 44*f*
    looking where you want to go, 53
    making progress visible, 30–31
    plan questionnaire before writing it, 173–174, 174*t*
    routine framework and, 24
    visualizing succeeding, 81
Graphic organizers
    building a foundation with, 103–104, 104–105, 104*f*
    communicating the big picture, 105–106, 106*f*
    explore structure, 104–105, 105*f*
Growth
    making progress visible, 30
    recognizing, 26–27
Guided practice
    individualized feedback, 82
    needs assessment, 86
    overview, 80
Guiding questions, 105, 105*f*

H

Handouts, 149–150
Hoops U website, 120
Humanistic approach to learning, 79

I

Improvisation, 91–92, 98
Interaction, 145
Interest levels, 157

J

Judgment
    choiceless awareness and, 63–64
    zen master insights into, 64

K

King, Billie Jean, 118
Knight, Bobby, 120

L

LaCroix, Darren, 152
Leadership skills
    energetic leadership, 31
    purposeful action and, 54–55
    recognizing accomplishment and, 27
Learner-centeredness approach, 79
Learning environment
    appearances of learning spaces, 25–26, 26*f*
    overview, 79
    respect, 25
Learning management system, 56
Letter of critique activity, 129
Leveling-up, 41–44, 42*f*, 43*f*, 44*f*
Library field trip, 56
Likert scale items, 175, 176*f*
Listening
    addressing the needs of students and, 15–16
    overview, 11–12
    respect, 24

M

Martial Arts Industry Association, 32
Martial arts master
    appearances of learning spaces, 25–26, 26*f*
    belt system, 26–27
    disguise repetition, 28–30, 29*f*
    energetic leadership, 31
    involving families, 30–31
    making progress visible, 30
    overview, 23–24, 31–32
    patience, 28
    practice, 27–28
    respect, 24–25
    routine framework, 24

Materials
- building confidence with, 158–160, 159*f*
- creating unity through repetition, 162–166, 163–166, 163*f*
- cultural differences in design principles and, 166–167
- making easy to use, 158
- overview, 167
- raising interest and curiosity of learners, 157
- using alignment to guide the reader's eyes, 161–162, 162*f*, 163–166
- using contrast to emphasize important information, 160, 160*f*, 163–166
- using proximity to group information, 161, 161*f*, 163–166

Means in data analysis, 175–177, 177*f*
Meditation, 24, 60
Metaphors for language teaching, 7
Mindfulness, 60
Minute Message activity, 146–147
Mode in data analysis, 176
Modeling
- photovoice activity and, 132
- practice and, 27

Montell, Gabriela, 120
Motivation, 23, 37–38, 117–118
Movement, 142
My Hero activity, 39–40, 41*f*, 45

N

Names of students, remembering, 12–13, 13*f*
National Association of Professional Martial Artists, 32
National Speakers Association, 152
Needs assessment, 53, 80
Needs of students
- addressing, 15–18
- needs assessment, 53, 80, 86
- understanding, 80
- variation among, 97–98

Nonverbal communication, 142–144

O

Objective
- character sheets, experience points, and leveling-up, 41–44, 42*f*, 43*f*, 44*f*
- identifying, 90
- looking where you want to go, 53
- making progress visible, 30–31
- needs assessment, 80
- plan questionnaire before writing it, 173–174, 174*t*
- practice and, 27
- routine framework and, 24
- visualizing succeeding, 81

Observation
- choiceless awareness and, 61
- concern and compassion for students and, 60–63
- unsolved mysteries, 95–96, 95*t*

Obstacles, 51–52
Online activities, 56
Oral responses, using picture books as springboards for, 127–131
Organization, 144–148

P

Patience, 28
Patterns, 103–104, 104*f*
Pele, 118
Personas, 39–40, 41*f*
Photovoice activity, 132–133, 133*f*
Physical components of communication, 112–114, 113*f*
Picture books, as springboards for oral and written responses, 127–131
Piggybook (Browne, 1986), 129–131
Planning
- delivering the message effectively, 144–148
- flexibility and, 53, 54
- needs assessment, 53
- overview, 53
- plan questionnaire before writing it, 173–174, 174*t*
- research and, 173–174, 174*t*

Play, 104–105, 105*f*
Portfolios of work, 27
Positivity, 18
Postcard activity, 14–15, 15*f*

Poster presentations, 106–108, 107f
Poster Tour activity, 83–84
Power, responsibilities involved in reviewing writing, 70–71
PowerPoint presentations, 151
Practicing
   delivering the message effectively, 144–148
   needs assessment, 86
   overview, 27–28
Praise, motivation and, 117
Preparation, 53, 54f, 55f
Prereading Brainstorming Exercise, 4–6, 5f
Progress
   character sheets, experience points, and leveling-up, 41–44, 42f, 43f, 44f
   making visible, 30
   recognizing, 26–27
   struggles and obstacles, 51–52
Props, 144–148
Proving a Proverb activity, 148
Public speaker
   delivering the message effectively, 144–148
   overview, 141, 150–151
   tailoring messages to the audience, 149–150
   use of body to deliver your message, 142–144
Purposeful action, 54–55
Pyramid of Success, 118–119, 119f

Q

Qualitative questioning, 177–179, 178f
Quest engagement, 37–38
Questionnaire
   classwork employed as qualitative data in addition to, 179–180, 179f
   open-ended questions and preparing students to respond, 177–179, 178f
   planning before writing, 173–174, 174t
   using Likert scale items, 175, 176f
Questions
   open-ended questions and preparing students to respond, 177–179, 178f
   overview, 105, 105f
   physical and verbal components of communication, 112–114, 113f
   using picture books as springboards for oral and written responses, 128–129, 131

R

Rapport building, 12–15, 13f, 15f
Recycling principle
   overview, 79, 81
   Poster Tour activity, 83–84
   Research Talks activity, 84–85
Reflection
   bartender insights, 18, 19–20, 19f
   coaching models and, 119–120
   facilitating in learners, 82–83
   staying positive and, 18
   videotaping technique and, 82–83, 85–86
Reflective observation, 78–79, 78f
Relaxing, 53–54
Repetition
   disguising, 28–30, 29f
   document design and, 162, 163f
Research Talks activity, 84–85
Researcher
   classwork employed as qualitative data, 179–180, 179f
   data analysis, 175–177, 177f
   open-ended questions and preparing students to respond, 177–179, 178f
   overview, 171–173, 180
   plan questionnaire before writing it, 173–174, 174t
   using Likert scale items, 175, 176f
Resources, 44–45
Responsibility, 31–32
Restaurant reviewer
   overview, 69–70, 73–74
   thick description, 72–73
   visiting more than once, 71–72, 72f
   wield power judiciously, 70–71
Rewarding students, motivation and, 117–118
Risk-taking
   anonymity and, 39–40, 41f
   moving on from unsuccessful attempts, 57
   by teachers, 56
Role-playing game master
   character sheets, experience points, and leveling-up, 40, 41–44, 42f, 43f, 44f
   equipment inventory, 44–45
   overview, 35–37, 45
   quest engagement, 37–38
   set-up and teamwork, 38–39
   use avatars, 39–40, 41f

Routine framework, 24
RPG.net, 46

S

Safe behaviors, risk-taking by teachers and, 56
Scaffolding
    photovoice activity and, 132
    practice and, 27
    zone of proximal development (ZPD) and, 79
Scientific approach, 171–173
Seldin, Peter, 120
Self-assessment, 64
Set-up, 38–39
Ski instructors
    guided practice, 80
    individualized feedback, 82
    learner reflection, 82–83
    learners' needs, 80
    overview, 77–80, 78f, 86
    recycle in different contexts, 81
    sample activities, 83–86
    theoretical basis, 78–80, 78f
    visualizing succeeding, 81
    warm up the gears, 81–82
Skills, 41–44, 42f, 43f, 44f
Small-group work
    physical and verbal components of communication, 114
    poster presentations, 106–108, 107f
Social activist
    documentary photography, 132–133, 133f
    overview, 125–126, 133–135
    use picture books as springboards, 127–131
Social injustice
    overview, 125–126, 133–135
    using picture books as springboards for oral and written responses, 127–131
Sociability, 11–12
Spitz, Mark, 118
Stories
    curiosity, 96–97
    overview, 92–93
    unsolved mysteries, 95–96, 95t
Strengths, 41–44, 42f, 43f, 44f
Struggles, 51–52
Student needs. *see* Needs of students
Student presentations, 106–108, 107f
Summary, 74
Survey activity, 13–15, 13f
Surveying students, 180. *see also* Questionnaire; Researcher

T

Task dependency, 79
Task-based instruction, 79
Teachable moments, flexibility and, 54
Teacher talk, addressing the needs of students and, 16
Teamwork, 38–39, 53
Technology, tailoring messages to the audience, 150
Three in One activity, 147–148
Toastmasters, 151–152
Trust, addressing the needs of students and, 16

U

Understanding, 105–106, 106f

V

Variety in activities, 28–30, 29f
Video clips, tailoring messages to the audience, 151
Videotaping technique, 82–83, 85–86
Visual aids
    building a foundation with, 103, 104f
    communicating the big picture, 105–106, 106f
    creating unity through repetition, 162–166, 163–166, 163f
    cultural differences in design principles and, 166–167
    explore structure, 104–105, 105f
    overview, 108–109, 167
    poster presentations, 106–108, 107f
    tailoring messages to the audience, 149
    using alignment to guide the reader's eyes, 161–162, 162f, 163–166
    using contrast to emphasize important information, 160, 160f, 163–166
    using proximity to group information, 161, 161f, 163–166
Visualization, 81

Vocabulary learning
    playbook of language drills, 114
    recycle in different contexts, 81
Vocal characteristics, 143–144
Vygotsky, Lev, 79, 127

W

Warm-up exercises, 81–82
Whitewater paddler
    adjusting courses, 54
    being prepared for the unplanned, 53, 54*f*, 55*f*
    enjoy the adventure, 57
    lean downstream, 56
    learn to roll, 57
    looking where you want to go, 53
    overview, 51–52, 57
    planning, 53
    reading the water, 53
    relaxing, 53–54
    taking risks with safety following, 56
    teamwork, 53
    using the current, 54
    using the paddle, 54–55
Wooden, John, 118–119, 119*f*
World Champion's Edge, 152

Writing skills
    communicating the big picture, 105–106, 106*f*
    overview, 69–70
    photovoice activity and, 132
    responsibilities involved in reviewing writing, 70–71
    reviewing throughout the writing process, 71–72, 72*f*
    thick description and, 72–73
Written responses, using picture books as springboards for, 127–131

Z

Zapotek, Emil, 117
Zazen meditation, 61–63
Zen master
    challenges to achieving choiceless awareness, 63–64
    choiceless awareness, 61–64
    concern and compassion for students, 60–61
    meditation, 61–63
    overview, 59–60, 64–65
Zone of proximal development (ZPD), 79, 80